365 plus one
Vegetarian Starters, Snacks and Savouries

365 plus one Vegetarian Starters, Snacks and Savouries

Delicious mini meals for every
day of the year

Janet Hunt

Thorsons
An Imprint of HarperCollinsPublishers

Thorsons
An Imprint of HarperCollins*Publishers*
77–85 Fulham Palace Road,
Hammersmith, London W6 8JB

Published by Thorsons 1992
1   3   5   7   9   10   8   6   4   2

Some recipes in this book have appeared in
Janet Hunt's previous books.

Janet Hunt asserts the moral right to
be identified as the author of this work

A catalogue record for this book
is available from the British Library

ISBN 0 7225 2686 5

Typeset by Harper Phototypesetters Limited,
Northampton
Printed in Great Britain by
The Bath Press, Bath, Avon

*The front cover shows (clockwise, from top left):
Spinach Cheesecake (p. 58); Layered Vegetable
Terrine (p. 30); Carrot Mousse (p. 27); Egg
and Avocado Pâté (p. 18).*

Contents

Introduction

What is a snack?

Ask a dozen people to define the word *snack* and chances are you'll get a dozen different definitions. To one person it is a packet of crisps, to another a bowl of soup and a buttered roll, to a dieter it's a stick of celery filled with a teaspoon of cottage cheese – and to someone who has just played squash and is about to go and cut the lawn, it could be a hearty risotto plus a pudding.

Appetites vary considerably, not just from one person to the next, but also at different times of year and of our lives. The calorific energy needs of a growing child are obviously higher than those of a middle-aged office worker, who in turn needs more than an elderly person who rarely leaves the house.

Age, life style, weather – all affect the way we eat, but there is one other very important factor.

As eating is something we do not just do to keep our bodies going, but also for the sheer pleasure of it, individual taste preferences play an important role, too. Ultimately they are responsible for *what* we choose, for helping us decide *how much* of it we need to satisfy us as well as *when* and *where* to consume it.

It is because definitions of the word 'snack' differ so much that this book offers such a wide and varied selection of recipes.

There are simple dishes that can be put together in minutes when you are tired and hungry, others that will take a little longer and those that are useful for a light lunch with the family. A few require more exotic ingredients and more time in the kitchen, but will result in something special to offer to guests – or to indulge in when you feel like pampering yourself. All of them would be great for a buffet party. Many of them could be taken on picnics, rambles or put into lunchboxes.

In order to cater for all tastes and pockets, each recipe is also followed by tips and ideas for adapting it, for turning it into a more substantial snack, for cutting corners to save both time and money. They will also, hopefully, help you discover what a creative challenge cookery can be and encourage you to experiment with ingredients and techniques so that you can develop recipes of your own.

Why snack?

Snacking is very much a phenomenon of the eighties and nineties. A hectic life, small kitchens, families where each individual is busy doing one thing or another and, therefore, wanting to eat at different times – these are just some of the reasons for the growing popularity of the snack. Though this way of eating is sometimes criticized as being unhealthy (which it is if you eat only crisps, chocolate bars and hamburgers), there is no reason at all why this has to be the case. In fact, other experts say the opposite.

It has been proven that many people function better by eating little and often, rather than going without all day and having one big compensatory meal in the evening. Smaller amounts of food will not overload your system so, if your digestion is poor, snacking can save you much discomfort. Because the calories are used up at once rather than stored, snacks are also thought to be less likely to make you put on weight – a theory that features in a number of diet plans these days. If you choose the ingredients with care, you'll find snacks can help you stay alert and energetic through the most demanding day.

If the recipes given in this book are very varied, they do have one important thing in common: they are all vegetarian.

These days, interest in vegetarianism is growing faster than a beansprout, and for every person who takes the plunge and gives up flesh foods completely, there are many more who are resolving to at least reduce their consumption of them. It is hard for anyone to remain ignorant of the health hazards associated with eating foods rich in saturated fats, or of increasing doubts about the overuse of drugs by the meat industry in an effort to make their product even more profitable. Such concerns as world hunger, the destruction of rainforests, the diminishing numbers of dolphins and other creatures are directly linked to the consumption of meat and fish – another factor that is causing caring people to stop and think.

What's more, being vegetarian gets easier and easier. The vast and delicious variety of ingredients now available makes it possible to ring the changes as never before; to eat not just well but wonderfully well. These can be found not just in health food and wholefood shops, but in supermarkets and even your corner shop!

Look out for free-range eggs, vegetarian cheeses in many varieties, organic vegetables and fruits, grains that haven't been stripped of their goodness and taste, fresh nuts and pulses from every corner of the world. Try your local ethnic store for even more goodies. If you miss meat, do try some of the excellent substitutes that are readily available. Mostly made from beans or other plants, they either taste of 'beef' or are unflavoured and are usually vegan. Quorn, relatively new on the market and very versatile, contains egg white.

If you cannot get an ingredient that is listed – try something else! When you make a habit of only using quality ingredients that are fresh and tasty, you know your snack will be as tasty as it is nutritious.

When is a snack not a snack?

When it's a starter.

In theory, most, if not all, of the recipes given here can be eaten as either snacks, complete on their own, or as the first courses of main meals. The choice is yours. It depends on when you want to serve it and who will be sharing it with you.

While a snack is intended to fill a gap, at least for a while, a starter must do the opposite. Its purpose is to stimulate the digestive juices so that the diner is ready to enjoy the dishes that follow and although you can serve something as simple as a chilled tomato soup or cinnamon grapefruit, this is also your opportunity to prepare a cordon vert masterpiece! Remember, too, that individual portions cooked and served in their own dishes or ramekins look particularly attractive.

Alternatively, do what many Continentals do and serve a pasta or risotto to start with, following it with something light, plus salad or young, lightly cooked vegetables. Remember that a meal should always be seen as a complete entity, with each course complementing the others, the whole thing being balanced in terms of taste and texture. The visual aspect is also important. Choose ingredients that offer a variety of colours and use garnishes to brighten any dish that would otherwise look a bit bland. (If you're trying to plan a dinner party menu – or *any* dinner menu for that matter – see *365 plus 1 Vegetarian Main Meals* for lots of ideas!)

What about vegans?

Many of the recipes given here contain no dairy products at all and are therefore suitable for vegans just as they are. Others can be easily adapted by replacing cow's milk with soya milk, cheese with one of the many excellent non-dairy cheeses now available in a range of flavours, and by using soya flour instead of eggs to bind. Make a creamy white sauce with oil, flour and vegetable stock and stir in some concentrated soya milk. Use nut butters or tahini instead of creamy cheeses, coconut cream instead of real cream, and yogurt and mayonnaise made from plant-derived ingredients instead of ones made with milk or eggs. Again, be adventurous and adapt recipes in your own unique way.

It is also worth taking a regular wander around your local wholefood shop as new 'alternative' products arrive regularly – some being specially developed to fill a gap, others being imported from overseas. Though they might sometimes seem rather expensive, the basics of a vegan diet are some of the cheapest foods (surprising when you consider they are often also the most nutritious) so you shouldn't be out of pocket.

Using this book

When fresh vegetables are not available, try frozen ones. Frozen vegetables are good alternatives as they are usually processed shortly after they are picked and contain few, if any, additives (check the packaging to be sure). If using them in a specific recipe you will need to adjust the amount. How much will vary from one variety to another. In general the firmer vegetables (those that contain less water) will be similar in weight. When using spinach, remember that about 680g (1½ lb) fresh spinach can be replaced with a 455g (1 lb) pack of frozen.

Cooking dried beans and pulses is very economical and, if you cook several batches at once and freeze them, very convenient, especially when just small quantities are required. All beans and pulses should be soaked overnight, then the soaking water is drained off. Then, simply cover them with plenty of fresh water, bring it to the boil, boil the beans or pulses fast for 10 minutes before lowering the heat, covering the pan, and simmering the beans until soft. Different beans and pulses take different lengths of time to cook: haricot (navy) beans take about 30 to 45 minutes after boiling, black beans the same, chick peas 25 to 30 minutes, aduki beans an hour, kidney beans about an hour, flageolets 20 minutes and soya beans 1½ to 2 hours. Make extra and freeze them as small quantities are required for quite a few recipes and cooking them yourself is much more economical. If using tinned beans instead of cooking them yourself, replace 115g (4 oz) dried beans with one 395g (14 oz) tin.

Many of the recipes list margarine in the ingredients. Use one made from vegetable oils, which are low in saturated fats and high in polyunsaturates. However, butter not only has a better taste, but is a more natural product, so do use it instead of margarine on those occasions when you feel the difference is important.

N.B. The quantities are given in metric and imperial (on the left of the ingredients) and in American measurements (on the right of the ingredients), but please follow just *one* system, not a mixture, as it could affect the result, especially with doughs, cakes and so on. **Items in brackets represent the equivalent American names/terms.**

All the recipes make four average servings. When serving the heavier dishes - those made with grains, pastas, pizzas - as starters, you might like to reduce the quantities.

For ease of reference, basic recipes referred to throughout the book have been grouped together at the end of the book.

1

Soups

Cashew and Carrot Soup

55g (2 oz)	cashew nut pieces	½ cup
30g (1 oz)	margarine	2½ tbsp
1 small	onion, finely chopped	1 small
2 large	carrots, finely chopped	2 large
55g (2 oz)	wholemeal (whole wheat) flour	½ cup
850ml (1½ pt)	vegetable stock	3¾ cups
285ml (½ pt)	milk	1⅓ cups
	seasoning to taste	
	single cream, dairy or soya (optional)	
	fresh parsley, to garnish	

1 Use a grinder to process the cashew pieces until they are reduced to a powder.
2 Melt the margarine and sauté the onion and carrot for a few minutes. Stir in the flour, cook until lightly browned, then add the ground cashew nuts, gradually add the vegetable stock and milk, stirring, and season generously.
3 Bring the soup to the boil, then lower the heat and simmer for 15 minutes. Serve it hot with a swirl of cream to give the soup a richer taste. Parsley used to garnish each bowl adds colour.

Note: For a creamier soup, blend all the ingredients just before serving. Try this basic recipe using peanuts instead of cashews.

Lemon Chowder

30g (1 oz)	margarine	2½ tbsp
1 large	onion, chopped	1 large
1 large	green pepper, chopped	1 large
30g (1 oz)	wholemeal (whole wheat) flour	¼ cup
570ml (1 pt)	vegetable stock	2½ cups
570ml (1 pt)	milk	2½ cups
170g (6 oz)	sweetcorn, fresh or frozen	1 cup
85g (3 oz)	wholemeal (whole wheat) spaghetti rings	¾ cup
1	lemon, juice of	1
140ml (¼ pt)	sour (soured) cream	⅔ cup
	seasoning to taste	
	fresh chives, snipped, to garnish	

1 Melt the margarine in a saucepan, add the onion and green pepper and cook for 5 minutes or until they begin to soften. Add the flour and brown over a low heat.
2 Pour in the stock and milk gradually, stirring, and bring the soup to the boil, then drop in the sweetcorn and pasta rings. Cook gently, uncovered, for about 10 minutes, or until both are just tender.
3 Add the juice of the lemon and grate in a little of the peel, then stir in the sour cream and heat the soup gently for a few minutes more (do not let it boil). Season to taste, then serve with the chives sprinkled over each bowl to garnish.

Note: Any pasta can be used in this unusual soup. It's an ideal way to use up those broken pieces of spaghetti that collect at the bottom of the pack!

Creamy Lentil Soup

225g (8 oz)	dried split red lentils, washed	1 cup
1 l (1¾ pt)	vegetable stock	4½ cups
1 medium	onion, chopped	1 medium
1 tsp	dried tarragon	1 tsp
	seasoning to taste	
55g (2 oz)	low-fat cream cheese	¼ cup
	celery leaves, to garnish	

1 Put the lentils into a saucepan with the vegetable stock and onion and bring to the boil. Simmer for 10 to 15 minutes or until the lentils are soft.
2 Remove the pan from the heat, add the tarragon and season to taste. Add the cream cheese, stirring until it has completely dissolved and serve at once, garnished with the celery leaves.

Note: This is an exceptionally quick and easy lentil soup. Whole lentils can be used instead of the split variety, but then allow at least twice as long for them to cook. A vegan version can be made by using concentrated soya milk instead of the cream cheese to give the soup a creamy texture.

Autumn Vegetable Soup with Barley

85g (3 oz)	pot barley (wholegrain barley)	⅓ cup
850ml (1½ pt)	vegetable stock	3¾ cups
2 medium	leeks, sliced	2 medium
2	sticks celery, sliced	2
2 large	carrots, sliced	2 large
1 large	parsnip, diced	1 large
1 large	onion, chopped	1 large
	bouquet garni	
	seasoning to taste	
1-2 tsp	yeast extract	1-2 tsp

1 If possible, soak the barley in water overnight and then drain it well before using.
2 Combine the barley and vegetable stock in a saucepan, bring to the boil, then reduce the heat and simmer the soup for 30 to 40 minutes, by which time the barley should begin to soften. Add the prepared vegetables and bouquet garnish and continue cooking for 15 minutes, or until all the ingredients are just tender.
3 Remove the bouquet garni, season to taste and stir in the yeast extract to enrich the soup (if you choose to use the larger amount of yeast extract, be careful with the seasoning or the final taste might be too salty).

Note: Any vegetables can be used in this soup – just add whatever you have handy. Pot barley is the whole grain, making it more nutritious than pearl barley, but slower to cook. You can speed up the process by using barley flakes (though the resulting texture will be different), or try replacing the barley with oatmeal.

Onion and White Wine Soup with Croûtons

2 tbsp	vegetable oil	2 tbsp
680g (1½ lb)	onions, chopped	4 cups
30g (1 oz)	wholemeal (whole wheat) flour	¼ cup
1 l (1¾ pt)	vegetable stock	4½ cups
200ml (⅓ pt)	white wine	¾ cup
	seasoning to taste	
4	thick slices wholemeal bread, diced	4
2 tbsp	vegetable oil	2 tbsp
55g (2 oz)	grated Parmesan cheese	½ cup

1 Heat the oil and gently sauté the onions for a few minutes to soften them. Add the flour, cook briefly, then gradually stir in the vegetable stock and wine. Cover the saucepan and cook the soup over a low heat for about 30 minutes. Season well.
2 Just before serving, fry the bread, stirring frequently, until brown and crisp. Divide the soup between the bowls, sprinkle the cheese and the croûtons over the top and serve at once.

Note: To make this into a meal in a bowl, cut a couple of potatoes into cubes and add them to the soup for the final 10 minutes of cooking. Extra cheese can be passed around at the table.

Spiced Almond Soup

1 tbsp	vegetable oil	1 tbsp
1 medium	onion, chopped	1 medium
1 large	apple, chopped	1 large
2 tsp	ground coriander	2 tsp
½ tsp	ground mace	½ tsp
½ tsp	ground turmeric	½ tsp
115g (4 oz)	almonds, ground	1 cup
850ml (1½ pt)	water	3¾ cups
	seasoning to taste	
1 small	lemon, juice of	1 small
140ml (¼ pt)	natural (unsweetened) yogurt	⅔ cup
	flaked almonds, lightly toasted	

1 Heat the oil and gently sauté the onion and apple in it for 5 to 10 minutes. Add the spices and cook a little

longer. Add the ground almonds and water, bring the soup to the boil and then simmer for 5 minutes.

2 Season the soup to taste and add the lemon juice. Off the heat, stir in enough of the yogurt to make the soup creamy. Serve with a few flaked almonds floated on top of each bowlful.

Note: If you do not have these spices, experiment with others. For example, you could stir 1–2 teaspoons of mild curry paste into the hot soup. To make it more filling, add a few spoonfuls of cooked brown rice. It also makes an unusual soup when served chilled – float some cucumber slices on top.

Brussels and Chestnut Soup

225g (8 oz)	chestnuts	8 oz
55g (2 oz)	margarine	¼ cup
1 large	onion, chopped	1 large
225g (8 oz)	Brussels sprouts, cleaned	8 oz
850ml (1½ pt)	vegetable stock	3¾ cups
200-g (7-oz)	tin (can) tomatoes	7-oz
good pinch	ground nutmeg seasoning to taste	good pinch
4 tbsp	single cream, dairy or soya parsley, chopped, to garnish	4 tbsp

1 Cut a cross in the top of each chestnut, then either bake them in a slow oven or boil them in a pan of water for about 10 minutes. When they are cool enough to handle, peel off the outer shell and inner skin and coarsely chop the nuts.

2 Melt the margarine in a saucepan and add the onion. Sauté it gently until it becomes transparent. Slice the Brussels sprouts and add them to the pan. Cook them briefly, then add the vegetable stock, the tomatoes and juice, breaking the tomatoes up if necessary. Stir in the chestnuts, cover the pan and simmer all the ingredients for 20 minutes or until they are tender.

3 Add the nutmeg and season to taste, stir in the cream and serve the soup at once (you can blend the ingredients if you prefer a smoother soup, adding a drop more stock or water if it is too thick). Garnish with the chopped parsley.

Note: Though fresh chestnuts are only available at certain times of the year, dried chestnuts can be used in their place. As these tend to have less flavour, you might like to add a sprinkling of soy sauce and a spoonful of olive oil. The herb thyme also goes well with these ingredients.

Sweet and Sour Borscht

2 tbsp	vegetable oil	2 tbsp
1 small	onion, chopped	1 small
3	raw beetroots (beets), peeled and grated	3
¼ small	white cabbage, grated	¼ small
1 medium	carrot, grated	1 medium
570ml (1 pt)	vegetable stock or water	2½ cups
2 tbsp	lemon juice	2 tbsp
2 tbsp	raw cane sugar seasoning to taste fresh parsley, chopped	2 tbsp

1 Heat the oil in a saucepan and sauté the onion for a few minutes until it has softened. Stir in the beetroot (beet), cabbage and carrot. Add the remaining ingredients, except the parsley, and bring to the boil. Lower the heat, cover the pan and cook it gently for about 20 minutes or until the vegetables are cooked.

2 Adjust the seasoning to taste and serve at once sprinkled with the parsley (if you like a smooth soup you can purée the ingredients just prior to serving).

Note: Traditionally, borscht is served with some sour cream stirred into it – vegans can use tahini instead. This soup makes a tasty lunch, accompanied by dark rye or pumpernickel bread and maybe some cheese.

Pistou Soup with Tofu

850ml (1½ pt)	vegetable stock	3¾ cups
2 medium	sticks celery, sliced	2 medium
225g (8 oz)	fine green beans, trimmed and sliced	½ cup
115g (4 oz)	vermicelli, broken into pieces	4 oz
200-g (7-oz)	tin (can) tomatoes	7-oz
2 tbsp	vegetable oil	2 tbsp
3	cloves garlic, peeled and crushed	3
285g (10 oz)	tofu, drained	1¼ cups
1 tsp	dried basil seasoning to taste parsley sprigs	1 tsp

1 Heat the vegetable stock in a saucepan, then add the celery, green beans and vermicelli and cook for 10 minutes.

2 Meanwhile, blend together the tomatoes, oil, garlic and tofu to make a smooth sauce. Stir this into the vegetable stock, add the basil and season to taste. Cook the soup gently for just a few minutes more.

3 Serve it hot, topped with plenty of fresh parsley.

Note: This is a meal-in-a-soup – just add French bread for a delicious midday snack. To ring the changes, try using tahini, peanut butter or yogurt instead of the tofu or simply stir in lots of grated (shredded) cheese.

Parsnip Vichysoisse

30g (1 oz)	*margarine*	*2½ tbsp*
2 large	*leeks, finely sliced*	*2 large*
1 medium	*onion, chopped*	*1 medium*
455g (1 lb)	*parsnips, peeled and chopped*	*3 cups*
850ml (1½ pt)	*vegetable stock*	*3¾ cups*
good pinch	*ground nutmeg*	*good pinch*
	seasoning to taste	
1	*free-range egg yolk*	*1*
140ml (¼ pt)	*single (light) cream*	*⅔ cup*
	fresh chives, chopped, to garnish	

1 Melt the margarine in a saucepan and gently sauté the leek and onion in it until they have softened. Add the parsnip, stock, nutmeg and season to taste. Bring the soup to the boil, then cover the pan and simmer for 30 minutes or until the vegetables are well cooked.

2 Blend the vegetables in a liquidizer or food processor and return the purée to the saucepan, heating it gently until it is almost boiling. Meanwhile, lightly whisk the egg yolk into the cream, then whisk this into the hot soup. Do not let it come to the boil. Serve at once with a generous sprinkling of the chopped chives.

Note: This recipe is traditionally made with potatoes – try it for a change. It's also unusual made with a mixture of root vegetables, such as carrots, turnips and parsnips. All versions can also be served chilled. They are good topped with croûtons, made by frying tiny cubes of stale wholemeal (whole wheat) bread, draining them well, then serving at once or letting them cool and storing them in an airtight container until needed.

Chinese Broth with Eggs

2 tbsp	*vegetable oil*	*2 tbsp*
1	*clove garlic, peeled and crushed*	*1*
1 tsp	*fresh ginger, grated*	*1 tsp*
1 l (1¾ pt)	*vegetable stock*	*4½ cups*
115g (4 oz)	*mushrooms, chopped*	*2 cups*
115g (4 oz)	*sweetcorn, cooked*	*1 cup*
small chunk	*Chinese cabbage, shredded*	*small chunk*
2	*spring onions (scallions), chopped*	*2*
1 tbsp	*soy sauce*	*1 tbsp*
	squeeze of lemon juice	
	seasoning to taste	
2	*free-range eggs, well beaten*	*2*
55g (2 oz)	*beansprouts (optional)*	*1 cup*

1 Heat the oil in a saucepan and sauté the garlic and ginger in it for a few minutes. Add the stock, bring it to the boil and stir in the mushrooms, sweetcorn, cabbage and spring onions (scallions). Simmer the soup for 5 minutes.

2 Flavour it with the soy sauce, lemon juice and season to taste. Then gradually trickle the egg into the hot soup, stirring continuously so that the eggs set in ragged shreds. If using bean sprouts, add them at this point and continue cooking the soup for literally a minute more, then serve it at once.

Note: Pasta can be added too – quick cooking noodles are best. The Italians make a similar soup, adding semolina and Parmesan cheese.

Jerusalem Artichoke Soup

2 tbsp	*vegetable oil*	*2 tbsp*
1 medium	*onion, sliced*	*1 medium*
680g (1½ lb)	*Jerusalem artichokes, peeled and chopped (see note)*	*1½ lb*
2 medium	*carrots, peeled and chopped*	*2 medium*
2	*sticks celery, chopped*	*2*
850ml (1½ pt)	*vegetable stock*	*3¾ cups*
	squeeze lemon juice	
	seasoning to taste	

1 Heat the oil in a saucepan and sauté the onion in it until it has softened. Add the prepared vegetables and vegetable stock, lemon juice and season to taste. Bring the soup to the boil then cover the pan and simmer for about 45 minutes or until the vegetables are well cooked.

2 Blend it in a liquidizer or food processor to make a thick, creamy soup, then reheat it gently and adjust the seasoning to taste before serving.

Note: Scrub the artichokes before peeling them, removing as little of the flesh with the skin as possible. This is easiest to do with the smoother tubers, so try to avoid those that are particularly lumpy. This soup can be turned into a filling snack by adding some cooked beans and/or grated (shredded) cheese and serving with fresh wholemeal (whole wheat) rolls.

Spicy Rice and Tomato Soup

85g (3 oz)	*raw brown rice*	*½ cup*
1 tbsp	*vegetable oil*	*1 tbsp*
1 medium	*onion, chopped*	*1 medium*
½ tsp	*ground turmeric*	*½ tsp*
½ tsp	*ground cumin*	*½ tsp*
¼ tsp	*ground cayenne*	*¼ tsp*

680g (1½ lb)	tomatoes, peeled and chopped	1½ cups
850ml (1½ pt)	vegetable stock	3¾ cups
115g (4 oz)	peas, fresh or frozen	⅔ cup
1 tsp	garam masala seasoning to taste	1 tsp

1 Cook the rice in boiling water for 30 minutes or until it is tender and then drain it.

2 Meanwhile, heat the oil in a saucepan, then fry the onion in it for a few minutes to soften. Sprinkle in the spices and cook for a few minutes more. Add the tomatoes, vegetable stock and peas. Bring the soup to the boil then lower the heat and simmer for 5 to 10 minutes or until the tomatoes have broken down and the peas are cooked. Stir in the rice and cook for a few minutes more to heat it through.

3 Stir in the garam masala, adjust the seasoning to taste, and serve at once.

Note: This is a good way to use up any leftover rice. Other grains can replace the rice – millet, for example, is an unusual but tasty ingredient for this soup. Alternatively, try bulgar, which, as it cooks so quickly, can be added raw at the same time as the vegetable stock, and will be ready in less than 15 minutes.

Spinach and Pine Nut Soup

455g (1 lb)	fresh spinach, well washed	1 lb
55g (2 oz)	margarine	¼ cup
1 large	onion, chopped	1 large
1	clove garlic, peeled and crushed	1
2 tbsp	wholemeal (whole wheat) flour	2 tbsp
1 l (1¾ pt)	vegetable stock	4½ cups
2 tbsp	single cream, dairy or soya	2 tbsp
55g (2 oz)	pine nuts seasoning to taste	½ cup
good pinch	ground nutmeg	good pinch

1 Wash, shred and steam the spinach in a covered saucepan – the water that remains on the leaves should be enough, but take care it does not burn. Cook it for 5 to 10 minutes until it is tender, then drain off any excess liquid, chop the spinach finely and set it aside.

2 Melt the margarine in a saucepan and gently cook the onion and garlic together for 5 minutes. Sprinkle in the flour, sauté it briefly, then slowly add the vegetable stock, stirring continually. Bring it to the boil, add the spinach and cook for a few more minutes.

3 Lower the heat and stir in the cream and pine nuts, then simmer the soup just long enough to heat it through, ensuring that it does not boil. Just before serving, season it to taste and add the nutmeg.

Note: Pine nuts are expensive so this is a good soup to serve on special occasions. To make an everyday version, replace them with chopped raw peanuts. Sesame seeds also go well with spinach, so try replacing the cream with a spoonful or two of light tahini (sesame paste) and sprinkle the soup with toasted sesame seeds just before serving.

Minestrone Verde

85g (3 oz)	dried haricot (navy) beans, soaked overnight (see page 9)	½ cup
3 tbsp	vegetable oil	3 tbsp
1-2	cloves garlic, peeled crushed	1-2
3 large	tomatoes, chopped	3 large
2 medium	leeks, chopped	2 medium
1 large	potato, scrubbed and diced	1 large
½ small	cauliflower, broken into large florets	½ small
1 l (1¾ pt)	vegetable stock	4½ cups
55g (2 oz)	wholemeal (whole wheat) pasta shells	1 cup
1 tbsp	fresh green herbs (including parsley) seasoning to taste grated Parmesan cheese, to garnish (optional)	1 tbsp

1 Cook and drain the beans and set them aside.

2 In another saucepan, heat the oil and cook the garlic for a few minutes before adding the tomatoes and leeks. Continue cooking until the tomatoes break down and form a sauce.

3 Add the potato, cauliflower and the vegetable stock. Bring the soup to the boil, cook it briefly, then stir in the pasta shells, the cooked beans and the herbs. Cook the soup for 10 minutes until the pasta is just tender.

4 Season to taste, then serve the soup very hot, with a sprinkling of the cheese for those who want it.

Note: To cut cooking time use ready-cooked beans, either left over from a previous recipe or tinned.

There are many different kinds of minestrone, but all of them use beans and vegetables as the basic ingredients. Some minestrones omit the pasta altogether. Try replacing it with potato dumplings made by mixing cooked mashed potatoes with a little flour, forming this into small balls and dropping them into the soup to cook for 10 minutes.

Chilled Avocado Soup

2 large	ripe avocados	2 large
570ml (1 pt)	vegetable stock	2½ cups
285ml (½ pt)	milk	1⅓ cups
½	clove garlic, peeled and crushed	½
½ tsp	onion, finely grated	½ tsp
1 tsp	lemon juice	1 tsp
225g (8 oz)	silken tofu, drained	1 cup
	Tabasco sauce to taste	
	seasoning to taste	
	fresh chives, snipped, to garnish	

1 Peel and stone (pit) the avocados and cut the flesh into chunks. Put it into a blender with the stock, milk, garlic, onion and lemon juice. When the mixture is smooth, gradually blend in the tofu, then add Tabasco and seasoning to taste.
2 Add more stock if it seems too thick then chill it well. Taste it again just before serving as chilled food may lose some of its flavour. Serve the soup with the chives sprinkled over the top.

Note: You can replace the tofu with natural (unsweetened) yogurt, if you prefer. For a milder flavoured soup, omit the garlic and onion and use instead herbs such as mint and parsley.

Curried Coconut Cream Soup

2 tbsp	vegetable ghee or margarine	2 tbsp
1 medium	onion, chopped	1 medium
1	clove garlic, peeled and crushed	1
1 tsp	ground coriander	1 tsp
1 tsp	garam masala	1 tsp
1 tsp	ground turmeric	1 tsp
½ tsp	ground ginger	½ tsp
115g (4 oz)	green beans, fresh or frozen	¼ cup
1 medium	carrot, diced	1 medium
1 medium	potato, diced	1 medium
850ml (1½ pt)	vegetable stock	3¾ cups
good squeeze	lemon juice	good squeeze
85g (3 oz)	creamed coconut, grated (shredded)	3 oz

1 Melt the fat in a saucepan and sauté the onion and garlic in it for 5 minutes, then stir in the spices and cook for a minute more. Add the vegetables and stock, bring it to the boil, cover the pan and simmer for 15 minutes or until the vegetables are tender.

2 Stir in the lemon juice and coconut. The coconut will dissolve, making the soup thick and creamy (adjust the amount you use to suit your own taste). Check the seasoning and adjust this if necessary. When the soup is piping hot, serve it at once.

Note: For a soup that is richer in protein, add split lentils at the beginning of the cooking time or peas half way through. Served with bread (Indian breads go especially well) and a side salad, this makes a perfectly balanced snack.

Pumpkin Soup

45g (1½ oz)	margarine	3½ tbsp
1 medium	onion, chopped	1 medium
1 tsp	freshly grated root ginger	1 tsp
1.15 k (2 lb)	pumpkin, peeled and diced	2 lb
1 large	apple, peeled and diced	1 large
1 l (1¾ pt)	vegetable stock	4½ cups
1 tsp	raw cane sugar	1 tsp
good pinch	ground cloves	good pinch
good pinch	ground cinnamon	good pinch
	seasoning to taste	

1 Melt the margarine and sauté the onion and ginger in it briefly.
2 Add the pumpkin, stirring it well, to mix it with the onion and ginger, and cook it for 5 minutes. Add the apple, vegetable stock, sugar and spices, bring it to the boil, then lower the heat and simmer until the pumpkin is tender. Mash or blend to make a thick purée. Season to taste. Serve it hot or cold.

Note: Pumpkin soup is sometimes thought of as rather bland, yet you can easily adjust the flavour to suit your own personal taste: try adding garlic and/or celery, a pinch of chilli powder or other spices, such as cumin or coriander; swirl a little cream, yogurt or tahini into the hot soup just before serving. Thicken it, if liked, with a spoonful of wholemeal (whole wheat) flour.

Chilled Tomato Soup

2 tbsp	vegetable oil	2 tbsp
1 large	onion, chopped	1 large
1	clove garlic, peeled and crushed	1
395-g (14-oz)	tin (can) tomatoes, chopped	14-oz
285ml (½ pt)	vegetable stock	1⅓ cups
1 tsp	fresh marjoram or chervil	1 tsp
	seasoning to taste	
4 tbsp	mayonnaise (dairy or soya)	4 tbsp
2 large	free-range eggs, hard-boiled (hard-cooked), chopped, to garnish	2 extra large

1 Heat the oil in a saucepan and sauté the onion and garlic in it until they have softened. Add the tomatoes, stock and herbs and season to taste. Bring the soup to the boil and then simmer for 5 to 10 minutes. Let it cool briefly, blend it until it is smooth, then stir in enough of the mayonnaise to make the soup creamy and chill it.

2 Divide the soup between 4 small bowls and garnish each one with a sprinkling of the chopped egg.

Note: A popular soup with everyone, but children in particular. It is good hot, too. Instead of the mayonnaise, try stirring in some sour cream or maybe some left over hummus.

Red Pepper Soup

3 large	red peppers, chopped	3 large
3 large	tomatoes, peeled and chopped	3 large
850ml (1½ pt)	vegetable stock	3¾ cups
1-2 tsp	dried tarragon	1-2 tsp
good pinch	chilli powder	good pinch
	seasoning to taste	
4 tbsp	tahini	4 tbsp
handful	fresh parsley, chopped	handful

1 In a saucepan, combine the red pepper and tomatoes with the stock, tarragon, and chilli powder and season to taste. Bring the mixture to the boil, then cover the pan and simmer for about 20 minutes or until the peppers have softened.

2 Blend all the ingredients in a liquidizer or food processor to make a light, smooth purée. Reheat the soup gently, stir in enough of the tahini to make the soup creamy, taste it and adjust the seasoning if necessary. Stir in the parsley just before serving.

Note: Replace the tahini with yogurt, sour cream or buttermilk if you prefer. You could also add tofu at the blending stage. Instead of parsley you could stir in some coarsely chopped watercress. For a thicker soup, add flour or cornflour just before you bring it to the boil.

Tofu and Celery Soup

30g (1 oz)	margarine	2½ tbsp
1	head celery, chopped	1
1 medium	onion, chopped	1 medium
1 l (1¾ pt)	vegetable stock	4½ cups
2 tbsp	tomato purée (paste)	2 tbsp
	bouquet garni	
	seasoning to taste	
225g (8 oz)	firm tofu, drained	1 cup
good squeeze	lemon juice	good squeeze
	soy sauce or miso to taste	

1 Melt the margarine and gently sauté the celery and onion together for 5 minutes. Pour the stock over, stir in the tomato purée, add the bouquet garni and season to taste. Bring the soup to the boil, then cover the pan and simmer for 20 minutes or until the celery is tender. (If liked, at this stage you can blend half the vegetables to make the soup thicker.)

2 Cut the tofu into small cubes, add them to the soup together with the lemon juice and heat the soup through very gently for just a few minutes. Remove the bouquet garni. For extra flavour, add a few drops of soy sauce or stir a spoonful of miso into cold water and add this to the soup.

Note: You can blend the finished soup for a creamy texture. Alternatively, gently fry the tofu cubes instead and sprinkle them over the bowls of the hot soup just before serving. Try adding garlic with the onion for a different taste altogether.

2
Dips and Pâtés

Egg and Avocado Pâté

2 medium	ripe avocados	2 medium
1 tbsp	lemon juice	1 tbsp
2 medium	tomatoes, finely chopped	2 medium
2	spring onions (scallions), chopped	2
3	free-range eggs, hard-boiled (hard-cooked)	3
2 tbsp	curd cheese (cottage cheese, mashed)	2 tbsp
1 tbsp	watercress, chopped seasoning to taste	1 tbsp
generous pinch	chilli powder	generous pinch
	extra watercress sprigs, to garnish	

1 Peel and stone (pit) the avocados and mash the flesh together with the lemon juice. Stir in the tomatoes and spring onions (scallions). Peel and mash the eggs and add them to the avocado mixture.
2 Soften the cheese slightly by mashing it with a fork, then add this to the other ingredients, making sure they are well mixed together. Season generously and add the chilli powder.
3 Pile the mixture into a small dish and chill. Garnish with the sprigs of watercress.

Note: This is good with tortilla chips or piled onto small, crisp biscuits for a party. Try sour (soured) cream or silken tofu instead of the curd (cottage) cheese.

Cheese Pâté with Olives

30g (1 oz)	margarine	2½ tbsp
30g (1 oz)	wholemeal (whole wheat) flour	¼ cup
140ml (¼ pt)	milk	⅔ cup
115g (4 oz)	Red Leicester cheese, grated	⅔ cup
1-2 tbsp	mayonnaise seasoning to taste	1-2 tbsp
12	pimiento stuffed olives fresh chives, snipped, to garnish	12

1 Melt the margarine in a pan, sprinkle in the flour and cook it briefly. Stir in the milk, gradually, and continue cooking until the sauce thickens. Add the cheese, mix it in well and then set the pan aside to cool.
2 Stir in the mayonnaise and season the mixture well. Chop the olives coarsely and stir them well into the mixture until they are distributed evenly. Spoon it into a dish, smooth the top and chill it well before serving sprinkled with the chives.

Note: Any cheese can be used in this recipe, though if you use a strongly flavoured variety, such as a blue cheese, adjust the quantity so that the flavour does not overpower that of the olives. Try black olives instead for a change.

Black Bean Pâté

170g (6 oz)	black beans, soaked overnight (see page 9)	1 cup
2 tbsp	vegetable oil	2 tbsp
1	clove garlic, peeled and crushed	1
1 large	leek, sliced	1 large
2 tbsp	tomato purée (paste)	2 tbsp
good squeeze	lemon juice	good squeeze
	vegetable stock or water	
	seasoning to taste	
generous handful	fresh parsley, chopped	generous handful
	parsley sprigs, to garnish	
	lemon twist, to garnish	

1 Drain the beans, cover them with fresh water and bring to the boil. Continue boiling for 10 minutes, then lower the heat and simmer the beans for 45 minutes or until they are tender, then drain them well.
2 Heat the oil in a pan and sauté the garlic in it for a few minutes, then add the leek and cook a little longer. Stir in the tomato purée and lemon juice.
3 Either mash the beans by hand or purée them in a blender (adding a drop of stock or water as necessary). Combine them with the sautéed mixture, adjust the seasoning to taste and add the parsley.
4 Transfer the pâté to a small dish, smooth the top and chill. Garnish with the sprigs of parsley and the twist of lemon.

Note: This simple pâté can be made using different varieties of beans. Experiment, too, with other herbs and/or spices. Alternatively, omit the lemon juice, using orange instead plus some grated peel. Serve with Melba toast.

Indian Marrow Pâté

1 large	marrow (summer squash)	1 large
1 medium	onion, finely grated	1 medium
1	red pepper, finely grated	1
½ tsp	whole cumin seeds	½ tsp
½ tsp	raw cane sugar	½ tsp
2 tbsp	lemon juice	2 tbsp
	seasoning to taste	

1 Peel and dice the marrow, then steam it briefly so that the flesh is just tender. Drain it very well, mash it, and then drain it again.
2 Combine the marrow with the onion, red pepper, cumin seeds, sugar and lemon juice and season generously. Spoon the pâté into a bowl, smooth the top and chill well.

Note: This is more like a thick vegetable purée than a pâté, although it can be served as a starter or snack and tastes very exotic with Indian breads such as chapatis and poppadoms. If you prefer it smoother, grind the cumin seeds and reduce the quantity a little so that the flavour is not then overpowering. Add a few spoonfuls of thick, natural (unsweetened) yogurt to make it creamier. Much the same recipe can be followed using aubergine (eggplant), cucumber or pumpkin as the main ingredient.

Hummus

225g (8 oz)	dried chick peas (garbanzos), soaked overnight (see page 9)	1⅓ cups
1-2	cloves garlic, peeled and crushed	1-2
2 tbsp	vegetable oil	2 tbsp
2 tbsp	lemon juice	2 tbsp
½ tsp	dried oregano	½ tsp
½ tsp	ground ginger	½ tsp
	seasoning to taste	
	alfalfa sprouts, to garnish	

1 Drain the chick peas (garbanzos) and put them into a saucepan with fresh water, bring it to the boil and continue boiling for 10 minutes. Lower the heat, cover the pan and simmer for 45 minutes or until they are tender. Drain them well (reserving some of the cooking water) and set them aside to cool.
2 Use a blender to grind the chick peas (garbanzos) to a powder, then gradually add in the garlic, oil, lemon juice, oregano and ginger. Add some of the reserved cooking liquid and beat until you have a thick, creamy paste. Season it generously, chill it briefly, then serve it garnished with a few alfalfa sprouts.

Note: Hummus is even better made with fresh ginger instead of ground. Try adding a few spoonfuls of tahini or some natural (unsweetened) yogurt. Traditionally it is served piled into pitta breads which are split open, topped with salad ingredients such as alfalfa sprouts, tomatoes, shredded cabbage. Although they are difficult to eat genteely, they are delicious. Hummus also makes an unusual stuffing for raw tomatoes or baked peppers.

Blue Cheese Dip

225g (8 oz)	Ricotta or cottage cheese	1 cup
115g (4 oz)	crumbled blue cheese	½ cup
1 tbsp	fresh chives, chopped	1 tbsp
2 tbsp	fresh parsley, chopped	2 tbsp
	seasoning to taste	
pinch	paprika	pinch
	milk or single (light) cream	
	walnut (English walnut) pieces, chopped	

1 Blend together the Ricotta or cottage and blue cheeses, add the herbs, paprika and season to taste. (If you do not have a blender, use a fork to mash all the ingredients instead – the resulting dip will be less smooth, but just as tasty.) Stir in just enough milk or cream to make a dipping consistency. Chill the dip briefly before serving, then sprinkle generously with the walnuts.

Note: Apart from being especially good with raw vegetables (try carrot and courgette sticks, cauliflower florets, celery, strips of pepper and fennel), this dip makes a great topping for jacket potatoes.

Mushroom Pâté

30g (1 oz)	margarine	2½ tbsp
1 medium	onion, chopped	1 medium
2	cloves garlic, peeled and chopped	2
340g (12 oz)	mushrooms, chopped	4½ cups
115g (4 oz)	wholemeal (whole wheat) breadcrumbs	2 cups
2 tbsp	lemon juice	2 tbsp
1 tsp	medium strength mustard	1 tsp
½ tsp	dried sage	½ tsp
	seasoning to taste	
	hot water or vegetable stock	
	lemon twists, to garnish	
	parsley sprigs, to garnish	

1 Melt the margarine and gently sauté the onion and garlic for 5 minutes. Stir in the mushrooms and cook them for a few minutes. Add the breadcrumbs, lemon juice, mustard, sage and season to taste.
2 The texture should be like a thick paste, but if it is too dry, stir in a drop or two of hot water or vegetable stock until you have the right consistency. Spoon the mixture into a small dish, smooth the top and chill. Garnish with the twists of lemon and parsley sprigs.

Note: To make this into a starter for a special meal, try adding a little white wine and replace some of the breadcrumbs with ground almonds.

Green Mayonnaise Dip

285ml (½ pt)	mayonnaise (dairy or soya)	1⅓ cups
1 tbsp	lemon juice	1 tbsp
2	spring onions (scallions), chopped	1 tbsp
2 tbsp	fresh parsley, chopped	2 tbsp
2 tbsp	fresh watercress, chopped	2 tbsp
1 tbsp	chives, snipped	1 tbsp
	seasoning to taste	

1 Simply stir all the ingredients together, transfer the mixture to a bowl or jar and chill it well. If possible chill it overnight so that the flavours blend together.

Note: This easy-to-make dip can be varied by the addition of any fresh herbs you have to hand. As you would imagine it is also excellent as a salad dressing and goes well with fried battered vegetables.

Aubergine Pâté with Soya Cheese

2 medium	aubergines (eggplants)	2 medium
1 small	green pepper, sliced	1 small
1 small	red pepper, sliced	1 small
1-2 tbsp	vegetable oil	1-2 tbsp
1 tbsp	fresh parsley, chopped	1 tbsp
	seasoning to taste	
115g (4 oz)	crumbled soya cheese	1 cup
	black olives, to garnish	

1 Pierce the skins of the aubergines (eggplants) with a fork, put them on a baking sheet tray and bake them at 400°F/200°C (Gas Mark 6) for 30 minutes. Then put the green and red pepper slices on the same sheet and cook for another 15 minutes or until the skins of both the aubergines (eggplants) and peppers are charred.
2 Leave them to cool slightly, then scrape or rub the skins off the peppers. Cut the aubergines (eggplants) in half and use a spoon to scoop out the flesh. Mash the vegetables together, put the mixture into a bowl, add the oil, parsley and season to taste. Mix well before adding the soya cheese. (If you have a blender, you can combine the ingredients in it to make a smoother pâté.)
2 Pile the pâté into a small bowl and chill. Dot the top with black olives just before serving.

Note: This pâté can be made without the cheese, or the cheese can be replaced with dairy cheese or a few spoonfuls of natural (unsweetened) yogurt.

Vegetable Guacamole

2 medium	ripe avocados	2 medium
2 tbsp	lemon juice	2 tbsp
1	clove garlic, peeled and crushed	1
½	stick celery, finely chopped	½
2	radishes, finely chopped	2
½	green pepper, finely chopped	½
1 large	tomato, finely chopped	1 large
½ tsp	chilli powder	½ tsp
¼ tsp	paprika	¼ tsp
	seasoning to taste	
70ml (⅛ pt)	sour (soured) cream	¼ cup

1 Peel and stone (pit) the avocado, then mash the flesh together with the lemon juice. Gradually add in the garlic and vegetables and spices and season to taste. Stir in the cream, making sure it is well blended into the mixture. Chill the guacamole well before serving.

Note: Instead of the cream, try adding a spoonful or two of olive oil. Both versions are tasty served with corn chips. Vegetable Guacamole also makes an unusual and tasty topping for jacket potatoes or try it as a filling for pancakes.

Peanut Butter Dip

115g (4 oz)	peanut butter	2 cups
60-90ml (2-3 fl oz)	hot vegetable stock	¼-⅓ cup
good pinch	mustard powder	good pinch
good pinch	cayenne pepper	good pinch
	seasoning to taste	
2 tbsp	tahini	2 tbsp

1 Dissolve the peanut butter in the hot vegetable stock. Add the mustard and cayenne and season to taste. Stir in the tahini, making sure all the ingredients are thoroughly blended (if the dip is too thick, you might need to add extra hot vegetable stock to achieve the right consistency). Set it aside to cool before serving.

Note: This dip is great with vegetable sticks, especially celery. Adapt it by using different spices and/or herbs. Different nut butters – used alone or in combination – can be prepared in the same way.

Spinach and Tofu Pâté

2 tbsp	vegetable oil	2 tbsp
1 medium	onion, sliced	1 medium
455g (1 lb)	fresh spinach, well washed	1 lb
170g (6 oz)	tofu, drained	¾ cup
1 tbsp	lemon juice	1 tbsp
½-1 tsp	dried marjoram	½-1 tsp
	seasoning to taste	
	garlic salt	
	salted peanuts, chopped, to garnish	

1 Heat the oil in a saucepan and sauté the onion in it for a few minutes until it has softened. Shred the spinach into the pan, stir and continue cooking gently until the spinach wilts.
2 Transfer the mixture to a blender, add the tofu and lemon juice and blend to make a creamy paste. Add the marjoram, seasoning and garlic salt to taste. Spoon the mixture into a small dish and chill it. Serve it with the peanuts sprinkled over the top.

Note: This is an unusual pâté that goes well with warm French bread. Its rich colour makes it particularly attractive and so it is ideal for buffet parties. It can also be made using curd (cottage cheese, mashed) or cream cheese instead of the tofu.

Skordalia

70ml (⅛ pt)	water	¼ cup
4	cloves garlic, peeled and chopped	4
2 medium	potatoes, peeled and cooked	2 medium
115g (4 oz)	blanched almonds	1 cup
70ml (⅛ pt)	white wine vinegar	¼ cup
	seasoning to taste	
200ml (⅓ pt)	olive oil	¾ cup
	parsley and black olives, to garnish	

1 In a blender combine the water, garlic, potato, almonds and wine vinegar and season to taste (the potatoes should still be hot, if possible). Then, very gradually, add the oil, drop by drop, making sure each one is completely absorbed before adding the next. Stop adding it when the oil is no longer being fully absorbed.
2 A mixture that is too dry can be softened by adding a drop of warm water and beating it in well.
3 Chill before serving in a bowl, garnished with the parsley and olives.

Note: This garlic sauce originates from Greece where it is served as an accompaniment to hot vegetables. Other equally tasty versions can be made by omitting the nuts, or replacing the potatoes with breadcrumbs, or using walnuts (English walnuts) instead of almonds.

Curried Lentil Pâté

115g (4 oz)	*dried lentils, soaked overnight*	*½ cup*
30g (1 oz)	*vegetable ghee* or *margarine*	*2½ tbsp*
1 medium	*onion, chopped*	*1 medium*
1 large	*carrot, coarsely grated*	*1 large*
55g (2 oz)	*creamed coconut, grated*	*2 oz*
1 tsp	*curry paste, or to taste*	*1 tsp*
	cucumber slices, to garnish	

1 Put the lentils into fresh water, bring to the boil and continue boiling for 10 minutes. Cover the pan, lower the heat and cook for 45 minutes or until the lentils are soft. Drain them well then either mash or blend them to make a thick purée.
2 In a separate pan, melt the ghee or margarine and sauté the onion in it for a few minutes. Stir in the carrot. Then add the coconut and stir it in until it has completely dissolved. Combine this mixture with the lentil purée, adding enough curry paste to give the pâté a good flavour.
3 Spoon the mixture into a small bowl, smooth the top and chill it well. Decorate it just before serving with a ring of overlapped cucumber slices.

Note: Ghee gives the pâté a better flavour than margarine, so keep a tin in the refrigerator for all Indian dishes. Split lentils could be used instead of whole ones, which reduces the cooking time considerably, or try split or whole dried peas. You might like to use more creamed coconut for a smoother taste or replacing it with soft mild cheese or natural (unsweetened) yogurt.

Nutty Cauliflower Dip

1 tbsp	*vegetable oil*	*1 tbsp*
1 small	*onion, chopped*	*1 small*
1 small	*red pepper, chopped*	*1 small*
½ small	*cauliflower*	*½ small*
good squeeze	*lemon juice*	*good squeeze*
85g (3 oz)	*walnut (English walnut) pieces, finely or coarsely ground*	*⅔ cup*
70ml (⅛ pt)	*sour (soured) cream*	*¼ cup*
2	*free-range eggs, hard-boiled, peeled and mashed*	*2*
½ tsp	*ground nutmeg*	*½ tsp*
	seasoning to taste	
	strips of red pepper, to garnish	
	extra walnut (English walnut) pieces	

1 Heat the oil and sauté the onion and red pepper in it for a few minutes to soften. Meanwhile, break the cauliflower into florets and steam them briefly.
2 Stir together the cooked vegetables, add the lemon juice, ground walnut (English walnut) and the sour cream. Mix in the mashed egg and the nutmeg and season to taste. (If a softer texture is required, stir in more sour cream or some milk.)
3 Transfer the mixture to a small bowl and chill it briefly. Just before serving, garnish it with the pepper and walnut (English walnut) pieces.

Note: This dip tastes good eaten with strips of pumpernickel bread. Try using curd (cottage cheese, mashed) or cream cheese instead of sour cream for a firmer consistency, more like a pâté.

Tahini Pâté with Herbs

140ml (¼ pt)	*tahini*	*⅔ cup*
70ml (⅛ pt)	*hot vegetable stock*	*¼ cup*
1 tbsp	*fresh parsley, chopped*	*1 tbsp*
1 tbsp	*fresh mint, chopped*	*1 tbsp*
dash	*soy sauce*	*dash*
good squeeze	*lemon juice*	*good squeeze*
	seasoning to taste	
55g (2 oz)	*wholemeal (whole wheat) breadcrumbs*	*1 cup*
	sesame seeds, to garnish	
	parsley sprigs, to garnish	

1 Stir the tahini into the hot stock so that it dissolves completely. Add the herbs, soy sauce and lemon juice and season to taste. Stir in the breadcrumbs to thicken the mixture (the amount given is approximate – adjust it as necessary).
2 Spoon the mixture into a dish, smooth the top and sprinkle some sesame seeds over the top. Chill it before serving garnished with the sprigs of parsley.

Note: This pâté can also be thickened with a few spoonfuls of cooked grains, such as oatmeal or bulgar instead of the breadcrumbs. The sesame seeds taste even nicer if they are lightly toasted first.

Sunflower Pâté

140g (5 oz)	sunflower seeds	1 cup
3 tbsp	vegetable oil	3 tbsp
1 small	red pepper, chopped	1 small
1 small	courgette (zucchini), chopped	1 small
good squeeze	lemon juice	good squeeze
½ tsp	mixed dried herbs	½ tsp
	seasoning to taste	
	watercress sprigs, to garnish	

1 Carefully dry roast the sunflower seeds in a heavy bottomed pan or in the oven, shaking them frequently so that they are lightly and evenly browned.

2 Heat the oil and sauté the red pepper for a few minutes. Stir in the courgette (zucchini) and continue cooking until the vegetables are soft.

3 In a blender, combine all the ingredients, except the watercress, adjusting the herbs and seasoning to suit your own taste. Alternatively, grind the seeds and then use a fork to mix them with the other ingredients. Add a drop more oil if necessary.

4 Pile the pâté into a small dish, smooth the top and chill it briefly. Using watercress to garnish the pâté makes an attractive colour contrast.

Note: Any vegetables can be used in this pâté. If liked you can add some breadcrumbs and a few spoonfuls of tahini or nut butter to make a more substantial pâté.

Olive Pâté

115g (4 oz)	black or green olives	1 cup
1 tbsp	vegetable oil	1 tbsp
1 tbsp	lemon juice	1 tbsp
30g (1 oz)	wholemeal (whole wheat) breadcrumbs	½ cup
	lemon twist, to garnish	
	fresh chives, snipped, to garnish	

1 Remove the stones (pits) from the olives then put them into a blender together with the oil and lemon juice and blend until the mixture is smooth. Add enough breadcrumbs to thicken it, then transfer the pâté to a small dish, smooth the top and chill it for a short time. Serve it garnished with the twist of lemon and chives.

Note: This Greek-style pâté goes well with pitta bread. It also makes an unusual but delicious stuffing for vegetables such as peppers and marrow (summer squash) rings.

3
Mousses, Moulds and Savoury Creams

Asparagus Mousse

12	asparagus spears, fresh (cooked) or tinned/canned	12
570ml (1 pt)	vegetable stock	2½ cups
2 tsp	agar agar	2 tsp
170g (6 oz)	curd (cottage cheese, mashed) or Ricotta cheese	¾ cup
pinch	paprika seasoning to taste	pinch

1 Rinse a medium-sized jelly mould in cold water. Arrange the well-drained asparagus spears in the bottom of the mould so that they radiate out from the centre like the spokes of a wheel. Trim as necessary, reserving and finely chopping any extra pieces.
2 Heat the vegetable stock, whisk in the agar agar and continue cooking for a few minutes more, whisking continually. Cool it slightly.
3 Beat the cheese until it is smooth, then add it to the vegetable stock mixture and mix it in well. Add the paprika and season to taste, plus the reserved asparagus.
4 Pour the mixture gently into the mould, taking care not to disturb the asparagus 'spokes'. Leave it to cool completely, then chill it for at least 2 hours or until it has set.
5 To remove the mousse from the mould, dip it quickly into hot water, then invert it over a flat serving plate.

Note: You can use other vegetables instead of the asparagus, of course, though this delicately flavoured vegetable is ideal when you want to make an impressive starter.

Egg and Chive Creams

3	free-range eggs, hard-boiled (hard-cooked), shells removed	3
140ml (¼ pt)	whipping cream soy sauce seasoning to taste	⅔ cup
2 tbsp	fresh chives, snipped	2 tbsp
2 tbsp	walnuts (English walnuts), coarsely chopped watercress sprigs, to garnish	2 tbsp

1 Halve the eggs, remove the yolks and mash them well. Coarsely chop the egg whites.
2 Whip the cream until it holds its shape, then mix in the egg yolk and white, soy sauce and season to taste. Add the chives, making sure that they are evenly distributed throughout the mixture.
3 Divide the mixture between 4 ramekins, top each with the nuts and chill the creams well before serving garnished with the sprigs of watercress.

Note: This is a really easy dish that makes a classy start to a special dinner. Use other fresh herbs if you prefer.

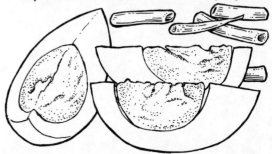

Avocado Nut Mousse

2 large	ripe avocados	2 large
1 tbsp	lemon juice	1 tbsp
30g (1 oz)	margarine	2½ tbsp
30g (1 oz)	wholemeal (whole wheat) flour	¼ cup
200ml (⅓ pt)	vegetable stock	¾ cup
1½ tsp	carrageen	1½ tsp
3 tbsp	cold water	3 tbsp
2 tsp	white wine vinegar	2 tsp
115g (4 oz)	silken tofu, drained seasoning to taste	½ cup
55g (2 oz)	almonds, coarsely chopped	½ cup

1 Peel the avocados and remove the stones (pits). Mash the flesh together with the lemon juice to form a smooth purée.
2 Melt the margarine in a saucepan, sprinkle in the flour and cook it gently for a few minutes. Add the stock gradually to the pan, stirring all the time and cook to make a sauce.
3 Whisk the carrageen into the cold water and add the mixture to the sauce. Bring it to the boil then lower the heat and simmer for a few minutes before setting it aside to cool slightly. Add the puréed avocados and the wine vinegar.
4 Mash the tofu by hand or blend it in a liquidizer or food processor to make a thick, smooth cream. Add this to the avocado mixture and season it generously. Stir in most of the nuts.
5 Rinse a jelly mould with cold water, spoon the mixture into it and leave it to cool. Stir it again to ensure that all the ingredients are well mixed, then chill it for at least 2 hours or until it has set.
6 When you are ready to serve, dip the mould briefly in hot water then unmould onto a flat plate. Decorate the top with the reserved nuts.

Note: Instead of tofu, you can use a soft white cheese such as Ricotta or cottage cheese pushed through a sieve (strainer) and you can replace the vegetable stock with milk. Like agar agar, carrageen is a setting agent derived from seaweed. Though it is ideal for this particular recipe, you could use agar agar instead.

Curried Cottage Cheese Mousse

455g (1 lb)	cottage cheese, strained	2 cups
140ml (¼ pt)	sour (soured) cream	⅔ cup
1 tbsp	lemon juice	1 tbsp
1 tbsp	mild curry paste, or to taste	1 tbsp
1 small	cucumber, thinly sliced	1 small

1 Mash together the cottage cheese and sour cream to make a smooth purée. Add the lemon juice and curry paste to taste.
2 Press the mixture down into 4 ramekins, then decorate the tops with a ring of overlapped slices of the cucumber. Cover the ramekins and chill for at least an hour.

Note: You can use other low-fat soft cheeses instead of the cottage cheese, if liked. This mixture is also delicious as a dip – just add milk to make the consistency more liquid.

Lemon Salad Mould

425ml (¾ pt)	diluted lemon juice	2 cups
2 tsp	agar agar	2 tsp
2 tbsp	raw cane sugar	2 tbsp
1 tbsp	finely grated lemon peel	1 tbsp
1 small	cucumber, thinly sliced	1 small
1 large	stick celery, chopped	1 large
1 large	carrot, diced	1 large
1 large	apple, diced	1 large
85g (3 oz)	walnuts (English walnuts), coarsely chopped watercress sprigs, to garnish	⅔ cup

1 Pour the lemon juice into a saucepan, bring it gently to boiling point, whisk in the agar agar and continue simmering and whisking for 5 minutes. Stir in the sugar and peel, heat the mixture for a minute more, then set it aside to cool slightly.
2 Rinse a medium-sized plain or decorated jelly mould in cold water. Line the base of the mould with the cucumber, overlapping the slices to make a pattern. Add the celery, carrot, apple and walnuts to the thickening lemon jelly and carefully pour it into the mould, taking care not to disturb the cucumber. Leave it to cool, then chill it for at least 2 hours or until it has set.
3 When you are ready to serve, dip the mould briefly in hot water, then turn it out onto a flat dish. Top it with the watercress and serve at once.

Note: This is a particularly refreshing jelly – ideal with salad and French bread for lunch on a hot summer's day. You can adjust the strength of the lemon flavour (and the sweetness) to suit yourself.

Spinach Ramekins

30g (1 oz)	*margarine*	*2½ tbsp*
½	*clove garlic, peeled and crushed*	*½*
½ small	*onion, sliced*	*½ small*
455g (1 lb)	*fresh spinach, well washed*	*1 lb*
1 tbsp	*lemon juice*	*1 tbsp*
115g (4 oz)	*cream cheese*	*½ cup*
¼ tsp	*ground nutmeg*	*¼ tsp*
	seasoning to taste	
30g (1 oz)	*pine nuts, roasted (see note)*	*3 tbsp*

1 Melt the margarine in a saucepan and sauté the garlic and onion in it for 5 minutes. Shred the spinach, shake off the excess water and add it to the pan. Cover and continue cooking for 5 minutes or until the spinach is soft. Drain it well, then either chop it very fine or purée it in a blender.
2 Mix together the lemon juice, cream cheese and nutmeg and season to taste. Combine this with the spinach, either by hand or in the blender.
3 Divide the mixture between 4 ramekins, smooth the top and chill well. Serve with the pine nuts sprinkled over the tops.

Note: To roast the pine nuts, put them into a dry, heavy bottomed pan over a medium heat and cook them for a few minutes, shaking the pan frequently until they begin to colour. Other nuts can be dry roasted in the same way, though the larger nuts will cook through better if they are baked in a 275–300°F/140–150°C (Gas Mark 1–2) oven. Roasted flaked (slivered) almonds also go well with spinach.

Tomato Aspic with Olives

30g (1 oz)	*margarine*	*2½ tbsp*
½ small	*onion, sliced*	*½ small*
2 tbsp	*tomato purée (paste)*	*2 tbsp*
395-g (14-oz)	*tin (can) tomatoes, chopped*	*14-oz*
1 tbsp	*lemon juice*	*1 tbsp*
1 tsp	*vegetarian Worcestershire sauce*	*1 tsp*
1 tsp	*dried tarragon*	*1 tsp*
	seasoning to taste	
2 tsp	*agar agar*	*2 tsp*
1 tbsp	*fresh parsley, chopped*	*1 tbsp*
140ml (¼ pt)	*vegetable stock*	*⅔ cup*
12	*pimiento stuffed green olives, sliced*	*12*
a few	*lettuce leaves, shredded*	*a few*
	mayonnaise (dairy or soya) to serve	

1 Melt the margarine and sauté the onion in it for 5 minutes until it has softened. Stir in the tomato purée, tomatoes, lemon juice, Worcestershire sauce and tarragon and season to taste. Mix them all together well, cook briefly and then blend in a liquidizer or food processor to make a smooth sauce. Return the sauce to the pan and sprinkle in the agar agar, stirring so that it dissolves, and cook it briefly. Stir in the parsley and vegetable stock, then set the sauce aside to cool.
2 Rinse 4 ramekins in cold water, then sprinkle some of the olive slices across the base of each. Carefully pour in the tomato mixture, taking care not to disturb the olives. Leave to one side until they are cold, before chilling for at least 2 hours or until they have set.
3 When you are ready to serve, make a bed of the shredded lettuce on 4 little plates, dip each ramekin briefly in hot water, then unmould the jelly onto the lettuce. Serve with mayonnaise.

Note: Aspic is usually made from meat jelly. Though similar, this version has a more subtle taste. The mayonnaise is a delicious addition, but if you don't like mayonnaise, try pouring a little sour (soured) cream over each portion.

Watercress Mousses

140ml (¼ pt)	*vegetable stock*	*⅔ cup*
1½ tsp	*agar agar*	*1½ tsp*
2 tbsp	*lemon juice*	*2 tbsp*
115g (4 oz)	*garlic and herb-flavoured cream cheese*	*½ cup*
140ml (¼ pt)	*natural (unsweetened) yogurt*	*⅔ cup*
½	*bunch watercress, washed and chopped*	*½*
1 tbsp	*chopped fresh parsley*	*1 tbsp*
	seasoning to taste	
4	*tomatoes, sliced*	*4*
	parsley sprigs, to garnish	

1 Heat the stock gently in a saucepan. Whisk in the agar agar, heat a few minutes more, then add the lemon juice. Set the mixture aside to cool.
2 Mash together the cheese and yogurt. Add the watercress and parsley. Gradually stir in the stock mixture, then season generously.
3 Rinse 4 ramekins in cold water and divide the mixture between them. Leave it to cool before chilling for at least 2 hours or until it has set.
4 Serve the mousses in the ramekins, topped with slices of tomato and the sprigs of parsley.

Note: This recipe is also good made with other cheeses. Try a blue cheese for a stronger tasting mousse or a mild Ricotta or curd cheese (strained cottage cheese) – maybe with spices and nuts added – for a more delicate flavour.

Russian Salad Ring

2	carrots, diced	2
1	stick celery, chopped	1
1 medium	potato, diced	1 medium
170g (6 oz)	peas, fresh or frozen	1 cup
2	gherkins, chopped	2
285ml (½ pt)	vegetable stock	1⅓ cup
2 tsp	agar agar	2 tsp
140ml (¼ pt)	mayonnaise (dairy or soya)	⅔ cup
1 tbsp	lemon juice seasoning to taste mustard and cress, to garnish	1 tbsp

1 Cook the carrot, celery, potato and peas until they are just tender (do not overcook them), then drain them well and stir them together. Add the gherkins.

2 In a saucepan, gently heat the vegetable stock. Whisk in the agar agar and cook it for a few minutes before setting the mixture aside to cool.

3 Stir the mayonnaise, lemon juice and seasoning into the stock, then add the vegetables. Rinse a small ring mould (tube pan) in cold water, then pour in the stock mixture, stirring it to distribute the vegetables evenly. Leave to cool, then chill it for at least 2 hours or until it has set.

4 To release the ring, dip the mould briefly in hot water, then place a flat serving dish over it and turn it upside down. Fill the centre of the mould with mustard and cress and serve at once.

Note: An unusual vegan version of this dish can be made by replacing the mayonnaise with leftover hummus. Stir it in well so that it dissolves and add a little extra stock.

Brie and Green Pepper Creams

114g (4 oz)	Brie cheese, diced	½ cup
55g (2 oz)	Ricotta or low-fat cream cheese	¼ cup
4 tbsp	whipping cream	4 tbsp
2	spring onions (scallions), chopped	2
1 medium	green pepper, chopped	1 medium
1 tbsp	fresh parsley, chopped seasoning to taste soya 'bacon' bits (optional)	1 tbsp

1 Mash the cheeses together by hand or in a liquidizer or food processor. Whip the cream and add it to the cheeses. Stir in the spring onions (scallions), green pepper and parsley and season well.

2 Transfer the mixture to 4 ramekins and chill them briefly. Sprinkle the 'bacon' bits over the tops, if using.

Note: This makes a rather elegant starter when served with fingers of warm wholemeal (whole wheat) toast or rye crackers. It is also a good dish to serve for a buffet.

Carrot Mousses

455g (1 lb)	carrots, peeled and chopped	2½ cups
1 tbsp	fresh chives, snipped, plus extra to garnish	1 tbsp
4 tbsp	single (light) cream	4 tbsp
2 large	free-range eggs, separated	2 extra large
½ tsp	ground cumin	½ tsp
½ tsp	paprika seasoning to taste	½ tsp
30g (1 oz)	margarine	2½ tbsp
55g (2 oz)	wholemeal (whole wheat) breadcrumbs	1 cup

1 Steam or boil the carrots until they are tender, then drain them well and mash them to a thick purée. Drain them again. Stir in the chives, cream, egg yolks and spices and season to taste. Whisk the egg whites until they are stiff and, using a metal spoon, fold them into the mixture.

2 Preheat the oven to 325°F/170°C (Gas Mark 3). Meanwhile, lightly grease 4 ramekins, divide the mixture between them and cover each one with a circle of foil. Stand the dishes in a baking tin (pan) and pour hot water round them until it comes half way up the sides of the ramekins.

3 Bake them in the preheated oven for 20 minutes or until the mousses have set. Meanwhile, melt the margarine and gently fry the breadcrumbs until they are crisp and brown. When the mousses are cooked, sprinkle the breadcrumbs over them and serve while they are still warm, garnished with the extra chives.

Note: Though not strictly a mousse, this dish has a light texture that is very reminiscent of one. This version is not just quick and easy to make, but very inexpensive. For a special occasion version, substitute a fennel bulb for some of the carrot.

Mushroom Paprika Timbale

55g (2 oz)	margarine	¼ cup
1	clove garlic, peeled and crushed	1
455g (1 lb)	mushrooms, chopped	6½ cups
1-2 tsp	ground paprika	1-2 tsp
¼ tsp	ground cayenne pepper	¼ tsp
200ml (⅓ pt)	milk	¾ cup
1 tbsp	lemon juice	1 tbsp
	seasoning to taste	
3 large	free-range eggs, beaten	3 extra large
	fresh parsley, chopped, to garnish	

1 Melt the margarine and sauté the garlic in it for a few minutes. Add the mushrooms and cook them gently until they have softened. Drain them well, then chop them very finely or blend them in a liquidizer or food processor. Combine them with the spices, milk and lemon juice and season to taste. Add the eggs to the mixture.

2 Preheat the oven to 350°F/180°C (Gas Mark 4). Pour the mixture into 4 lightly greased ramekins and stand them in a baking tin (pan), then pour enough boiling water around them to come half way up the ramekins. Bake in the preheated oven for about 45 minutes or until when a knife or skewer is inserted in the middle it comes out clean.

3 Leave them to cool, then sprinkle the parsley over each one to garnish and serve with fingers of pumpernickel bread or wholemeal (whole wheat) rolls.

Note: The word 'timbale' originally referred to a certain kind of dish, though nowadays it is used to describe vegetable purées cooked with milk and eggs to make a sort of savoury custard. You can use other vegetables instead of the mushrooms.

Potted Aubergine Creams

2 medium	aubergines (eggplants)	2 medium
1	clove garlic, peeled and crushed	1
2 tbsp	tahini, or to taste	2 tbsp
1 tbsp	lemon juice	1 tbsp
1 tbsp	olive oil	1 tbsp
30g (1 oz)	sesame seeds, toasted	¼ cup
	seasoning to taste	
	watercress, to garnish	

1 Wash the aubergines, prick them lightly with a fork, then bake them in a 400°F/200°C (Gas Mark 6) oven for 1 hour or until they are soft. Leave them to cool briefly, then cut them open and scoop out as much of the flesh as you can.

2 Mash the flesh and mix in the garlic, tahini, lemon juice and olive oil to make a thick, creamy purée. If preferred, blend them in a liquidizer or food processor. Stir in most of the sesame seeds and season generously.

3 Spoon the cream in to 4 small dishes or ramekins, sprinkle the remaining sesame seeds over the tops and chill. Garnish the creams with the watercress just before serving.

Note: Garlic salt gives a more subtle flavour than fresh garlic and is especially useful when you are serving these creams to guests and are not sure whether or not they like garlic. Instead of tahini you can try stirring in sour (soured) cream.

Egg Mayonnaise Mousse

4	free-range eggs, hard-boiled and peeled	4
2 tsp	agar agar	2 tsp
4 tbsp	water	4 tbsp
140ml (¼ pt)	mayonnaise	⅔ cup
140ml (¼ pt)	natural (unsweetened) yogurt	⅔ cup
½ small	onion, finely chopped	½ small
1 tsp	lemon juice	1 tsp
¼ tsp	Tabasco sauce, or to taste	¼ tsp
	seasoning to taste	
55g (2 oz)	beansprouts	1 cup
	fresh chives, snipped, to garnish	

1 Chop the eggs and set them aside.

2 Whisk the agar agar into the water in a saucepan, then bring it to a gentle boil, stirring continually. Combine the mayonnaise and yogurt, then add the agar agar mixture to it and stir them together well. Add the lemon juice and Tabasco and season to taste.

3 When the mixture begins to set, stir in the eggs and beansprouts. Rinse a small jelly mould in cold water, pour the mixture into it and leave it to cool, then chill it for at least 2 hours or until it has set.

4 To serve, dip the mould briefly in hot water, then cover it with a flat serving dish and turn it upside down. Sprinkle the chives over the mousse just before serving.

Note: This is a soft, creamy mousse that is perfect for special meals. To make it look as good as it tastes, use a decorative mould if you have or can borrow one.

Spicy Cauliflower Mousses

2 tbsp	*vegetable oil*	*2 tbsp*
1 medium	*onion, sliced*	*1 medium*
¼ tsp	*ground turmeric*	*¼ tsp*
¼ tsp	*ground coriander*	*¼ tsp*
¼ tsp	*mustard powder*	*¼ tsp*
1 medium	*cauliflower, broken into florets*	*1 medium*
140ml (¼ pt)	*cold water*	*⅔ cup*
200ml (⅓ pt)	*thick, set, natural (unsweetened) yogurt*	*¾ cup*
1	*free-range egg white*	*1*
	seasoning to taste	
1 small	*packet crisps (potato chips), lightly crushed*	*1 small*

1 Heat the oil in a saucepan and gently sauté the onion in it for 5 minutes until it has softened. Add the spices, stirring, and cook a few minutes more. Add the cauliflower, cover them with the water (use a little more if necessary), cover the pan and cook until the cauliflower is soft. Leave it to cool for a few minutes before draining it. Mash it by hand or blend it in a liquidizer or food processor to make a purée.
2 Combine the purée with the yogurt. Whisk the egg white until it is stiff and fold it gently into the cauliflower and yogurt mixture, using a metal spoon, and season well. Divide it between 4 ramekins, smooth the tops and chill them briefly. Serve the mousses with the crisps (potato chips) sprinkled over them.

Note: A mousse for serving in the winter as it is spicy and satisfying. Ring the changes by using sour (soured) cream or a low-fat cream cheese instead of the yogurt.

Tofu and Leek Mousse

1 medium	*leek, cleaned and sliced*	*1 medium*
4 tbsp	*vegetable stock*	*4 tbsp*
2 tsp	*carrageen*	*2 tsp*
1 tbsp	*fresh parsley, chopped*	*1 tbsp*
1 tbsp	*fresh chives, snipped*	*1 tbsp*
4	*spring onions (scallions), chopped*	*4*
good squeeze	*lemon juice*	*good squeeze*
225g (8 oz)	*silken tofu*	*1 cup*
¼ tsp	*cayenne pepper*	*¼ tsp*
	seasoning to taste	
½ small	*red pepper, finely chopped, to garnish*	*½ small*

1 Steam the leek until it is just tender, then drain it well.
2 In a saucepan, heat the vegetable stock and whisk in the carrageen, bring it to the boil and cook for 3 minutes, then leave it to cool.
3 Chop the leek as fine as possible, then add to the stock mixture with the herbs, spring onions (scallions) and lemon juice. Drain the tofu, mash or blend it to a purée, add it to the other ingredients with the cayenne and season to taste.
4 Spoon the mixture into 4 ramekins and chill them for at least 2 hours or until the mousses have set. Top them with the red pepper for a lovely splash of colour.

Note: You can use cream cheese or a low-fat cheese, yogurt or sour (soured) cream instead of the tofu if you prefer. Instead of adding the red pepper as a garnish at the end, try steaming it with the leek and mixing it in with the other ingredients, then top each ramekin with some chopped, roasted hazelnuts.

Cucumber Cumin Ring

425ml (¾ pt)	*vegetable stock*	*2 cups*
2 tsp	*agar agar*	*2 tsp*
115g (4 oz)	*Ricotta cheese*	*½ cup*
70ml (⅛ pt)	*natural (unsweetened) yogurt*	*½ cup*
1 large	*cucumber, grated (shredded)*	*1 large*
½ tsp	*ground cumin, or to taste*	*½ tsp*
	seasoning to taste	

1 Bring the stock to a gentle boil, then whisk in the agar agar and cook it briefly. Blend the Ricotta and yogurt together, drain the cucumber very well and stir it in together with the cumin, and season to taste. Add this mixture to the stock mixture and combine them well.
2 Rinse a small ring mould (tube pan) with cold water, then pour the mixture into it. Leave it to cool, then chill it for at least 2 hours or until it has set.
3 When you are ready to serve the ring, dip the mould into hot water, hold a flat serving plate over the top, then invert them together.

Note: For special occasions, try filling the ring with a salad of fresh fruit and nuts.

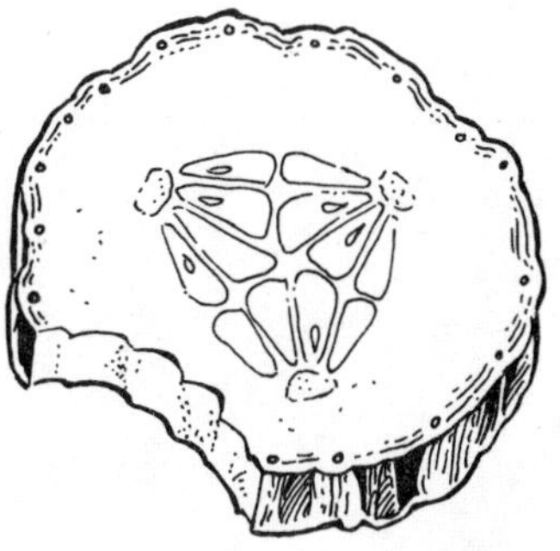

Layered Vegetable Terrine

First layer

2 tbsp	vegetable oil	2 tbsp
1	clove garlic, peeled and crushed	1
½ small	onion, sliced	½ small
680g (1½ lb)	fresh spinach, well washed	1½ lb
55g (2 oz)	wholemeal (whole wheat) breadcrumbs	1 cup
2	free-range eggs	2
3 tbsp	single (light) cream	3 tbsp
¼ tsp	ground nutmeg	¼ tsp
	seasoning to taste	

Second layer

455g (1 lb)	carrots, sliced	2½ cups
1 tbsp	lemon juice	1 tbsp
1	free-range egg	1

Third layer

1 medium	cauliflower, broken into florets	1 medium
285ml (½ pt)	thick White Sauce (see page 156)	1⅓ cups
1	free-range egg	1
1 large	red pepper, sliced	1 large
115g (4 oz)	walnut (English walnut) pieces, coarsely chopped	¾ cup

1 Make the first layer. Heat the oil and sauté the garlic and onion in it for a few minutes. Coarsely shred the spinach and add it to the pan. Cover the pan and cook for 5 minutes or until the spinach is soft. Drain it well, then chop it and blend it with the breadcrumbs, eggs, cream and nutmeg and season to taste. Set the mixture aside.

2 Now make the second layer. Steam the carrots until they are soft, drain them well, mash them to a purée, then mix in the lemon juice and egg. Set the mixture aside.

3 Now make the third layer. Steam the cauliflower and, when it is tender, drain it thoroughly. Mash it well and mix in the White Sauce and egg.

4 Drop the pepper slices into a pan of boiling water and cook them literally for a few minutes to soften them, then drain them.

5 Preheat the oven to 350°F/180°C (Gas Mark 4).

6 Line a small loaf tin (pan) with greased greaseproof (waxed) paper. Spread a layer of the spinach mixture across the base, top it with some of the pepper strips and some of the chopped walnuts. Next, spread a layer of the carrot mixture and top it with pepper strips and walnuts as before. Then spread a layer of the cauliflower mixture and top it with pepper and walnuts as before. Repeat the layers using up the remaining ingredients.

7 Cover the tin (pan) with greaseproof (waxed) paper or foil. Stand it in a baking tin (pan) and pour hot water around it until it comes half way up the sides of the loaf tin (pan). Bake in the preheated oven for about an hour or until the terrine is firm. Leave it to cool completely and, if possible, chill it overnight. Unmould the terrine very carefully from the tin and serve it cut in slices.

Note: Layered terrines are always very attractive to look at and so make an inviting start to a meal or centrepiece at a buffet. They can be made using a variety of vegetable purées, but the important thing is to have a good contrast of colours. Experiment with ideas of your own, remembering to add an egg to each layer to help it set firm and to think about the combination of flavours, too.

4
Vegetable Dishes

Root Vegetable Bake

1 medium	parsnip, peeled and diced	1 medium
1 medium	carrot, peeled and diced	1 medium
1 medium	swede (rutabaga), peeled and diced	1 medium
1 medium	turnip, peeled and diced	1 medium
2 large	free-range eggs	2 large
285ml (½ pt)	milk	1⅓ cups
115g (4 oz)	wholemeal (whole wheat) breadcrumbs	2 cups
good pinch	ground nutmeg	good pinch
2 tbsp	fresh parsley, chopped, plus extra to garnish seasoning to taste	2 tbsp
55g (2 oz)	Double Gloucester cheese, grated	½ cup

1 Very lightly steam the vegetables until they just begin to soften, then drain them well.
2 Meanwhile, preheat the oven to 350°F/180°C (Gas Mark 4).
3 Stir together all the ingredients except the cheese and extra parsley and pour the mixture into a greased, shallow ovenproof dish and smooth the top. Sprinkle the cheese evenly over the top. Stand the dish in a roasting tin half filled with hot water. Bake in the preheated oven for 1 hour or until the mixture has set. Serve it garnished with the extra parsley.

Note: You could use other cheese instead of the Double Gloucester – Gruyère or Red Leicester, for example. A lighter summer vegetable bake can be made in the same way, but instead of the root vegetables use spinach, cauliflower, green beans, peppers or whatever you happen to have.

Sweet and Sour Cabbage

285ml (½ pt)	Sweet and Sour Sauce (see page 157)	1⅓ cups
2 tbsp	vegetable oil	2 tbsp
455g (1 lb)	white cabbage, shredded	4 cups
225g (8 oz)	red cabbage, shredded	2 cups
4	free-range eggs, hard-boiled (hard-cooked), peeled	4

1 Make the Sweet and Sour Sauce as given in the recipe.
2 Heat the oil and stir in the white and red cabbage, then cover the pan and simmer for 2 minutes. Add the Sweet and Sour Sauce, stir again and continue cooking for 3 to 5 minutes until the cabbage is just beginning to soften (it should still be crisp) and the sauce has thickened.
3 Serve it topped with the eggs, either chopped or cut into quarters.

Note: Other vegetables can be cooked in much the same way. Instead of adding egg for protein, you can stir in a handful of nuts or some cooked pulses (legumes) such as kidney beans or chick peas (garbanzos).

'Bacon'-stuffed Aubergines

2 medium	aubergines (eggplants)	2 medium
	sea salt, as required	
2 tbsp	vegetable oil	2 tbsp
1 medium	onion, sliced	1 medium
1 medium	green pepper, sliced	1 medium
4 tbsp	bulgar, cooked	4 tbsp
2 tbsp	tomato purée (paste)	2 tbsp
1 tbsp	lemon juice	1 tbsp
4 tbsp	soya 'bacon' bits	4 tbsp
	seasoning to taste	
1×recipe	Tomato Sauce (see page 156), to serve	1×recipe

1 Slice the aubergines (eggplants) in half lengthways, then scoop out the flesh leaving 4 shells. Chop the flesh and put it into a bowl. Sprinkle both the flesh and the shells lightly with salt and leave for 30 minutes until the bitter juices have oozed out, then rinse with cold water and drain well.
2 Preheat the oven to 400°F/200°C (Gas Mark 6).
3 Heat the oil and sauté the onion and green pepper in it for 5 minutes. Add the prepared aubergine (eggplant) flesh and continue cooking for 5 minutes more or until all the vegetables are cooked. Off the heat stir in the bulgar, tomato purée, lemon juice and soya 'bacon' bits and season to taste.
4 Arrange the aubergine (eggplant) shells side by side in a small, shallow ovenproof dish and divide the prepared mixture between them. Pour 2 or 3 tablespoons of water into the dish around the shells, then cover the dish with its lid or foil and bake them in the preheated oven for 30 minutes or until they are cooked.
5 Meanwhile, heat the tomato sauce. Serve 1 shell to each person with hot sauce poured over the top.

Note: Bulgar is excellent with aubergine (eggplant), and it can be cooked very quickly (or simply soaked in hot water). However, you can also use any other leftover cooked grains in this recipe (rice, for instance, is also good) or wholemeal (whole wheat) breadcrumbs. The soya 'bacon' bits add texture and a taste contrast, but if you prefer, use fried and then crumbled strips of tempeh.

Deep-fried Mushrooms with Yogurt Mint Sauce

Sauce

285ml (½ pt)	natural (unsweetened) yogurt	1⅓ cups
1 tbsp	fresh mint, chopped	1 tbsp
	seasoning to taste	

Batter

225g (8 oz)	button mushrooms	4 cups
55g (2 oz)	wholemeal (whole wheat) flour	½ cup
good pinch	sea salt	good pinch
1 tbsp	vegetable oil	1 tbsp
4 tbsp	warm water	4 tbsp
1	free-range egg white	1
	vegetable oil, for frying	

1 Prepare the sauce in advance so that the flavours have time to mingle. To the yogurt add the mint and season to taste, then chill it until you are ready to serve.
2 Gently wipe the mushrooms with a damp cloth then set them aside.
3 Now make the batter. Sift together the flour and salt, then gradually add the oil and water and mix them all together well. Beat the egg white until it is stiff and, using a metal spoon, fold it into the first mixture.
4 Pour enough oil into a small pan to be able to deep fry the mushrooms, and heat it gently. When it is very hot, coat the mushrooms with the batter, then drop them into the oil a few at a time. Cook them for 5 minutes or until they are crisp and golden brown. Drain them on a paper towel and keep them hot while you cook the remaining mushrooms in the same way.
5 Serve small portions of the mushrooms on individual plates and hand the sauce around at the table to either pour over them or dip into.

Note: Other vegetables can be used instead of mushrooms. Try large florets of cauliflower or broccoli, for example, or carrot and celery (if liked, steam them briefly first, then dry them well before dipping them into the batter mix).

Leek and Pecan Loaf

2 medium	leeks, trimmed and cleaned	2 medium
170g (6 oz)	pecan nuts, finely chopped	1½ cups
2 tbsp	fresh parsley, chopped	2 tbsp
1 large	free-range egg, lightly beaten	1 extra large
½ tsp	dried sage	½ tsp
½ tsp	dried tarragon	½ tsp
	seasoning to taste	
6 tbsp	milk, to bind	6 tbsp

1 Preheat the oven to 350°F/180°C (Gas Mark 4).
2 Lightly steam the leeks until they are just tender, then drain them well and chop them coarsely.
3 Mix together the leeks, nuts, parsley, egg and herbs and seasoning. Stir in just enough of the milk to moisten the other ingredients and bind them into a thick paste.
4 Spoon the mixture into a greased, small loaf tin (pan) and smooth the top. Stand the tin in a roasting tin (pan) half filled with hot water and bake in the preheated oven for about an hour or until it has just set.

Note: Turn this into a delicious snack meal by serving with a green salad and warm French bread or wholemeal baps. Substitute other nuts if you prefer – walnuts are the closest to pecans in flavour, though brazils have a creamier texture.

Creamed Spinach with Oat Crumble

30g (1 oz)	margarine	2½ tbsp
4	spring onions (scallions), chopped	4
1.15 k (2 lb)	fresh spinach, well washed and trimmed	2 lb
115g (4 oz)	curd (cottage cheese, mashed) or *Ricotta* cheese	½ cup
½ tsp	ground nutmeg seasoning to taste	½ tsp

Crumble

85g (3 oz)	rolled oats	¾ cup
55g (2 oz)	margarine	¼ cup
55g (2 oz)	Cheddar cheese, grated	½ cup
2 tbsp	sesame seeds	2 tbsp

1 Melt the margarine and gently sauté the onion in it for a few minutes. Add the drained spinach, stir, then cover the pan and cook the spinach gently for 10 minutes. Drain and chop the spinach, then return it to the pan, together with the cheese and stir until it melts to make a creamy sauce. Flavour it with the nutmeg and season to taste. Pile the mixture into 4 ramekins.
2 Preheat the oven to 400°F/200°C (Gas Mark 6).
3 Now make the crumble. Put the oats in a bowl and use your fingertips to rub (cut) the margarine into the oats so that everything is well mixed. Stir in the cheese, add the sesame seeds and season it well. Sprinkle the mixture over the spinach and bake in the preheated oven for about 20 minutes or until the top is crisp and golden brown.

Note: The crumble topping can also be made with flour instead of the oats. As an alternative to cheese, try mixing crumbled tofu in with the spinach.

Carrot Curry

30g (1 oz)	vegetable ghee	2½ tbsp
2	cloves garlic, peeled and crushed	2
1 tsp	ground turmeric	1 tsp
1 tsp	ground paprika	1 tsp
½ tsp	ground ginger	½ tsp
455g (1 lb)	carrots, scrubbed and chopped	2½ cups

2 tbsp	lemon juice	2 tbsp
1 tsp	garam masala	1 tsp
55g (2 oz)	cashew nut pieces	½ cup

1 Melt the ghee and fry the garlic in it for a few minutes, then add the spices and cook for a few more minutes.
2 Stir in the carrot, making sure that the pieces are coated with the spices. Add the lemon juice, cover the pan and simmer the carrot for 5 minutes or until they are just tender (if you need to cook them a little longer, take care that they do not burn, adding a little water if necessary).
3 Sprinkle the garam masala and then the nuts over the curry and serve at once.

Note: If you have no ghee, use vegetable oil instead. Curry powder can be used instead of the individual spices. A few spoonfuls of natural (unsweetened) yogurt added shortly before serving make the curry creamier. Serve it in small dishes with Indian breads such as parathas or poppadoms as accompaniments.

Peppers with Fruit Stuffing

2 medium	red peppers	2 medium
2 medium	green peppers	2 medium

Filling

1 tbsp	vegetable oil	1 tbsp
½ small	onion, sliced	½ small
1 oz (30g)	sultanas (golden seedless raisins)	2 tbsp
1 oz (30g)	prunes, stoned (pitted) and chopped	2 tbsp
1 small	apple, chopped	1 small
55g (2 oz)	almonds, chopped	½ cup
1 tbsp	lemon juice	1 tbsp
4 tbsp	brown rice, cooked	4 tbsp
1-2 tsp	ground mixed spices seasoning to taste	1-2 tsp

1 Carefully slice off the stalks at the top of the peppers (reserving them), then spoon out the seeds. Put the peppers under a hot grill, turning them often, until their skins blister. Let them cool briefly then rub off the skins. Stand the peppers upright in a small, ovenproof dish.
2 Preheat the oven to 350°F/180°C (Gas Mark 4).
3 Now make the filling. Heat the oil and sauté the onion until it has softened. Then stir in all the remaining ingredients, making sure that they are well mixed together. Divide the filling between the peppers, replace the tops and bake them in the preheated oven for 40 minutes.

Note: Removing the skins in this way makes the peppers softer, but doing so does require more time and effort. If you are rushed, boil them briefly instead (to soften the skins) then drain them well before stuffing them.

Individual Courgettes Parmesan

4 tbsp	vegetable oil	4 tbsp
4 medium	courgettes (zucchini), sliced	4 medium
85g (3 oz)	wholemeal (whole wheat) breadcrumbs	1½ cups
285ml (½ pt)	Tomato Sauce (see page 156)	1⅓ cup
1 tbsp	fresh basil, chopped	1 tbsp
85g (3 oz)	Parmesan cheese, grated, plus extra for sprinkling	¾ cup
170g (6 oz)	Mozzarella cheese, thinly sliced	6 oz
2	free-range eggs, hard-boiled (hard-cooked), peeled and sliced seasoning to taste	2

1 Preheat the oven to 375°F/190°C (Gas Mark 5).
2 Heat half the oil and gently sauté the courgette (zucchini) slices until they have just softened, turning them so that they colour evenly.
3 In a separate pan, heat the remaining oil and gently fry the breadcrumbs until they are crisp.
4 In 4 lightly greased, small, ramekins, arrange layers of half the courgette slices, Tomato Sauce, basil, Parmesan, Mozzarella and egg, seasoning as you go. Repeat the layers then cover the top with the remaining Tomato Sauce (if necessary make up extra). Finally, sprinkle the fried breadcrumbs and a little extra Parmesan cheese over the top.
5 Bake in the preheated oven for about 20 minutes or until it is hot and bubbling.

Note: Other vegetables can be used in this recipe. Aubergine (eggplant) is a traditional alternative, but why not try peppers? You can omit the eggs if you like, maybe replacing them with a sprinkling of walnuts (English walnuts).

Tahini Vegetable Crumble

2 medium	leeks, cleaned and trimmed	2 medium
2 medium	carrots, scrubbed and sliced	2 medium
55g (2 oz)	peas, fresh or frozen	⅓ cup
2 tbsp	vegetable oil	2 tbsp
115g (4 oz)	mushrooms, thickly sliced	2 cups
1 tbsp	wholemeal (whole wheat) flour	1 tbsp
200ml (⅓ pt)	vegetable stock	¾ cup
3 tbsp	tahini, or to taste	3 tbsp
1 tsp	dried parsley	1 tsp

Crumble

30g (1 oz)	margarine	2½ tbsp
55g (2 oz)	wholemeal (whole wheat) breadcrumbs	1 cup
55g (2 oz)	sunflower seeds seasoning to taste	⅓ cup

1 Cut the leeks into chunks and steam them for 5 minutes. Add the carrots and continue cooking for 5 to 10 minutes or until the vegetables are just tender. Cook the peas.
2 Heat half the oil and gently fry the mushrooms for just a few minutes, turning them so that they are evenly coloured.
3 Preheat the oven to 350°F/180°C (Gas Mark 4).
4 Heat the remaining oil in another pan, add the flour and cook it briefly, then gradually add the stock, stirring continually until the sauce thickens. Stir in enough tahini to give the sauce a rich flavour, then add the parsley. Gently combine the sauce with the vegetables and pile the mixture into a small ovenproof dish.
5 Now make the crumble. Melt the margarine and mix it with the breadcrumbs. Stir in the sunflower seeds and season generously. Sprinkle the mixture over the vegetables.
6 Bake it in the preheated oven for 10 minutes to heat it through.

Note: As a change from tahini, try dissolving smooth peanut butter into the sauce to make a lovely nutty vegetable crumble. You can also, of course, make a cheese sauce to mix the vegetables into.

Quick Cheesy Fennel

4 small	fennel bulbs	4 small
170g (6 oz)	Gruyère cheese, grated	1½ cups
2 small	packets crisps (potato chips), lightly crushed seasoning to taste watercress sprigs, to garnish	2 small

1 Preheat the oven to 375°F/190°C (Gas Mark 5).
2 Trim the fennel bulbs, then cut them in half lengthways and arrange them in an ovenproof dish. Bake in the preheated oven for about 15 minutes or until they have just softened.
3 Top each one with some of the cheese and crisps (potato chips) and season to taste, then either return them to the oven for 5 minutes or put them under a hot grill.
4 Serve them at once, garnished with the watercress.

Note: Fennels can also be steamed, but baking them in the oven tends to result in them retaining their flavour better. Served this way they are delicious at the start of a meal.

Autumn Stir-fry with Egg Strips

2 tbsp	vegetable oil	2 tbsp
1	clove garlic, peeled and crushed	1
2 small	onions, peeled and quartered	2 small
2 small	carrots, scrubbed and sliced (see below)	2 small
1 medium	marrow (summer squash) soy sauce to taste seasoning to taste	1 medium
½ bunch	watercress, trimmed and cleaned	½ bunch
30g (1 oz)	margarine	2½ tbsp
3	free-range eggs	3

1 The first secret of a good stir-fry is to have all the ingredients ready before you start cooking. Carrots look especially attractive, if they are sliced at an angle. To prepare the marrow, peel and de-seed it, cut into thick rings, then cut these into even-sized cubes.

2 The second is to make sure that the oil is very hot so that the vegetable juices are sealed in. As each vegetable will take a different length of time to cook, and as this will also depend on the size you have cut it to, you will need to add them to the pan carefully.

3 Start by heating the oil and cooking the garlic briefly in it so that it flavours the oil. Add the onion and carrot, cooking them gently and stirring continually for a few minutes. Add the marrow and continue stirring. Flavour the vegetables with soy sauce and seasoning to taste, then stir in the watercress and cook for 1 minute.

4 The omelette is best cooked at the same time as the vegetables. Melt the margarine. Beat the eggs together with a few spoonfuls of water and season the mixture to taste. Pour this into the pan and continue cooking until the egg has set firm. Roll up the omelette and use a sharp knife to cut across the roll to form thin strips. Use these to decorate the vegetables and serve at once.

Note: If you have no one to help you, cook the omelette *before* you start cooking the vegetables, then keep it warm on a covered plate over a pan of boiling water.

For a different flavour, sprinkle nuts over your stir-fried vegetables or add tofu cubes to the pan as its soft, creamy texture goes well with the crisp vegetables.

Grilled Aubergine and Mozzarella

1 large	aubergine (eggplant)	1 large
2 tbsp	vegetable oil seasoning to taste	2 tbsp
225g (8 oz)	Mozzarella cheese, thinly sliced	8 oz
4 medium	tomatoes, quartered fresh mint sprigs, to garnish French bread, to serve	4 medium

1 Cut the aubergine (eggplant) lengthways into 8 thin slices. Sprinkle salt over them and leave them for 30 minutes until the bitter juices have oozed out, then rinse them and drain them well. Arrange them on a baking sheet and brush them with some of the oil. Grill them for about 10 minutes, turning them over carefully half way through cooking and brush the second side with oil. Season them well.

2 Top each one with a slice of the Mozzarella and put them back under the grill for a few minutes more or until the cheese has melted.

3 Decorate them with the tomato wedges and sprigs of mint. Serve them with French bread (the bread can also be sliced lengthways and the aubergine (eggplant) slices placed on top of it).

Note: If liked, the tomatoes can be sliced, arranged on top of the melted cheese and put back under the grill for a further minute. Try, too, toasting the French bread before topping it with the aubergine (eggplant) slices.

Tofu Creole

3 tbsp	vegetable oil	3 tbsp
2 medium	onions, sliced	2 medium
2	sticks celery, chopped	2
1 medium	red pepper, sliced	1 medium
1 medium	green pepper, sliced	1 medium
225g (8 oz)	tomatoes, chopped	1½ cups
1 tsp	dried basil	1 tsp
½ tsp	paprika seasoning to taste Tabasco sauce to taste	½ tsp
285g (10 oz)	smoked tofu, crumbled	1¼ cups

1 Heat the oil and sauté the onions, celery and peppers in it for 5 minutes, stirring frequently, then cover the pan and simmer them for 10 minutes or until they are just tender. Add the tomatoes, basil, paprika, seasoning and Tabasco to taste. Stir in the tofu and continue cooking just long enough to heat it through, then serve at once.

Note: To make this a more filling snack, stir a few spoonfuls of cooked rice in with the tofu or serve it with squares of home-made corn bread.

Tomatoes with Pesto Sauce

4	beefsteak (extra large) tomatoes	4
½ oz	wholemeal (whole wheat) breadcrumbs	¼ cup
Pesto		
1-2	cloves garlic, peeled and crushed (minced)	1-2
2 tbsp	pine nuts	2 tbsp
30g (1 oz)	Parmesan cheese, grated	¼ cup
2 tbsp	fresh basil, chopped	2 tbsp
4 tbsp	vegetable oil	4 tbsp
	seasoning to taste	
	crisp lettuce, shredded, to serve	

1 Cut a slice off the top of each tomato and scoop out the flesh. Stand the shells upside down on a plate to drain. Drain the flesh, chop it, and mix it with the breadcrumbs.

2 Now make the pesto sauce. Put the garlic, pine nuts, Parmesan and basil into a blender and process until they are well mixed together. Then gradually add enough of the oil, a spoonful at a time, to make a thick smooth sauce. Stir the tomato and breadcrumb mixture into the pesto sauce, season to taste, then spoon the mixture back into the tomato shells. Serve them nestling on a bed of the shredded lettuce.

Note: Pesto is so useful that it is a good idea to make extra and keep it in the refrigerator, where it should stay fresh for weeks, ready to be added to soups or stews, or stirred into cooked pasta.

Kohlrabi Polonaise

455g (1 lb)	kohlrabi, washed and peeled	1 lb
55g (2 oz)	margarine	¼ cup
	seasoning to taste	
2	free-range eggs, hard-boiled, peeled	2
55g (2 oz)	wholemeal (whole wheat) breadcrumbs	1 cup
285ml (½ pt)	hot White Sauce (see page 156)	1⅓ cups
1-2 tbsp	fresh parsley, chopped	1-2 tbsp

1 Halve the kohlrabi and steam them until they are just tender, then drain them well and chop them into dice. Melt half the margarine and fry the kohlrabi briefly in it, then put the kohlrabi into a shallow, heatproof dish, season well and keep it warm.

2 Rub the egg yolks through a sieve (strainer) and chop up the whites. Fry the breadcrumbs in the remaining margarine until they are crisp and golden brown. Pour the White Sauce over the kohlrabi and sprinkle the egg yolks and white over the top, making patterns. Sprinkle the fried breadcrumbs and the parsley over the top, and serve at once.

Note: It is more usual to serve cauliflower in this way, but kohlrabi makes an unusual alternative. It is especially good as a starter for a winter dinner party.

Potted Mushrooms

55g (2 oz)	margarine	¼ cup
455g (1 lb)	mushrooms, chopped	8 cups
	seasoning to taste	
1 tsp	fresh parsley, chopped	1 tsp
1 tsp	fresh marjoram, chopped	1 tsp
	seasoning to taste	
	wholemeal (whole wheat) toast, to serve	

1 Melt half the margarine, add the mushrooms and herbs, cover and cook them gently for 10 minutes, shaking the pan now and again so that the mushrooms do not stick.

2 Using a slotted spoon, lift the mushrooms from the pan and set them aside. Boil the liquid in the pan until it has reduced to only a spoonful or two, then return the mushrooms and season them generously. Divide them between 4 small ramekins, and press the mixture down evenly.

3 Melt the remaining margarine, pour this over the top of the mushrooms, leave them to cool, then chill them well. Serve the pots with warm toast.

Note: This is a traditional way of preparing potted mushrooms, though the original recipes usually recommend butter instead of margarine. It makes an original starter for a summer dinner party.

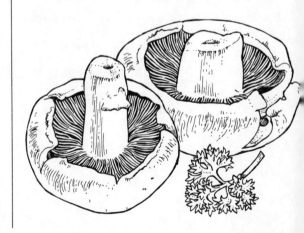

Cucumber Ratatouille with Chick Peas

4 tbsp	vegetable oil	4 tbsp
1	clove garlic, peeled and crushed	1
2 small	onions, peeled and chopped	2 small
395-g (14-oz)	can tomatoes, chopped	14-oz
1 medium	cucumber, diced	1 medium
1 medium	green pepper, diced	1 medium
1 small	aubergine (eggplant), diced	1 small
	seasoning to taste	
225g (8 oz)	cooked or canned chick peas (garbanzos), drained (see page 9)	8 oz
	fresh parsley, chopped, to garnish	

1 Heat the oil, add the garlic and onion and cook them gently in it for 5 minutes. Stir in the remaining vegetables, cover the pan and simmer them for about 20 minutes or until they are tender. Season generously.
2 Add the chick peas (garbanzos) and cook just long enough to heat them through. Serve the dish with a generous sprinkling of parsley over the top.

Note: Aubergine (eggplant) can be bitter, though in a dish where it is mixed with a number of other flavours this is rarely a problem. If, however, you prefer to be sure, sprinkle the cubed flesh with salt and leave it for 30 minutes for the bitter juices to ooze out, then rinse and drain it before cooking. Instead of chick peas (garbanzos), try topping the ratatouille with grated (shredded) cheese just before serving. Soya 'bacon' bits also go well with this dish.

Tempeh and Vegetable Stir-fry

3 tbsp	vegetable oil	3 tbsp
½ tsp	ground ginger	½ tsp
½ small	white cabbage, shredded	½ small
2	sticks celery, sliced diagonally	2
1 medium	carrot, sliced diagonally	1 medium
55g (2 oz)	mange-tout (snow peas), trimmed	2 oz
115g (4 oz)	beansprouts	2 cups
225g (8 oz)	tempeh, drained	1 cup
	rice cakes, to serve	

1 Prepare all the vegetables before you start.
2 Heat 2 tablespoons of the oil and cook the ginger for a minute. Add the cabbage and cook it briefly, stirring continually, then add the celery and carrot and continue cooking in the same way for a few minutes more. Add the mange-tout (snow peas), cook them for 3 minutes, then stir in the beansprouts and cook them just long enough to heat them through.
3 Meanwhile, cook the tempeh, first slicing it into thin domino rectangular shapes. Heat the remaining oil and fry the tempeh shapes until they are crisp and golden brown. Drain them well before stirring them into the stir-fried vegetables. Serve at once, accompanied by rice cakes.

Note: Fresh ginger, peeled and finely grated (shredded), can be used instead of the ground variety – the flavour will be much richer. Use 1 teaspoon or to taste.

Tempeh originates from Indonesia and is made by incubating cooked beans or grains to make a curd-like food that is high in protein, essential amino acids and fibre. It has a unique and rather strong flavour. If you cannot find it in the shops or do not like it, use smoked tofu instead and omit the ginger.

5
Ways with Potatoes

Jacket Potatoes with Various Fillings

4 medium	potatoes, scrubbed	4 medium
	vegetable oil	

1 Preheat the oven to 400°F/200°C (Gas Mark 6).
2 Try to choose potatoes that are the same size as each other, well shaped and free from blemishes. Pat them dry and then brush them lightly with oil. Prick them well with a fork, then put them directly onto the bars of the oven shelves. Bake them in the preheated oven for 1-1½ hours. To test if they are cooked, press gently (protect your fingers with a cloth). Cut a large cross in each one and gently split apart.

Mushroom, Sweetcorn and 'Bacon' Filling

85g (3 oz)	sweetcorn, fresh or frozen	½ cup
2 tbsp	vegetable oil	2 tbsp
1 small	onion, sliced	1 small
115g (4 oz)	mushrooms, chopped	2 cups
	soya 'bacon' bits to taste	
	fresh parsley, chopped, to garnish	

1 Cook the sweetcorn in boiling water or use leftover sweetcorn, in which case, just warm it through.
2 Heat the oil and sauté the onion in it for a few minutes. Add the mushrooms, stir and cook them gently for 5 more minutes.
3 Mix together the drained sweetcorn, onion and mushrooms. Spoon in a generous amount of soya 'bacon' bits to taste, then spoon some of the mixture into each of the potatoes and top with a sprinkling of the parsley.

Creamy Green Filling

1 tbsp	fresh chives, snipped	1 tbsp
1 tbsp	fresh parsley, chopped	1 tbsp
½ bunch	watercress, trimmed and chopped	½ bunch
30g (1 oz)	butter or margarine	2½ tbsp
140ml (¼ pt)	fromage frais	⅔ cup
	seasoning to taste	
55g (2 oz)	flaked (slivered) almonds	½ cup

1 When the potatoes are cooked, cut a cross in the top of each one and carefully scoop out most of the flesh. In a bowl, mash this together with the chives, parsley, watercress and butter or margarine. Stir in the fromage frais, season to taste, then spoon the soft, creamy mixture back into the potato shells. Return them to the oven for 5 to 10 minutes, to heat them through.
2 Top each one with some flaked almonds and serve at once.

Curried Egg Filling

2 tbsp	vegetable oil	2 tbsp
1 small	onion, chopped	1 small
1 small	cooking (tart) apple, peeled, cored and chopped	1 small
1-2 tsp	curry powder water	1-2 tsp
4	free-range eggs, hard-boiled (hard-cooked), peeled and quartered	4

1 Heat the oil and sauté the onion for 5 minutes. Stir in the apple and cook for 5 more minutes, or until the onion and apple are soft. Add the curry powder, stir it in well and continue cooking. Add a few spoonfuls of water to make a thick sauce.
2 Share the egg between the cooked potatoes, then spoon some of the curry sauce over each one (alternatively, chop the eggs and add them to the sauce before dividing it between the potatoes).

Celery à la Grecque Filling

285ml (½ pt)	water	1⅓ cup
1 small	onion, sliced	1 small
2 tbsp	vegetable oil	2 tbsp
2 tbsp	lemon juice	2 tbsp
1 tsp	black peppercorns	1 tsp
½ tsp	ground coriander	½ tsp
4 medium	sticks celery, chopped seasoning to taste	4 medium
12	black olives	12
55g (2 oz)	walnuts (English walnuts), coarsely chopped	½ cup

1 In a saucepan, combine the water, onion, oil, lemon juice, peppercorns and coriander. Bring the mixture to the boil, cover the pan and simmer for 10 minutes.
2 Add the celery and cook it until it softens, then remove it from the pan using a slotted spoon and keep it to one side. Continue fast boiling the remaining sauce to reduce it. Strain the thickened sauce, stir in the celery, season to taste, then reheat it gently.
3 Divide the filling between the cooked potatoes, decorating each one with black olives and a sprinkling of the walnuts.

Butter Bean and Tomato Filling

395-g (14-oz)	can butter (lima) beans (see note)	14-oz
1 small	onion, finely chopped	1 small
395-g (14-oz)	can tomatoes, chopped fresh parsley, chopped seasoning to taste	14-oz
good pinch	chilli powder (optional) fresh chives, snipped, to garnish	good pinch

1 Drain the beans.
2 In a saucepan combine all the ingredients, except the chives, and cook over a medium heat until the sauce begins to thicken and is piping hot.
3 Spoon the mixture over the cooked potatoes, garnish with the chives and serve at once.

Note: You can use leftover beans for this filling. In fact, it is always a good idea, when cooking beans, to prepare more than you need and keep the extra amount in the refrigerator for a day or so, or the freezer if you want to keep them longer.

Broccoli Yogurt Filling

455g (1 lb)	fresh broccoli	1 lb
30g (1 oz)	margarine	2½ tbsp
30g (1 oz)	wholemeal (whole wheat) flour	¼ cup
200ml (⅓ pt)	milk	¾ cup
200ml (⅓ pt)	natural (unsweetened) yogurt	¾ cup
good pinch	ground nutmeg seasoning to taste Parmesan cheese, grated, to taste	good pinch

1 Break the broccoli, into large florets, trimming off any tough stalks and leaves. Steam the broccoli briefly until it is just cooked.
2 Meanwhile, melt the margarine and stir in the flour, cooking it for a minute or two before gradually adding the milk, stirring continually until the sauce thickens. Add the yogurt and nutmeg and season the sauce well. Mix the prepared broccoli into the sauce and use the mixture to top the baked potatoes (you might find it necessary to spoon out some of the potato flesh, reserving it to use in another recipe, in order to accommodate the filling).
3 Top each potato with a good sprinkling of the Parmesan cheese and pop them under a hot grill (broiler) for a few minutes to melt the cheese, then serve.

Crunchy Peanut Filling

115g (4 oz)	peanuts, roasted (see note)	¾ cup
1 large	carrot, coarsely chopped	1 large
1 large	stick celery, coarsely chopped	1 large
3-4 tbsp	mayonnaise (dairy or soya)	3-4 tbsp
½-1 tbsp	fresh chives, snipped	½-1 tbsp
	seasoning to taste	

1 Simply combine the nuts, carrot and celery with enough mayonnaise to bind them together. Flavour the mixture with the chives and season to taste, then divide the mixture between the cooked potatoes.

Note: To dry roast the peanuts, spread them across a baking sheet and cook them in a 350°F/180°C (Gas Mark 4) oven for about 20 minutes, stirring them occasionally so they colour evenly. This can be done when you are using the oven to cook another dish at this temperature, and the roasted peanuts can be cooled and then stored in an airtight jar.

You can fill jacket potatoes with almost any ingredients you might have to hand. Ready cooked vegetables, beans, grated (shredded) cheese, sour (soured) cream, yogurt, nuts – or simply a little butter or margarine, lots of freshly ground black pepper and maybe a sprinkling of herbs. See also Chapter 2 as some of the dips there will make great toppings for baked potatoes.

Potato, Spinach and Sour Cream Bake

1.15 k (2 lb)	fresh spinach, well washed	2 lb
3 large	potatoes, scrubbed and halved	3 large
1 medium	onion, thinly sliced	1 medium
½ tsp	ground nutmeg	½ tsp
1 tbsp	fresh parsley, chopped	1 tbsp
285ml (½ pt)	sour (soured) cream	1⅓ cup
	seasoning to taste	
115g (4 oz)	Red Leicester cheese, grated	1 cup
55g (2 oz)	wholemeal (whole wheat) breadcrumbs	1 cup

1 Put the spinach into a saucepan, cover and cook it gently (in just the water that remains on the leaves) for 10 minutes or until it has wilted. Drain it well then coarsely chop it.
2 Steam the potatoes, let them cool, then cut them into even-sized slices.
3 Preheat the oven to 350°F/180°C (Gas Mark 4).
4 In a greased ovenproof dish, layer the potato, onion and

spinach, adding the nutmeg, parsley and a few spoonfuls of the cream and seasoning to taste between each layer. Repeat the layers until all the ingredients have been used, finishing with a layer of potatoes. Sprinkle first the cheese, then the breadcrumbs over the top.
5 Bake it in the preheated oven for 20 minutes.

Note: When fresh spinach is not available, use frozen, or for a winter dish, omit both the spinach and onion and use leeks instead.

Caraway Potato Squares

1.15 k (2 lb)	potatoes, peeled and diced	5 cups
1 small	onion, finely chopped	1 small
30g (1 oz)	butter or margarine	2½ tbsp
2 tbsp	whole caraway seeds, or to taste	2 tbsp
115g (4 oz)	wholemeal (whole wheat) flour	1 cup
	seasoning to taste	

1 Steam the potatoes until they are soft, then drain them well, mash them and stir them in a dry pan until any remaining moisture has evaporated. Drain the onion so that it, too, is as dry as possible.
2 Preheat the oven to 375°F/190°C (Gas Mark 5).
3 In a bowl, stir together the potato, onion, butter or margarine, caraway seeds and flour and season to taste, making sure all the ingredients are well mixed.
4 Lightly grease a shallow tin (pan) and press the mixture evenly down into it (it should be about 6mm/¼ in thick). Smooth the top before marking it into squares. Bake it in the preheated oven for 40 to 50 minutes or until the top is crisp and golden brown. Remove it from the tin (pan) and divide it into squares while still hot.

Note: These can be used as a base for other ingredients such as ratatouille, baked beans or cauliflower cheese. They can also be left to cool then spread with butter and served rather like bread to accompany soup or a salad. If you do not like caraway, you can replace the seeds with herbs of your choice.

Chilli Potatoes with Beans

225g (8 oz)	dried kidney beans, soaked overnight (see page 9)	1⅓ cups
680g (1½ lb)	small new potatoes, scrubbed	1½ lb
2 tbsp	vegetable oil	2 tbsp
4	spring onions (scallions), chopped	4
1	clove garlic, peeled and finely chopped	1
1 tbsp	chilli powder, or to taste	1 tbsp
1 tsp	ground cumin	1 tsp
1 tsp	dried oregano seasoning to taste fresh parsley, to garnish	1 tsp

1 Cook and drain the beans. Meanwhile, steam the potatoes for 10 minutes or until they are just beginning to soften, then drain them well.
2 Heat the oil and sauté the spring onions (scallions) and garlic in it for a few minutes before adding the spices, oregano and seasoning to taste. Continue cooking the mixture for a few minutes, then stir in the potatoes, making sure to coat them evenly with the spices. Add the beans and simmer the mixture gently for 5 to 10 minutes, stirring frequently, to heat it through. Serve it garnished with lots of parsley.

Note: The quantities given for the spices are purely there as a guideline so adjust them to suit your own taste. Those who eat dairy products might like to top the potatoes, just before serving, with a spoonful or two of sour (soured) cream, fromage frais or natural (unsweetened) yogurt.

Almond Cheese Croquettes

455g (1 lb)	potatoes, peeled and diced	2½ cups
115g (4 oz)	Cheddar cheese, grated	1 cup
2	free-range egg yolks	2
2 tsp	dried sage seasoning to taste	2 tsp
30g (1 oz)	flaked (slivered) almonds, lightly crushed vegetable oil, for frying	¼ cup

1 Steam the potatoes and, when they are cooked, drain them well. Mash them to a smooth purée and cook it gently in a pan to dry it out.
2 Mix together the potato, cheese, egg yolks and sage and season to taste. (If time allows, chill the mixture for an hour or so - this will make it easier to shape.)
3 Flour your hands, divide the mixture into small pieces

and shape them into croquettes. Roll these in the almonds and shallow fry them briefly, turning them so that they brown evenly. Serve the croquettes at once.

Note: Vegans can make these croquettes using ground nuts instead of the cheese and omitting the egg yolks. (As these two ingredients make the mixture hold together better, replace them with a spoonful or two of soya flour.) Any vegetables can be added to the croquettes, providing they are finely chopped.

Corn-stuffed Potato Skins

6 medium	potatoes, scrubbed vegetable oil, for brushing	6 medium
Filling		
170g (6 oz)	sweetcorn, fresh or frozen	1½ cups
4 medium	tomatoes, chopped	4 medium
2 tbsp	tomato purée (paste)	2 tbsp
30g (1 oz)	sunflower seeds	¼ cup
1 tbsp	fresh parsley, chopped seasoning to taste	1 tbsp
30g (1 oz)	wholemeal (whole wheat) breadcrumbs	½ cup
15g (½ oz)	margarine	1 generous tbsp

1 Preheat the oven to 400°F/200°C (Gas Mark 6).
2 Dry the potatoes, prick them and bake them in the preheated oven for 1 hour or until they are tender. Leave the oven on. Leave them to cool, then cut them in half and carefully scoop out as much of the flesh as possible, leaving a shell of skin. Brush the skins with vegetable oil, then put them on a baking sheet, cut side up. Bake them in the oven at the same temperature for 10 minutes. Reduce the oven temperature to 350°F/180°C (Gas Mark 4). (The scooped out potato can be used in other dishes such as cottage pie, potato soup or croquettes.)
3 Meanwhile cook the sweetcorn and drain it well. Mix it with the tomatoes, tomato purée, sunflower seeds and parsley and season to taste. Divide this between the prepared potato skins, top them with the breadcrumbs and dot with the margarine. Bake them in the oven for 10 minutes or until the breadcrumbs are golden brown and crisp, then serve them at once.

Note: Any filling can be used in the potato skins. Vegetables in a creamy sauce go especially well with the crisp skins. This recipe can also be served cold, which makes it ideal for buffets.

Spanish-style Fried Potatoes

2 tbsp	vegetable oil	2 tbsp
15g (½ oz)	margarine	1 generous tbsp
1 medium	onion, chopped	1 medium
1	clove garlic, peeled and crushed	1
1 small	green pepper, sliced	1 small
½ tsp	paprika	½ tsp
4 medium	potatoes, cooked and diced	4 medium
4	vegetarian 'sausages' (see note), sliced seasoning to taste	4

1 Heat the oil and margarine together, then sauté the onion, garlic and green pepper in them for 5 minutes or until they begin to soften. Add the paprika, potato and 'sausage', season to taste, stir, and cook the mixture gently for 10 minutes until hot and lightly browned.

Note: Frying is a traditional way to use up leftover cooked vegetables – potatoes in particular. This version turns them into a balanced snack with the addition of the vegetarian 'sausages'. You can use tinned or frozen ones or make them up from a dry mix. Alternatively, add chopped hard-boiled (hard-cooked) eggs or some beans.

Potato and Cauliflower Curry

2 tbsp	vegetable oil	2 tbsp
2 large	potatoes, scrubbed and diced	2 large
1 small	cauliflower, broken into florets	1 small
½ tsp	ground ginger	½ tsp
½ tsp	ground paprika	½ tsp
½ tsp	ground turmeric	½ tsp
1 tsp	ground cumin	1 tsp
1 tbsp	ground coriander sea salt to taste	1 tbsp
200ml (⅓ pt)	water	¾ cup
55g (2 oz)	peanuts, for sprinkling fresh parsley, chopped, for sprinkling	⅓ cup
4	tomatoes, quartered, to garnish	4

1 Heat the oil and sauté the potato and cauliflower in it for a few minutes, stirring continually. Mix the spices and salt together, add them to the pan and cook for 2 more minutes.
2 Pour the water over the vegetables and bring the mixture to the boil. Lower the heat, cover the pan and simmer it for 10 minutes or until the vegetables are tender. Serve the curry in soup bowls, sprinkling some

nuts and parsley over each bowl and decorating them with the tomato.

Note: For a curry with a creamier texture, stir in some grated (shredded) creamed coconut or a few spoonfuls of natural (unsweetened) yogurt. Any curry benefits from being left to cool overnight as the flavours mingle – just gently reheat it when needed the next day.

Rosti with Mushrooms

455g (1 lb)	potatoes	1 lb
55g (2 oz)	margarine or butter	¼ cup
1 small	onion, grated	1 small
2	cloves garlic, peeled and crushed seasoning to taste	2

Mushroom and tomato sauce

2 tbsp	vegetable oil	2 tbsp
225g (8 oz)	mushrooms, sliced	4 cups
4 medium	tomatoes, chopped seasoning to taste soya 'bacon' bits to taste	4 medium

1 Scrub and then parboil the potatoes for only 5 minutes. Drain them well, leave them to cool slightly, then grate (shred) them into a bowl.
2 Melt half the margarine or butter and sauté the onion and garlic in it until they have softened, then season to taste and stir the mixture into the potato, mixing them together well.
3 Melt half the remaining margarine in a frying pan (skillet), spread it across the bottom, then add the potato mixture, pressing it down so that it forms a flat, even cake and the top is smooth. Cook it gently for 5 to 10 minutes or until it is golden brown underneath. Using a wide spatula, turn the rosti over, adding the remaining margarine to the pan first. Continue cooking until the second side is also golden brown.
4 Meanwhile make the topping. Heat the vegetable oil and fry the mushrooms very gently until they are just cooked. Stir in the tomato, season to taste and cook the mixture for a few minutes longer to heat it through.
5 Cut the rosti into 4 wedges and serve them topped with the mushroom and tomato sauce and sprinkled with the soya 'bacon' bits.

Note: An alternative way to turn the rosti is to put a flat plate over the pan, then invert the pan so that the rosti falls onto the plate. Then, simply slide the rosti back into the pan to cook the second side.

Oven-baked Chips

455g (1 lb)	potatoes	1 lb
2 tbsp	vegetable oil	2 tbsp
	sea salt (optional)	

1 Cut the potatoes into chips (fries) about 1 cm (½ in) thick. Drop them into a saucepan of boiling water and cook them for just a few minutes, then drain them well and put them to one side until they have dried.
2 Preheat the oven to 475°F/240°C (Gas Mark 9).
3 Put the chips (fries) into a bowl and trickle the oil over them, then toss gently until all of them are lightly coated with the oil.
4 Spread them across a non-stick baking sheet and bake them in the preheated oven for about 15 minutes or until they are nicely browned. If you like them salted, serve them with sea salt, using a minimal amount.

Note: These low-fat chips (fries) are much better for you than the deep-fried variety *and* they are easy to make. Cut and parboil some potatoes and keep them in the refrigerator ready for when a quick and filling snack is needed.

Pepper, Hazelnut and Potato Loaf

4 large	potatoes	4 large
2	free-range eggs	2
1 large	yellow pepper, chopped	1 large
115g (4 oz)	hazelnuts, roasted and coarsely chopped	¾ cup
3 medium	tomatoes, chopped	3 medium
2 tsp	mixed dried herbs	2 tsp
	seasoning to taste	
15g (½ oz)	margarine	1 generous tbsp
285ml (½ pt)	Tomato Sauce (see page 156) (optional)	1⅓ cups

1 Preheat the oven to 350°F/180°C (Gas Mark 4).
2 Peel, quarter and then steam the potatoes until they are soft. Mash them well and drain off any excess liquid. Lightly beat the eggs.
3 Combine the potato, egg, yellow pepper, hazelnuts, tomato and herbs and season to taste. Mix the ingredients together thoroughly. Transfer the mixture to a lightly greased small loaf tin (pan), dot the top with the margarine and bake in the preheated oven for 30 minutes or until the mixture has set. Serve the loaf sliced, with the Tomato Sauce, if using.

Note: This loaf is also good cold, so serve any leftovers with a salad. The same mixture can be shaped into small balls and fried.

Potato Ratatouille

2 tbsp	vegetable oil	2 tbsp
30g (1 oz)	margarine	2½ tbsp
1 small	aubergine (eggplant), diced (see note)	1 small
2 small	courgettes (zucchini), sliced	2 small
1 medium	onion, sliced	1 medium
1	clove garlic, peeled and crushed	1
1 small	green pepper, sliced	1 small
1 small	red pepper, sliced	1 small
3 medium	potatoes, scrubbed and diced	3 medium
395-g (14-oz)	can tomatoes, chopped	14-oz
1 tsp	dried basil	1 tsp
1 tsp	dried oregano	1 tsp
1	bay leaf	1
	seasoning to taste	
115g (4 oz)	Cheddar cheese, grated	1 cup
	parsley sprigs, to garnish	

1 In a large frying pan (skillet), heat the oil together with the margarine. Add the aubergine (eggplant), courgettes (zucchini), onion, garlic, green and red peppers and potatoes. Stir them together well and cook them briefly. Add the tomatoes and herbs and season to taste. Bring the mixture to the boil, then cover the pan and simmer the mixture for about 15 minutes or until the vegetables are tender.
2 Taste and, if necessary, adjust the seasoning, remove the bay leaf, then serve the ratatouille at once, topped with the cheese and garnished with the parsley.

Note: This is an all-in-one dish that makes a quick and tasty snack. Though the vegetables given are those traditionally used in ratatouille, others can be used in much the same way. If time allows, salt the diced aubergines (eggplant) and leave it for 30 minutes until the bitter juices ooze out, then rinse it in clean water and pat it dry before cooking.

Latkes (Potato Fritters)

45g (1 lb)	potatoes, peeled and shredded	2 cups
30g (1 oz)	matzo meal	¼ cup
1 large	free-range egg, beaten	1 large
	seasoning to taste	
	vegetable oil, for frying	

1 Drain the potatoes well, squeezing to make sure that the mixture is as dry as possible. Stir together with all the remaining ingredients, except the oil, making sure that they are thoroughly blended.

2 Heat enough oil in a pan to deep fry spoonfuls of the potato mixture. Drop them in a few at a time and fry for a few minutes until they are golden brown. Drain them on paper towels so that they are dry and light, and serve while they are hot.

Note: Latkes are traditionally eaten with sour (soured) cream and apple sauce. However, they can also be used as a base for whatever you like – sweet or savoury. Matzo meal gives them their distinctive lightness (it is available from wholefood and speciality shops and some supermarkets), but you can use flour instead.

6
Things on Bread

Yogurt Rarebit

30g (1 oz)	margarine	2½ tbsp
15g (½ oz)	wholemeal (whole wheat) flour	2 tbsp
225g (8 oz)	Cheddar cheese, grated	2 cups
140ml (¼ pt)	natural (unsweetened) yogurt	⅔ cup
good pinch	mustard powder	good pinch
good pinch	cayenne pepper seasoning to taste	good pinch
4 thick	slices wholemeal (whole wheat) bread	4 thick
2	tomatoes, sliced mustard and cress or watercress, to garnish	2

1 Melt the margarine, sprinkle in the flour and cook it gently for a few minutes, stirring. Add the cheese, gradually stir in the yogurt, then add the mustard and cayenne and season to taste. Cook it over a medium heat, stirring continually until you have a thick, smooth sauce.
2 Meanwhile, lightly toast the bread. Spoon a generous amount of sauce over each slice, top with the tomato slices and cook them under a hot grill (broiler) for 2 minutes. Garnish them with mustard and cress and serve.

Note: This is also surprisingly good when it is cold, so try cutting the finished rarebits into smaller pieces and serving them at a buffet.

Indian Scrambled Eggs on Toast

8	free-range eggs seasoning to taste	8
½ tsp	ground ginger	½ tsp
1 tsp	garam masala, or to taste	1 tsp
4 tbsp	milk	4 tbsp
55g (2 oz)	margarine	¼ cup
½ small	onion, sliced	½ small
2 tbsp	mango chutney, chopped	2 tbsp
4 thick	slices wholemeal (whole wheat) bread parsley sprigs, to garnish	4 thick

1 Lightly beat the eggs, season to taste, then beat in the ginger, garam masala and milk.
2 Melt the margarine and gently fry the onion until it begins to brown. Add the egg mixture and cook it over a low heat, stirring continually, until it is just beginning to set (do not overcook – scrambled eggs should be soft and moist). Remove the pan from the heat immediately and stir in the chutney.
3 At the same time, toast the bread slices. Spoon the scrambled eggs onto them, garnish with the parsley and serve at once.

Note: Scrambled eggs are a nutritious and quick to prepare snack, though they can become rather boring. This version makes an interesting change. Other additions to try are fresh herbs and a spoonful or two of sour (soured) cream, chopped nuts, chilli powder and crumbled tortilla chips.

Leeks with Sesame Sauce on Toast

2 medium	leeks, cleaned and sliced	2 medium
4 tbsp	tahini	4 tbsp
1 tbsp	lemon juice	1 tbsp
4 tbsp	water	4 tbsp
¼ tsp	garlic salt, or to taste	¼ tsp
30g (1 oz)	sesame seeds	¼ cup
6 thick	slices wholemeal (whole wheat) bread	6 thick
3 tbsp	wholemeal (whole wheat) breadcrumbs	3 tbsp
30g (1 oz)	margarine	2½ tbsp
	tomato salad, to serve	

1 Steam the leeks gently until tender, then drain them very well before transferring to a bowl. Combine the tahini, lemon juice and water and stir this mixture into the leeks, together with the garlic salt and sesame seeds.

2 Toast the bread, cut each slice across diagonally and put 3 pieces on each plate. Top them with the leek mixture, then the breadcrumbs, dot with the margarine and cook under the grill (broiler) for a minute to heat each serving through and brown the tops.

Note: This is an excellent lunch snack for a busy day. You can use any other vegetables, or mix of vegetables, instead of the leek - cauliflower, for example, goes especially well with the sesame sauce. For a change, try using a nut butter instead of the tahini.

Spicy Tomatoes with Fennel

2 tbsp	vegetable oil	2 tbsp
1 small	fennel bulb, trimmed	1 small
¼ tsp	ground nutmeg	¼ tsp
¼ tsp	ground cinnamon	¼ tsp
4 large	ripe tomatoes, coarsely chopped	4 large
1 tbsp	lemon juice	1 tbsp
	seasoning to taste	
4 thick	slices wholemeal (whole wheat) bread	4 thick
2 tbsp	fresh chives, snipped	2 tbsp

1 Heat the oil, chop the fennel and sauté it gently for 5 minutes or until it has softened. Add the spices and cook them for a few minutes, then stir in the tomatoes and lemon juice and season to taste. Simmer the mixture for 10 to 15 minutes or until the vegetables have broken down to form a thick sauce.

2 Toast the bread and top each slice with some of the fennel and tomato sauce. Sprinkle the chives over each serving for a dash of colour and then serve.

Note: This versatile dish is ideal for breakfast, a light lunch or an evening snack. Add protein, if liked, by sprinkling chopped nuts, some mashed tofu or grated (shredded) cheese over the sauce. Cook double the amount of this spicy sauce and keep the rest in the refrigerator or freeze it to use another day. This sauce can also be blended and served with pasta.

Cheesy Crostini

8 thick	slices French bread - white or wholemeal (whole wheat), cut on the diagonal	8 thick
3 tbsp	olive oil	3 tbsp
2	spring onions (scallions), chopped	2
1	clove garlic, peeled and crushed	1
170g (6 oz)	Mozzarella cheese, thinly sliced	6 oz

1 Lightly toast the bread on one side only.

2 Mix together the oil, onion and garlic and spread the mixture over the uncooked side of each slice of bread. Arrange the slices of cheese on top of the onion and garlic mixture and cook under a hot grill (broiler) until the cheese melts, then serve the crostini at once.

Note: An Italian-style snack. For a change, use other cheeses. Blue cheese mixed with celery, for example, is good. Alternatively, top the onion and garlic mixture with chopped tomatoes mashed with tofu and chives.

Vegetable Toasties

85g (3 oz)	margarine	⅓ cup
1	onion, sliced	1
1	courgette (zucchini), chopped	1
1	red pepper, chopped	1
½ tsp	yeast extract, or to taste	½ tsp
	seasoning to taste	
30g (1 oz)	sunflower seeds	¼ cup
4 thick	slices wholemeal (whole wheat) bread	4 thick
55g (2 oz)	Cheddar cheese, grated (optional)	½ cup

1 Melt the margarine, add the vegetables and sauté them gently for 5 minutes, then add a spoonful or two of water and simmer the vegetables until cooked. Stir in the yeast extract and season to taste. Lightly mash the vegetables to make a chunky purée, season it to taste, then add the sunflower seeds.

2 Meanwhile, toast the bread. Spoon some of the mixture onto each slice and serve at once. If you are using the cheese, sprinkle some over each and cook the toasties under the grill (broiler) until the cheese has melted before serving.

Note: This vegetable purée can be made with any vegetables. It is also an excellent way to use up leftovers. Flavour it as you like. For example, by also adding herbs.

Scrambled Tofu Crispies

1 tbsp	vegetable oil	1 tbsp
285g (10 oz)	smoked tofu, drained and mashed	1¼ cups
55g (2 oz)	sweetcorn, cooked	⅓ cup
	soy sauce to taste	
	seasoning to taste	
1 tbsp	fresh parsley, chopped	1 tbsp
30g (1 oz)	margarine	2½ tbsp
4	slices wholemeal (whole wheat) bread	4
	parsley sprigs, to garnish	

1 Heat the oil and add the tofu, stirring it continually. Cook it for a few minutes, then stir in the drained sweetcorn, soy sauce, seasoning to taste and the parsley and continue cooking the mixture gently to heat it through.
2 At the same time, melt the margarine in another pan and fry the bread, turning the slices so that both sides are crisp and brown. Drain them well on paper towel. Spread the tofu mixture on the slices of bread and serve them at once garnished with the sprigs of parsley.

Note: The distinctive taste of smoked tofu means that it does not *need* anything else, but the sweetcorn makes this topping more satisfying. You could use peas instead or stir some lightly fried mushrooms into the tofu. The crispies make an original starter, with tomato and cucumber to garnish them.

Split Pea Rarebit

115g (4 oz)	dried split green peas	½ cup
30g (1 oz)	margarine	2½ tbsp
1 tbsp	wholemeal (whole wheat) flour	1 tbsp
200ml (⅓ pt)	milk or vegetable stock	¾ cup
1 tsp	vegetarian Worcestershire sauce	1 tsp
	seasoning to taste	
4 thick	slices wholemeal (whole wheat) bread	4 thick
	soya 'bacon' bits to taste	

1 Cook the split peas in boiling water for 30 minutes or until they are soft, then drain them and mash them coarsely.
2 Melt the margarine, add the flour and cook it for a few minutes, then gradually add the milk or stock, stirring continuously until the sauce thickens. Add the Worcestershire sauce and season to taste, before stirring in the split pea mixture. Keep the sauce warm while you toast the bread.
3 Spread the topping on the 4 slices and sprinkle 'bacon' bits over them, then serve them at once.

Note: This is an excellent way to use up leftover peas. You can also use split red lentils (which are ready in half the time) or cooked and mashed fresh peas. For extra protein, stir some cheese into the sauce (a soft, low-fat cheese makes it extra creamy) or add a few spoonfuls of tahini or nut butter.

Cheese and Apple on Toast

2 medium	apples, peeled and cored	2 medium
55g (2 oz)	margarine	¼ cup
4 thick	slices wholemeal (whole wheat) toast	4 thick
115g (4 oz)	Red Leicester cheese, sliced	4 oz

1 Slice the apples into thick rings. Melt the margarine and fry the apple rings until they are soft, turning them once so that both sides are evenly cooked.
2 Toast the bread, then top each slice with some of the apple rings, arrange slices of the cheese on top and grill (broil) them until the cheese begins to melt. Serve at once.

Note: This is an unusual snack that is especially popular with children. It also helps use up a glut of autumn apples!

Curried 'Chicken' and Pepper Toasts

2 tbsp	vegetable oil	2 tbsp
1 small	red pepper, sliced	1 small
225g (8 oz)	Quorn, shredded (see note)	8 oz
4 tbsp	natural (unsweetened) yogurt	4 tbsp
1 tbsp	mild curry paste	1 tbsp
	seasoning to taste	
4 thick	slices wholemeal (whole wheat) bread	4 thick
30g (1 oz)	flaked (slivered) almonds, roasted	3 tbsp

1 Heat the oil, add the red pepper slices and cook them gently for 5 minutes, stirring them occasionally. Add the shredded Quorn, stir it in and cook it for a few minutes more. Add the yogurt and curry paste and season to taste, then simmer gently.

2 Meanwhile, toast the bread. Spoon some of the mixture onto each slice, then top them with the almonds and eat at once.

Note: Quorn is a mild-flavoured vegetarian substitute for meat and is available at many large supermarkets. If you cannot get it, unflavoured TVP chunks have a similar texture, though they will need to be rehydrated first.

Hot Peanut Butter and Avocado Toasties

Peanut butter

170g (6 oz)	peanuts, lightly roasted	1⅓ cups
3 tbsp	vegetable oil seasoning to taste	3 tbsp
4 thick	slices wholemeal (whole wheat) bread	4 thick
2 small	avocados, peeled and stoned (pitted)	2 small
good squeeze	lemon juice	good squeeze

1 Make the peanut butter first. Grind the peanuts, then gradually mix in enough oil to make a thick cream. Season to taste. Store the peanut butter in a screw top jar in the refrigerator where it will stay fresh for at least a few weeks.

2 Toast the bread and spread a generous amount of the peanut butter over them. Grill (broil) them briefly. Meanwhile, cut the avocado flesh into thick slices and brush them with the lemon juice. Arrange the slices on top of the peanut buttered toasts and return them to the grill (broiler) for just a minute to heat the avocado through, then serve them at once.

Note: Other nut butters can be made in the same way, or make your own unique butter by combining your favourite kinds, raw or roasted. You can alter the flavour, too, by mixing in some yeast extract, miso or garlic salt or make a sweet butter by adding a little honey, maple syrup and/or vanilla essence (extract). For speed, you can, of course, use a ready-made peanut butter instead.

Eggs in Onion Sauce on Toast

1 large	onion	1 large
285ml (½ pt)	White Sauce (see page 156)	1⅓ cups
6	free-range eggs, hard-boiled (hard-cooked), peeled and quartered	6
1 tsp	dried sage seasoning to taste	1 tsp
1 tbsp	vegetable oil	1 tbsp
4 thick	slices wholemeal (whole wheat) bread parsley sprigs, to garnish	4 thick

1 Chop the onion in half: finely chop one half; thickly slice the other half. Drop the chopped onion into hot water, boil it briefly, then drain it and add it to the White Sauce. Heat the sauce gently. Stir the egg into the sauce, together with the sage, and season to taste. Continue heating the sauce for a few more minutes.

2 Meanwhile, heat the oil in a separate pan, add the sliced onion and cook it until it has browned nicely.

3 Also toast the bread. Divide the sauce between the toasts, topping each one with some of the onion and garnish with the parsley.

Note: This is a tasty way to serve eggs. As a change, try adding the eggs to Parsley or Cheese Sauce (see page 156). Tomato Sauce can be served in much the same way (see page 156).

French Toast with Maple Syrup

2 tbsp	milk	2 tbsp
2	free-range eggs seasoning to taste	2
6	slices wholemeal (whole wheat) bread vegetable oil, for frying maple syrup, to serve	6

1 Beat together the milk and eggs and season to taste. Cut the slices of bread in half on the diagonal and dip each piece in the milk and egg mixture. Heat some oil in a frying pan (skillet) and fry the dipped bread in it for a minute or two, then turn the slices over and cook the other side.

2 Drain on paper towels and serve them at once. Either trickle some maple syrup over each slice or hand it round at the table for everyone to help themselves.

Note: This is a favourite American breakfast dish, but it tastes equally good any time of day. For a savoury version, you can replace the maple syrup with fried mushrooms and tomatoes, or poached eggs, or fried onion with walnuts.

Garlic Yogurt Toasts with Pine Nuts

15g (½ oz)	margarine	1 generous tbsp
30g (1 oz)	pine nuts	3 tbsp
1-2	cloves garlic, peeled and crushed	1-2
1 tbsp	wholemeal (whole wheat) flour	1 tbsp
285ml (½ pt)	natural (unsweetened) yogurt	1⅓ cups
	seasoning to taste	
4 thick	slices wholemeal (whole wheat) bread	4 thick

1 Melt the margarine and gently fry the pine nuts until they are golden brown. Remove them with a slotted spoon and add the garlic, cooking it gently until it begins to soften. Stir in the flour, cook it briefly, then carefully stir in the yogurt and season to taste.
2 Toast the bread. Pile some of the garlic yogurt sauce onto each slice, top with the pine nuts and serve at once.

Note: This dish would make a tasty start to a meal and it is light, leaving space for the courses that follow. If you are serving it as a snack, you could add some grated (shredded) cheese and/or some breadcrumbs and cook them under the grill (broiler) for a few minutes.

Braised Tofu Toasties

225-g (8-oz)	can braised tofu	8-oz
30g (1 oz)	margarine	2½ tbsp
55g (2 oz)	beansprouts	1 cup
	seasoning to taste	
4 thick	slices wholemeal (whole wheat) bread	4 thick

1 Drain the tofu and reserve the liquid. Shred the tofu coarsely. Melt the margarine and cook the beansprouts briefly, stirring them continually. Add the tofu and season to taste, then cook for just a few minutes more to heat through.
2 Toast the bread and top with the tofu and beansprout mixture. Pour some or all of the reserved liquid over the toasties and serve them at once.

Note: Made from soya beans, braised tofu has a unique taste and texture. It can be eaten cold as well as cooked in this way, or grilled (broiled).

Bel Paese Triangles

30g (1 oz)	margarine	2½ tbsp
1 tbsp	vegetable oil	1 tbsp
6	slices wholemeal (whole wheat) bread	6
115g (4 oz)	Bel Paese cheese (see note), sliced	4 oz
	watercress, to garnish	

1 Heat the margarine and oil together. Cut each slice of bread diagonally into triangles and fry, turning them once, until they are crisp and golden brown. Drain them on paper towels.
2 Top each one with some of the Bel Paese cheese slices and grill (broil) long enough to melt the cheese. Serve them hot, garnished with the watercress.

Note: Perfect for parties, these triangles also make a delicious nibble to accompany pre-dinner drinks. Other cheeses can be used instead of the Bel Paese.

Mushroom Purée on Toasted Baps

1 tbsp	vegetable oil	1 tbsp
4	spring onions (scallions), chopped	4
½ small	red pepper, chopped	½ small
115g (4 oz)	mushrooms, chopped	2 cups
¼ tsp	chilli powder	¼ tsp
	seasoning to taste	
4	wholemeal (whole wheat) baps (burger buns)	4
30g (1 oz)	walnuts (English walnuts) coarsely chopped	3 tbsp
	fresh parsley, chopped, to garnish	

1 Heat the oil and sauté the spring onions (scallions) and red pepper for 5 minutes. Stir in the mushrooms and cook them for 5 to 10 minutes more or until they have softened. Add the chilli powder and season to taste.
2 Split the baps (burger buns) and toast the cut side. Pile the hot pepper and mushroom mixture on the other side, top with the walnuts and sprinkle the parsley over them. Serve them at once.

Note: If you have a blender you can use it to make a really smooth mushroom purée. Prepare more than you need and freeze the extra for another time or in another recipe. For a creamier purée, stir in some yogurt or sour (soured) cream.

Tofu Almond Spread on Toast

225g (8 oz)	tofu, drained	1 cup
55g (2 oz)	roasted almonds, ground	½ cup
1 tbsp	lemon juice	1 tbsp
	soy sauce to taste	
	seasoning to taste	
4 thick	slices wholemeal (whole wheat) bread	4 thick
	mustard and cress or snipped fresh chives, to garnish	

1 Mash the tofu and mix it well with the almonds, lemon juice, soy sauce and season to taste (for a smooth sauce use a blender to combine the ingredients). Adjust the seasoning as necessary.
2 Toast the bread. Spread the tofu and almond mixture generously over the toast, then grill (broil) for just a minute or two to heat through. Serve garnished generously with the mustard and cress or chives.

Note: Other nuts can be added to the tofu instead of the almonds.

Onion Stroganoff on Toast

55g (2 oz)	margarine	¼ cup
2 large	onions, sliced	2 large
good pinch	paprika	good pinch
140ml (¼ pt)	sour (soured) cream	⅔ cup
	seasoning to taste	
4 thick	slices wholemeal (whole wheat) bread	4 thick
	soya 'bacon' bits or salted peanuts to garnish	
	fresh parsley, chopped, to garnish	

1 Melt the margarine and sauté the onions, stirring them frequently, for 10 minutes or until they have softened. Add the paprika and gently stir in the cream. Season the mixture generously and heat it gently.
2 Meanwhile, toast the bread. Spoon the onion mixture onto the toast and top with the 'bacon' bits or peanuts and plenty of the parsley. Serve at once.

Note: This is an unusual topping for toast that makes a surprisingly good lunchtime snack. Other vegetables can be used instead of the onions and although mushrooms are a traditional choice, try green vegetables such as broccoli or cauliflower, or colourful, tasty combinations such as courgettes (zucchini) and red peppers.

Cottage Cheese Toasties

225g (8 oz)	cottage cheese	1 cup
1	stick celery, chopped	1
1	apple, peeled and diced	1
30g (1 oz)	almonds, coarsely chopped	¼ cup
1 tbsp	runny (liquid) honey	1 tbsp
	freshly ground black pepper to taste	
4 thick	slices wholemeal (whole wheat) bread	4 thick

1 Mix together all the ingredients except the bread, seasoning the mixture generously with the pepper.
2 Lightly toast the bread slices, then spread them evenly with the cottage cheese mixture. Cook them under a hot grill (broiler) for just a few minutes, then serve.

Note: This topping is a different and delicious combination, equally good hot or cold. Try it spread on fingers of toast or small biscuits for a buffet.

7
Flans, Quiches and Cheesecakes

Asparagus Tofu Flan

225g (8 oz)	pastry of your choice (see pages 152-153)	8 oz
Filling		
285g (10 oz)	fresh asparagus	10 oz
30g (1 oz)	margarine	2½ tbsp
30g (1 oz)	wholemeal (whole wheat) flour	¼ cup
285ml (½ pt)	milk	1⅓ cups
1 tsp	dried tarragon seasoning to taste	1 tsp
170g (6 oz)	drained tofu, coarsely crumbled	¾ cup
55g (2 oz)	wholemeal (whole wheat) breadcrumbs	1 cup
30g (1 oz)	grated Cheddar cheese	¼ cup

1 Preheat the oven to 400°F/200°C (Gas Mark 6).
2 Roll out the pastry and line a medium-sized flan dish (quiche pan) or ring (ring from a loose-bottomed quiche pan) standing on a baking sheet. Prick it with a fork, then bake it blind (see page 153) in the preheated oven for 10 minutes. Leave the oven on, but lower the temperature to 375°F/190°C (Gas Mark 5).
3 Meanwhile, make the filling. Wash and trim the asparagus spears, then tie them in bunches, stand them in a special tall pan (or use an ordinary pan and make a lid with foil) and cook them gently for 15 minutes or until they are just tender. Then drain them well.
4 Make a sauce by melting the margarine and stirring in the flour, then gradually adding the milk, stirring continually until the sauce has thickened. Stir in the tarragon and season to taste.
5 Arrange the cooked asparagus across the base of the pastry case (shell). Spread the tofu over the asparagus, then pour the sauce evenly over the top. Mix the breadcrumbs with the cheese and scatter the mixture evenly over the top. Bake the flan for about 20 minutes or until it is cooked, then serve it at once.

Note: This flan is also good cold – serve it for lunch out in the garden or wrap it carefully in foil and pack it for a picnic.

If fresh asparagus is not available, use frozen or tinned spears instead.

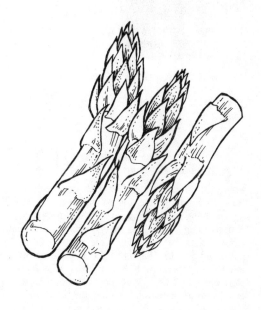

Cheese and Onion Tarts

225g (8 oz)	pastry of your choice (see pages 152-153)	8 oz

Filling		
2 tbsp	vegetable oil	2 tbsp
2 large	onions, sliced	2 large
170g (6 oz)	Gruyère cheese, grated	1½ cups
2	free-range eggs, beaten seasoning to taste fresh parsley, chopped, to garnish	2

1 Preheat the oven to 400°F/200°C (Gas Mark 6).
2 Roll the pastry out and line 6 to 8 small tart tins (tartlet molds). Prick the pastry with a fork, then bake them blind (see page 152) in the preheated oven for 5 minutes. Leave the oven on, lowering the temperature to 375°F/190°C (Gas Mark 5).
3 Now make the filling. Heat the oil and sauté the onions until they have just softened. Drain them well, then stir in the cheese and egg and season to taste. Pour the mixture into the tart cases (tartlet shells).
4 Cook the little tarts for about 20 minutes or until the filling has set, sprinkle the parsley over them and serve.

Note: For variety add 1 or 2 cloves of garlic together with the onion, if you like it. You can also replace the hard cheese with a soft type. These little tarts make excellent buffet fare.

Chilli Pumpkin Flan

225g (8 oz)	pastry of your choice (see pages 152-153)	8 oz

Filling		
680g (1½ lb)	pumpkin, peeled, diced and cooked	1½ lb
1 tbsp	vegetable oil	1 tbsp
1 large	onion, sliced	1 large
1-2 tsp	chilli powder, or to taste seasoning to taste	1-2 tsp
2	free-range eggs, beaten	2
3 tbsp	cooked brown rice	3 tbsp

1 Preheat the oven to 400°F/200°C (Gas Mark 5).
2 Roll out the pastry and line a medium-sized flan dish (quiche pan) or ring (ring from a loose-bottomed tart pan) standing on a baking sheet. Prick the pastry with a fork, then bake it blind (see page 152) in the preheated oven for 10 minutes. Leave the oven on, but lower the temperature to 375°F/190°C (Gas Mark 5).
3 Now make the filling. Drain the pumpkin. Heat the oil and cook the onion in it for 5 minutes, then stir in the chilli powder and cook it for a few more minutes. Stir in the pumpkin and season the mixture well. Cool it briefly, then add the egg and rice. Pour the mixture into

the pastry case (shell).
4 Bake the flan (savoury tart) in the oven for 20 to 30 minutes or until the filling has set.

Note: A filling dish, it is perfect for lunch on a winter's day and is also good with a topping of grated (shredded) cheese that has been added just before the filling is baked. It is an ideal way to use up leftover rice (or any other cooked grain), but if you prefer, you can use breadcrumbs instead. You can omit this ingredient altogether, though, for a lighter, smoother filling.

Avocado Flan

Crust		
170g (6 oz)	wholemeal (whole wheat) savoury crackers	6 oz
85g (3 oz)	margarine, melted	⅓ cup

Filling		
3 large	ripe avocados	3 large
1 tbsp	lemon juice	1 tbsp
1 tsp	fresh parsley, chopped	1 tsp
1 tsp	fresh chives, snipped	1 tsp
1 tbsp	watercress, chopped	1 tbsp
55g (2 oz)	curd cheese (cottage cheese, mashed)	¼ cup
55g (2 oz)	sweetcorn, cooked	½ cup
2-3 tbsp	mayonnaise seasoning to taste watercress sprigs, to garnish	2-3 tbsp

1 Preheat the oven to 350°F/180°C (Gas Mark 4).
2 First, make the crust. Grind the crackers finely and mix in the melted margarine. Stand a medium-sized flan ring (ring from a loose bottomed quiche pan) on a baking sheet and press the mixture evenly across the base and sides. Bake it in the preheated oven for 15 minutes. Leave to cool, then carefully slide it onto a serving plate and remove the ring.
2 Now, make the filling. Peel and mash the avocados together with the lemon juice, herbs and watercress. Soften the curd (cottage) cheese and add it to the avocado, then stir in the sweetcorn and add enough mayonnaise to make the mixture creamy but not too soft. Season the mixture well, then pour it into the pastry case (shell) and chill for at least a few hours. Serve the flan garnished with the watercress.

Note: As it has not been cooked and contains no setting ingredient, the filling for this flan (savoury deep tart) is especially soft. Ring the changes by adding mashed, hard-boiled (hard-cooked) eggs instead of the sweetcorn, which will also make the filling firmer. Soya 'bacon' bits make a delicious crisp and salty contrast when sprinkled over the top. This is a lovely dish to serve as a starter.

Parsnip Quiches

225g (8 oz)	pastry of your choice (see pages 152-153)	8 oz
Filling		
455g (1 lb)	parsnips, peeled and cooked	1 lb
55g (2 oz)	Edam cheese, grated	½ cup
2	free-range eggs, separated	2
¼ tsp	ground nutmeg seasoning to taste	¼ tsp
30g (1 oz)	sunflower seeds, roasted	¼ cup

1 Preheat the oven to 400°F/200°C (Gas Mark 6).
2 Roll the pastry out and line 6 to 8 small quiche tins (pans). Prick the pastry with a fork, then bake the cases (shells) blind (see page 152) for 5 minutes. Leave the oven on, but lower the temperature to 375°F/190°C (Gas Mark 5).
3 Meanwhile, make the filling. Drain the parsnips well, mash them to a smooth purée, then mix in the cheese, egg yolks and nutmeg and season to taste. Beat the egg whites until they are stiff and then fold them into the parsnip mixture using a metal spoon. Spoon the mixture into the pastry cases (shells), top with a sprinkling of the sunflower seeds and bake the quiches in the oven for 15 to 20 minutes or until the filling has set.

Note: These delicately flavoured quiches are popular with most people – even those who claim not to like parsnips! They are at their best served hot.

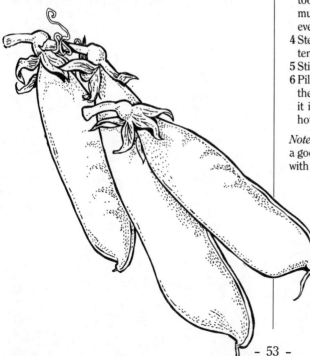

Creamy Vegetable Flan

225g (8 oz)	pastry of your choice (see pages 152-153)	8 oz
Filling		
55g (2 oz)	margarine	¼ cup
6 small	spring onions (scallions), chopped	6 small
1 medium	courgette (zucchini), sliced	1 medium
55g (2 oz)	button mushrooms	1 cup
115g (4 oz)	fine green beans, trimmed and sliced	¼ cup
115g (4 oz)	peas, shelled	⅔ cup
1 small	crown broccoli, broken into florets	1 small
140ml (¼ pt)	plain yogurt	⅔ cup
1 tbsp	wholemeal (whole wheat) flour seasoning to taste fresh parsley, chopped, to garnish	1 tbsp

1 Roll the pastry out and line a medium-sized flan dish (quiche pan) or ring (ring from a loose-bottomed quiche pan) standing on a baking sheet.
2 Preheat the oven to 400°F/200°C (Gas Mark 6).
3 Now make the filling. Melt some of the margarine and cook the onions in it for 5 minutes until they have softened. Lift out with a slotted spoon and set to one side. Add more margarine if necessary and cook the courgettes (zucchini) in the same way, removing them, too, from the pan. Do the same with the button mushrooms, stirring them so that they are lightly and evenly browned.
4 Steam the beans, peas and broccoli until they are just tender, then drain them well.
5 Stir the flour into the yogurt and season to taste.
6 Pile the vegetables into the pastry case (shell), smooth the top, then pour the yogurt over them evenly. Bake it in the preheated oven for 30 minutes then serve it hot, garnished with a sprinkling of the parsley.

Note: Take care not to overcook the vegetables. This is a good dish for a family lunch. You can flavour the sauce with fresh herbs or spices for a more powerful taste.

Curried Spinach and Lentil Flan

225g (8 oz)	pastry of your choice (see pages 152-153)	8 oz

Filling		
2 tbsp	vegetable oil	2 tbsp
1 large	onion, finely chopped	1 large
1	clove garlic, peeled and crushed	1
1 tsp	ground coriander	1 tsp
½ tsp	ground cumin	½ tsp
1 tsp	garam masala	1 tsp
140g (5 oz)	dried brown lentils, soaked overnight and drained	¾ cup
455g (1 lb)	spinach, well washed seasoning to taste	1 lb
2	tomatoes, sliced, to garnish	2

1 Preheat the oven to 400°F/200°C (Gas Mark 6).
2 Roll the pastry out and line a medium-sized flan dish (quiche pan) or ring (ring from a loose-bottomed quiche pan) standing on a baking sheet. Prick the pastry with a fork, then bake the case (shell) blind (see page 152) in the preheated oven for 10 minutes. Leave the oven on, but lower the temperature to 350°F/180°C (Gas Mark 4).
3 Meanwhile prepare the filling. Heat the oil and gently sauté the onion and garlic together for a few minutes. Add the spices and cook them for a few more minutes. Add the lentils together with just enough water to cover them. Bring the liquid to the boil and continue boiling for 10 minutes, then lower the heat, cover the pan and simmer for about 20 minutes or until the lentils are just tender.
4 In another saucepan cook the spinach with just the water that remains on the leaves, covering it and simmering gently for 10 minutes or until it has wilted. Then drain it and chop it coarsely.
5 Stir the spinach into the lentil mixture, season to taste, add more garam masala if you want a stronger curry flavour. Drain the mixture well, then spoon it into the flan case (pastry shell), smooth the top, decorate it with the tomato slices and bake it for 20 minutes or until the pastry has cooked. Serve it hot.

Note: For a creamier filling, add some coconut cream or yogurt to the spinach and lentil mixture. Although whole lentils do add a better texture to this flan, they take longer to cook than split lentils, so, if you are in a hurry, either save time by using lentils cooked in advance (maybe left over from another dish) or use split red lentils.

Carrot and Walnut Quiche

Crust		
85g (3 oz)	margarine	⅓ cup
170g (6 oz)	rolled oats seasoning to taste	1½ cups

Filling		
2 large	carrots, peeled and sliced	2 large
170g (6 oz)	quark (see note)	¾ cup
½ tsp	ground nutmeg	½ tsp
1 tsp	dried oregano	1 tsp
2 large	free-range eggs, separated seasoning to taste	2 large
55g (2 oz)	walnuts (English walnuts), coarsely chopped fresh parsley, chopped, to garnish	½ cup

1 Preheat the oven to 400°F/200°C (Gas Mark 6).
2 First make the crust. Using your fingertips, rub the margarine into the oats until it is evenly distributed then season the mixture well. Press the mixture down as evenly as possible, lining the sides and base of a flan ring (ring from a loose-bottomed quiche pan) standing on a baking sheet. Bake it blind (see page 152) in the preheated oven for 10 minutes. Leave the oven on, but reduce the temperature to 375°F/190°C (Gas Mark 5).
3 Meanwhile prepare the filling. Steam the carrots until they are soft. Drain them well then mash or blend them until they form a thick purée. Mix it into the quark (cottage cheese), nutmeg, oregano and egg yolks. Whisk the egg whites lightly and, using a metal spoon, gently fold them into the carrot mixture. Pour the mixture into the oat crust, smooth the top and sprinkle with the nuts.
4 Bake in the oven for 20 to 30 minutes or until the oat crust is cooked and the filling has set. Serve the quiche garnished with the parsley.

Note: Quark is a delicately flavoured but tangy low-fat, soft, white cheese that is perfect for this dish, but if you cannot find it in the shops, use sieved cottage cheese or Ricotta instead.

Though delicious hot, this quiche is also good served cold.

Chilled Apple and Celery Flan

225g (8 oz)	pastry of your choice (see pages 152-153)	8 oz
Filling		
3	sticks celery, finely chopped	3
1 medium	red apple, coarsely chopped	1 medium
2	spring onions (scallions), finely chopped	2
115g (4 oz)	curd cheese (cottage cheese), mashed	½ cup
2 tbsp	thick, set natural (unsweetened) yogurt	2 tbsp
2 tbsp	fresh parsley, chopped seasoning to taste watercress, to garnish	2 tbsp

1 Preheat the oven to 400°F/200°C (Gas Mark 6).
2 Roll the pastry out and line a flan dish (quiche pan) or ring (ring from a loose-bottomed quiche pan) standing on a baking sheet. Prick the pastry with a fork, then bake the pastry case (shell) blind (see page 152) in the preheated oven for 20 minutes or until it is cooked. Leave it to cool.
3 Now make the filling. Mix the chopped celery with the apple, onion, cheese, yogurt and parsley, and season to taste. Spoon the filling into the flan case (pastry shell), smooth the top and chill for at least an hour.
4 Before serving, garnish the top with the reserved cucumber, sliced, and the watercress.

Note: Serve this as a light lunch meal. For a filling with a firmer texture add 2 teaspoons of agar agar dissolved in a little milk. The cheese can be replaced with silken tofu and soya yogurt or mayonnaise to make it suitable for vegans. For extra flavour, stir in a spoonful or two of tahini.

Provençal-style Tofu Tarts

225g (8 oz)	pastry of your choice (see pages 152-153)	8 oz
Filling		
2 tbsp	vegetable oil	2 tbsp
2 medium	onions, sliced	2 medium
1	clove garlic, peeled and crushed	1
½ tsp	dried thyme	½ tsp
½ tsp	dried tarragon	½ tsp
170g (6 oz)	tofu, drained and mashed	¾ cup
	seasoning to taste	
4	tomatoes, sliced	4
6-8	black olives, to garnish	6-8

1 Preheat the oven to 400°F/200°C (Gas Mark 6).
2 Roll the pastry out, and line 6 to 8 small tart tins (tartlet molds). Prick the pastry with a fork, then bake the tarts (tartlets) blind (see page 152) in the preheated oven for 10 minutes. Do not turn the oven off as it will be needed later.
3 Meanwhile make the filling. Heat the oil and sauté the onions and garlic in it for 5 minutes. Add the herbs, cover the pan and cook them gently for 10 minutes. Stir in the mashed tofu, season it well and cook it for a minute longer.
4 Using a slotted spoon, lift the filling mixture from the pan, pressing it with another slotted spoon to remove as much moisture as possible. Put a couple of spoonfuls of the mixture into each of the tart cases (shells). Decorate the tops with the tomato slices, putting a black olive in the centre. Bake the tarts (tartlets) in the oven for 15 minutes.

Note: These tarts (tartlets) are great for a summer lunch in the garden or for a buffet.

Oriental Vegetables in a Rice Case

Rice case

170g (6 oz)	brown rice	¾ cup
2	free-range eggs, beaten	2
30g (1 oz)	sesame seeds	2 tbsp

Filling

2 tbsp	vegetable oil	2 tbsp
1 tsp	fresh ginger, peeled and grated (shredded)	1 tsp
6	spring onions (scallions), chopped	6
1	stick celery, finely chopped	1
1 medium	courgette (zucchini), chopped	1 medium
115g (4 oz)	mushrooms, chopped	2 cups
115g (4 oz)	mange-tout (snow peas)	4 oz
115g (4 oz)	baby sweetcorn	4 oz
55g (2 oz)	mung beansprouts	1 cup
55g (2 oz)	pumpkin seeds	⅓ cup
	soy sauce to taste	

1 Preheat the oven to 400°F/200°C (Gas Mark 6).

2 Boil the rice for 20 to 30 minutes until it is tender, then drain it well. Mix in the egg and the sesame seeds. Press the mixture evenly against the base and sides of a flan ring (from a loose-bottomed quiche pan) standing on a baking sheet. Bake the rice case in the preheated oven for 20 minutes or until it is firm.

3 Meanwhile, make the filling. Heat the oil and sauté the ginger and spring onions (scallions) briefly in it. Add the celery and cook it for a few minutes, stirring continually. Add the courgette (zucchini) and mushrooms and cook them in the same way for 5 minutes. Add the mange-tout (snow peas) and baby sweetcorn, cook them for a minute, then add the mung beansprouts and pumpkin seeds and just heat them through. Sprinkle soy sauce over the pan as you cook to moisten. All the vegetables should still be crisp at the end of this cooking time.

4 Carefully unmould the warm rice case onto a serving dish, pile in the filling and serve at once.

Note: Not truly a flan (savoury tart), this is more like a fancy way to serve vegetables! However, it is also a good way to use up leftover rice and it looks spectacular – ideal for a special lunch.

Cashew Nut Flan

225g (8 oz)	pastry of your choice (see pages 152-153)	8 oz
1 tbsp	finely chopped onion	1 tbsp

Filling

30g (1 oz)	margarine	2½ tbsp
1 small	leek, sliced	1 small
1 small	red pepper	1 small
115g (4 oz)	cashew nuts, finely ground	1 cup
140ml (¼ pt)	milk	⅔ cup
1 tsp	dried marjoram	1 tsp
1 tsp	dried parsley	1 tsp
	seasoning to taste	
1 large	free-range egg, beaten	1 extra large
	parsley sprigs, to garnish	

1 Make the pastry, mixing in the onion, ensuring that any excess moisture has been removed first, and line a medium-sized flan dish (quiche pan) or ring (ring from a loose-bottomed quiche pan) standing on a baking sheet.

2 Now make the filling. Melt the margarine and sauté the leek in it for a few minutes. Cut the pepper into half crossways and scoop out the seeds and ribs. Reserve half for garnishing, but chop the rest, add it to the leek and cook until both the leek and pepper begin to soften.

3 Preheat the oven to 350°F/180°C (Gas Mark 4).

4 Stir in the cashew, milk and herbs and season to taste. Mix all the ingredients together well. Remove the pan from the heat, cool the mixture briefly, then add the egg. Pour the mixture into the pastry case (shell) and smooth the top. Cut the reserved pepper into rings and arrange these on top of the mixture, pressing them down into it gently. Bake it in the preheated oven for 35 to 40 minutes. Garnish the cooked flan (savoury tart) with the parsley and serve it hot.

Note: This filling is quite rich, so if you are serving this flan (savoury tart) as a starter, follow it with something light.

Cauliflower Cheese Meringue

Pastry

75g (3 oz)	margarine	⅓ cup
200g (7 oz)	wholemeal pastry (whole wheat) flour	1¾ cups
75g (3 oz)	grated Cheddar cheese	¾ cup
	cold water, to mix	
1-2 tbsp	whole caraway seeds	1-2 tbsp

Filling

30g (1 oz)	margarine	2½ tbsp
1 small	cauliflower, broken into florets	1 small

Topping

2	*free-range egg whites*	2
	seasoning to taste	
55g (2 oz)	*grated Cheddar cheese*	*½ cup*

1 Preheat the oven to 375°F/190°C (Gas Mark 5).
2 First make the pastry. Rub the margarine lightly into the flour until the mixture resembles breadcrumbs, add the cheese, then stir in enough water to bind the mixture to a dough. Sprinkle the caraway seeds over the dough, knead it lightly, wrap it in polythene and chill it for at least 30 minutes. Then roll the dough out and line a medium-sized flan dish (tart pan) or ring (loose-bottomed tartlet pan) standing on a baking sheet. Prick it with a fork, then bake it blind (see page 152) in the preheated oven for 15 minutes. Leave the oven on, but lower the temperature to 325°F/170°C (Gas Mark 3).
3 Meanwhile, make the filling. Melt the margarine and add the cauliflower. Stir and cook it briefly, then cover the pan and cook it for 5 minutes more or until it is just tender, before draining it well.
4 Next, make the meringue topping by beating the egg whites until they are stiff and seasoning them to taste. Then fold in the cheese.
5 Put the cauliflower into the pastry case (shell), top it with the meringue mixture then put it straight into the oven and bake it for 20 minutes or until it is well risen. Serve at once.

Note: A very attractive-looking dish, serve it to guests who arrive unexpectedly for lunch. Other vegetables can be used instead of the cauliflower.

Ricotta and Pepper Cheesecakes

225g (8 oz)	*pastry of your choice (see pages 152-153)*	*8 oz*

Filling

1 tbsp	*vegetable oil*	*1 tbsp*
1 medium	*red pepper, sliced*	*1 medium*
1 medium	*green pepper, sliced*	*1 medium*
1 medium	*yellow pepper, sliced*	*1 medium*
225g (8 oz)	*Ricotta cheese*	*1 cup*
3	*free-range eggs, beaten*	*3*
pinch	*ground nutmeg*	*pinch*
	seasoning to taste	
55g (2 oz)	*Parmesan cheese, grated*	*½ cup*

1 Preheat the oven to 400°F/200°C (Gas Mark 6).
2 Roll the pastry out and line 6 or 8 small tart tins (tartlet molds). Prick them with a fork, then bake them blind (see page 152) in the preheated oven for 5 minutes.
3 Now make the filling. Heat the oil and sauté the red, green and yellow peppers for a few minutes, then cover the pan and simmer them for 10 more minutes or until they have softened (add a spoonful of water if they seem to be drying out). Leave the oven on, but lower the temperature to 350°F/180°C (Gas Mark 4).
4 Drain the peppers well, then mix them with the cheese and eggs. Add the nutmeg and season the mixture generously. Divide the mixture between the prepared cases, top each one with a sprinkling of the Parmesan and bake them in the oven for 30 minutes or until the filling has set.

Note: These little cheesecakes are perfect for a light lunch. If you serve them as the first course of an evening meal, garnish them with some radicchio leaves and parsley for a splash of colour.

Blue Cheese Cheesecake

Crust

170ml (6 oz)	digestive biscuits (Graham crackers)	6 oz
85g (3 oz)	margarine	⅓ cup

Filling

4 tbsp	milk	4 tbsp
1½ tsp	carrageen	1½ tsp
140g (5 oz)	Ricotta cheese	⅔ cup
85g (3 oz)	blue cheese	3 oz
2	free-range eggs, separated	2
	seasoning to taste	
½	cucumber, sliced	½
30g (1 oz)	walnuts (English walnuts), coarsely chopped	¼ cup

1 First, make the crust. Crush the biscuits (crackers) into fine crumbs. Melt the margarine and mix it into the biscuits. Press the mixture in an even layer across the base of a lightly greased, medium-sized loose-bottomed quiche tin (pan).

2 Now make the filling. Heat the milk, whisk in the carrageen and cook it, without boiling, for 2 minutes, then set the mixture to one side to cool.

3 Mash both the cheeses, blend them together, add the egg yolks and season the mixture to taste. Stir in the milk and carrageen mixture. Beat the egg whites until they are stiff, then, using a metal spoon fold them into the cheese mixture, making sure that everything is well blended. Pour the mixture into the tin (pan) and smooth the top. Garnish the top by arranging the cucumber slices, overlapping, in a ring around the outer edge, then sprinkle the nuts in the middle.

4 Chill the cheesecake for at least 2 to 3 hours, then very carefully remove it from its tin (pan) and transfer it to a serving plate. To cut, first dip the knife in hot water.

Note: This is a splendid dish to serve at a party. If you don't already have one, do invest in a loose-bottomed tin (pan) as it makes it so much easier to keep the cheesecake in one piece.

Spinach Cheesecake

Crust

170ml (6 oz)	savoury crackers (see note)	6 oz
85g (3 oz)	margarine	⅓ cup

Filling

455g (1 lb)	fresh spinach, well washed and shredded	10 cups
285g (10 oz)	curd cheese (cottage cheese, mashed)	1¼ cups
3	free-range eggs, separated	3
1 tbsp	wholemeal (whole wheat) flour	1 tbsp
¼ tsp	ground nutmeg	¼ tsp
140ml (¼ pt)	natural (unsweetened) yogurt	⅔ cup
	seasoning to taste	
2	tomatoes, sliced, to garnish	2
	fresh parsley, to garnish	

1 First, make the crust. Crush the crackers, melt the margarine and mix them together. Spread the mixture evenly across the base of a lightly greased medium-sized loose-bottomed tin (pan). Set it to one side.

2 Preheat the oven to 325°F/170°C (Gas Mark 3).

3 Now make the filling. Cook the spinach (in just the water still on the leaves from when it was washed), then drain it well and chop it as finely as possible. Press it down in a sieve (strainer) to remove any remaining water. Soften the cheese then mix in the spinach, egg yolks, flour, nutmeg and yogurt and seasoning to taste. Whisk the egg whites until they are stiff, then, using a metal spoon, gently fold them into the spinach and cheese mixture.

4 Pour the mixture over the biscuit base, smooth the top and bake the cheesecake in the oven for about 1½ hours or until the cheesecake feels firm (do not let it cook too long or it will be hard). Remove it carefully from the tin and garnish it with the tomato slices and parsley. Serve it either hot or cold.

Note: This is a perfect dish for either a summer or winter lunch (use frozen spinach when fresh is not available).

Use whatever savoury biscuits you like, but those with sesame or poppy seeds are especially good.

As it takes a little time and care to prepare, why not make two at the same time and keep one in the freezer for when unexpected guests arrive?

8
Pasta

Pasta Tricolore

225g (8 oz)	dried wholemeal (whole wheat) pasta spirals	4 cups
2 tbsp	vegetable oil	2 tbsp
½ medium	onion, sliced	½ medium
6	tomatoes, coarsely chopped	6
1 tbsp	fresh basil, chopped	1 tbsp
	seasoning to taste	
1 large	avocado	1 large
170g (6 oz)	Ricotta cheese	¾ cup

1 Cook the pasta in a saucepan of boiling water and, when it is *al dente**, drain it.
2 Meanwhile, heat the oil and sauté the onion for a few minutes. Stir in the tomatoes and basil and season to taste. Cook them for 5 more minutes, then add the pasta.
3 Peel the avocado, remove the stone (pit) and dice the flesh. Stir this into the pasta mixture and continue cooking over a gentle heat for just a minute or two to heat the avocado through.
4 Pile the pasta into a serving dish or onto 4 small plates, top it with the cheese and extra freshly ground black pepper and serve at once.

Note: Avocado is an original addition to pasta, but do not cook it too long or it becomes bitter. You could use Mozzarella instead of the Ricotta cheese.

* The term *al dente* ('firm to the teeth' in Italian) indicates the cooking of pasta until just tender, i.e. not too soft.

Tagliatelle with Cauliflower and Lentils

55g (2 oz)	margarine	¼ cup
1 small	onion, sliced	1 small
½ medium	cauliflower, broken into florets	½ medium
140g (5 oz)	dried split red lentils	¾ cup
140ml (¼ pt)	vegetable stock or milk	⅔ cup
½ tsp	dried oregano	½ tsp
	seasoning to taste	
225g (8 oz)	green tagliatelle	8 oz
	fresh chives, snipped, to garnish	

1 Melt the margarine and sauté the onion in it until it begins to soften. Stir in the cauliflower, cook it briefly, then add the lentils, stock or milk and oregano and season to taste. Bring to the boil, then cover the pan and simmer gently for 10 minutes or until the cauliflower and lentils are cooked. Adjust the seasoning to taste.
2 Meanwhile, drop the pasta into a pan of boiling water and cook it until it is *al dente*, then drain it well.
3 Divide the pasta between 4 plates, top each with some of the cauliflower and lentil sauce, garnish with a sprinkling of the chives and serve at once.

Note: This sauce can be made creamier by adding a few spoonfuls of yogurt. It is also good topped with some curd (cottage cheese, mashed) or low-fat cream cheese just before serving. You can use other pulses (legumes) instead of the lentils, such as ground chick peas (garbanzos). It is also an excellent way of using up leftover hummus.

Greek-style Lasagne

140g (5 oz)	TVP 'mince' (TVP 'ground round')	5 oz
170g (6 oz)	wholemeal (whole wheat) lasagne sheets	6 oz
1 medium	aubergine (eggplant), diced	1 medium
	sea salt, as required	
2 tbsp	vegetable oil	2 tbsp
1 medium	onion, sliced	1 medium
1	clove garlic, crushed (minced)	1
4	tomatoes, chopped	4
1 tbsp	fresh parsley, chopped	1 tbsp
1 tbsp	fresh oregano, chopped	1 tbsp
	seasoning to taste	
140ml (¼ pt)	sour (soured) cream	⅔ cup
2	free-range eggs, lightly beaten	2
55g (2 oz)	Feta cheese, crumbled	½ cup

1 Rehydrate the TVP 'mince' (TVP 'ground round').
2 Cook the lasagne in boiling salted water until it is *al dente*. Remove them from the pan, rinse them in cold water, then lay them out, side by side, on a clean tea towel (dish towel).
3 The TVP mince may well be tender enough to use, but if it is still hard, cook it briefly before draining it.
4 Spread the aubergine (eggplant) on a baking sheet, sprinkle sea salt over it and leave it for 30 minutes or until the bitter juices have oozed out. Rinse it in cold water, drain it very well then pat dry.
5 Heat the oil and sauté the onion and garlic in it for 5 minutes or until they have softened. Add the aubergine (eggplant) and continue cooking for 5 more minutes, stirring the mixture frequently. Then add the tomatoes, herbs, TVP mince (TVP ground round) and season to taste. Continue to cook it gently and if it starts to become dry, add a very little water.
6 Preheat the oven to 375°F/190°C (Gas Mark 5).
7 Combine the cream and eggs.
8 Lay a third of the lasagne sheets in the base of a greased, heatproof dish, top with half the 'meat' mixture, trickle a few spoonfuls of the cream mixture over it, then repeat these layers once more. Top with the rest of the lasagne sheets, the rest of the sour cream and sprinkle the cheese over the top.
9 Bake the lasagne in the preheated oven for 30 minutes or until the top is bubbling and golden brown.

Note: This makes a very satisfying lunch. To serve it as a starter, though, cook it in individual dishes or ramekins.

Rigatoni all'Amatriciana

2 tbsp	vegetable oil	2 tbsp
1 medium	onion, sliced	1 medium
70ml (⅛ pt)	dry white wine	¼ cup
4 large	tomatoes, peeled and chopped	4 large
approx. 4 tbsp	soya 'bacon' bits	approx 4 tbsp
	seasoning to taste	
1 tsp	fresh rosemary, chopped fine	1 tsp
285g (10 oz)	rigatoni (ribbed pasta)	5 cups
55g (2 oz)	Parmesan cheese, grated	½ cup

1 Heat the oil and gently fry the onion until it begins to soften. Add the white wine and tomatoes, stir well, and cook gently for about 10 minutes to make a sauce. Add the 'bacon' bits, season generously and add the rosemary.
2 Meanwhile, cook the pasta in boiling water for 10 minutes, or until just tender. Drain well, transfer to a serving dish, and pour the sauce over the top. Sprinkle with cheese and serve at once.

Note: Easy to make, filling, this is an ideal lunchtime snack. Although traditionally made with bacon, this dish also tastes good with nuts. Alternatively, stir in some cooked peas to add colour as well as protein. If you cannot find *rigatoni* in your local shops, use wholemeal (whole wheat) macaroni instead.

Fennel and Egg Vermicelli

2 small	fennel bulbs, trimmed and cut into chunks	2 small
1 tbsp	vegetable oil	1 tbsp
1	clove garlic, peeled and crushed	1
2 tbsp	single (light) cream	2 tbsp
1 tbsp	lemon juice	1 tbsp
	seasoning to taste	
225g (8 oz)	vermicelli	8 oz
6	free-range eggs, hard-boiled, peeled and quartered, to garnish	6
	fresh parsley, chopped, to garnish	

1 Drop the fennel into a pan of boiling water and cook it for just a few minutes, then remove it and drain well.
2 Heat the oil and sauté the garlic in it until it begins to soften. Add the fennel, stir and cook briefly. Stir in the cream, lemon juice and season well.
3 At the same time, cook the vermicelli in boiling water. As this pasta is very fine, it should be ready in just 5 minutes. Drain it well.
4 Pile the pasta into a small serving dish, top with the

fennel mixture and garnish with the egg and parsley. Serve at once.

Note: Artichoke hearts can be prepared in much the same way. If fresh ones are not available, use the ones sold in jars (although they are also available in tins (cans) these are rather tasteless).

Brazil Nut and Leek Ravioli

225g (8 oz)	pasta dough (see page 153)	8 oz

Filling

115g (4 oz)	brazil nuts, coarsely ground	1 cup
85g (3 oz)	wholemeal (whole wheat) breadcrumbs	1½ cups
30g (1 oz)	wheatgerm	¼ cup
1 tbsp	vegetable oil	1 tbsp
1 medium	leek, washed, trimmed and finely chopped	1 medium
1 tsp	dried sage	1 tsp
	soy sauce to taste	
	seasoning to taste	
55g (2 oz)	margarine	¼ cup
	parsley sprigs, to garnish	

1 Roll the pasta dough out thinly, cut it into small ravioli-sized squares. Place half of them on a flat, lightly floured surface and put the rest to one side.
2 Now make the filling. Mix together the nuts, breadcrumbs and wheatgerm.
3 Heat the oil and sauté the leek for a few minutes until it has softened. Add the nut mixture, then the sage and soy sauce and seasoning to taste. Use a wooden spoon to mash all the ingredients into a thick smooth paste (add either more soy sauce or a little water if the mixture is too thick).
4 Drop a spoonful of the mixture in the middle of each of half of the squares. Cover each one with one of the squares you put to one side, dampening the edges and pressing them firmly together.
5 Bring a large pan of salted water to the boil and drop in the ravioli, a few at a time, stirring once. Cook each batch gently for 8 to 10 minutes or until they rise to the surface. Use a slotted spoon to remove the cooked ravioli from the water, drain them well and keep them warm until all of them have been cooked. Serve them dotted with margarine and garnished with the parsley.

Note: This ravioli is a good starter to a winter meal, followed by something light, like a soufflé with a salad. Other nuts can be used instead of brazil nuts or simply mash leftover nut roast and use it as a filling.

Red Pepper Lasagne with Tahini

170g (6 oz)	lasagne verde sheets	6 oz
2 tbsp	vegetable oil	2 tbsp
1 medium	onion, sliced	1 onion
2	sticks celery, chopped	2
2 large	red peppers, sliced	2 large
55g (2 oz)	wholemeal (whole wheat) flour	½ cup
	cold water, as required	
115g (4 oz)	peas, cooked	⅔ cup
2 tbsp	tahini, or to taste	2 tbsp
	seasoning to taste	
55g (2 oz)	margarine	¼ cup
55g (2 oz)	wholemeal (whole wheat) breadcrumbs	1 cup
2 tbsp	fresh parsley, coarsely chopped	2 tbsp

1 Cook the lasagne in boiling salted water until it is *al dente*. Then, remove it at once from the heat and rinse it in cold water. Drain it well, laying the sheets out side by side on a clean tea towel (dish towel).
2 Preheat the oven to 400°F/200°C (Gas Mark 6).
3 Heat the oil and sauté the onion, celery and red pepper together for 5 minutes, stirring occasionally. Sprinkle and stir in the flour, cooking it briefly, then add just enough cold water to cover the vegetables and continue cooking until the vegetables are tender. Gently stir in first the peas, then the tahini to taste and season generously (the sauce should be quite liquid, so, if it seems too dry, add more water or some vegetable stock at this point).
4 In a shallow, ovenproof dish, layer the lasagne alternately with the vegetable mixture, finishing with a layer of lasagne. Mix the margarine, breadcrumbs and parsley together and sprinkle the mixture over the top. Bake the lasagne in the preheated oven for 20 to 30 minutes.

Note: This sauce can also be flavoured with different herbs, soy sauce or yeast extract. A delicious winter version of this lasagne can be made with leeks and parsnip.

Spaghetti Tempeh Bolognese

30g (1 oz)	margarine	2½ tbsp
2 tbsp	vegetable oil	2 tbsp
1	clove garlic, peeled and crushed	1
½ tsp	chilli powder, or to taste	½ tsp
1 large	onion, finely chopped	1 large
1 large	green pepper, finely chopped	1 large
55g (2 oz)	mushrooms, finely chopped	¾ cup
395-g (14-oz)	tin (can) tomatoes, chopped	14-oz
2 tbsp	tomato purée (paste)	2 tbsp
½ tsp	dried parsley	½ tsp
	seasoning to taste	
225g (8 oz)	tempeh	1 cup
225g (8 oz)	wholemeal (whole wheat) spaghetti	8 oz

1 Melt the margarine with half the oil, add the garlic and cook it briefly before adding the chilli powder, onion and green pepper. Cook gently until the vegetables begin to soften. Stir in the mushrooms and cook them for 3 minutes, then add the tomato, tomato purée and parsley and season to taste. Continue simmering the mixture gently.
2 In a separate pan, heat the remaining oil. Chop the tempeh into small cubes and fry them gently, stirring so that all the sides are evenly browned, then stir them into the sauce.
3 Meanwhile, cook the spaghetti in a pan of boiling water. When it is just *al dente*, drain it well and transfer it to a serving dish. Top it with the sauce and serve at once.

Note: A different and tasty version of everyone's favourite spaghetti sauce. Make up twice as much as you need and freeze the extra, ready for an instant light lunch another day. Traditionally, Bolognese Sauce contains meat, but tempeh is just as rich in protein and flavour with the added advantages of being low in saturated fats and especially easy to digest. If you cannot find tempeh, use tofu instead or TVP mince (TVP ground round), first rehydrating it in a flavoured stock.

Cheese and Pea Lasagne

170g (6 oz)	wholemeal (whole wheat) lasagne sheets	6 oz
55g (2 oz)	margarine	¼ cup
55g (2 oz)	wholemeal (whole wheat) flour	½ cup
850ml (1½ pt)	milk	3¾ cups
115g (4 oz)	blue cheese, crumbled	1 cup
115g (4 oz)	Cheddar cheese, grated	1 cup
115g (4 oz)	peas, cooked	1 cup

1 Cook the lasagne in boiling salted water until it is *al dente*. Rinse it in cold water then lay the sheets out side by side on a clean tea towel (dish towel).
2 Preheat the oven to 400°F/200°C (Gas Mark 6).
3 Melt the margarine, stir in the flour and let it cook for a minute, stirring. Gradually add the milk, cooking gently and stirring continually. Stir in most of the cheeses. The sauce should be of a pouring consistency, so, if necessary, add a little more milk.
4 Layer the prepared lasagne alternately with the sauce in 4 small dishes or ramekins, sprinkling some of the peas over each layer. Finish with a pasta layer and sprinkle the remaining cheese over the tops. Bake them in the preheated oven for 20 minutes or until they are cooked with the cheese bubbling and just browning. Serve them at once.

Note: A very rich lasagne, it is perfect for a snack – just add French bread and follow with fruit. You can make the flavour more subtle by using a soft cheese, such as cottage or Ricotta, instead of the Cheddar.

Crunchy Bean, Egg and Macaroni Bake

115g (4 oz)	wholemeal (whole wheat) macaroni	2 cups
455g (1 lb)	fresh broad (fava) beans, shelled (see note)	1 cup
285ml (½ pt)	White Sauce (see page 156)	1⅓ cups
115g (4 oz)	Cheddar cheese, grated	1 cup
4	free-range eggs, hard-boiled	4
1 small	packet plain crisps (potato chips), lightly crushed	1 small

1 Cook the macaroni in boiling salted water until it is *al dente*, then drain it well.
2 Preheat the oven to 400°F/200°C (Gas Mark 6).
3 Meanwhile, cook the beans for 15 minutes or until they are tender, then drain them too. Heat the White Sauce, add most of the cheese and stir the sauce until the cheese melts.
4 Spread half the macaroni across the base of a small, greased, ovenproof dish, top it with half the beans, 2 of the eggs, cut into slices, then with half of the cheese sauce. Repeat the layers with the rest of the ingredients. Sprinkle the remaining cheese and the crisps (chips) over the top.
5 Bake it in the preheated oven for 15 minutes, then serve it at once.

Note: This is an inexpensive and filling dish that is ideal for lunch. Use frozen or tinned beans if you prefer, and add any vegetables you have to hand. Try other cheeses, too, or use soya 'bacon' bits instead of the crisps.

Cannelloni Florentine with Tofu

455g (1 lb)	*fresh spinach, well washed*	*1 lb*
2 tbsp	*vegetable oil*	*2 tbsp*
1 small	*onion, chopped*	*1 small*
½	*clove garlic, peeled and crushed*	*½*
285g (10 oz)	*tofu*	*1¼ cups*
¼ tsp	*ground nutmeg*	*¼ tsp*
	seasoning to taste	
8	*dried cannelloni tubes*	*8*
285ml (½ pt)	*Tomato Sauce (see page 156)*	*1⅓ cups*

1 Coarsely shred the spinach and put it into a saucepan. Cook it gently, covered in only the water remaining on the leaves, for a few minutes until they have wilted. Drain off any remaining liquid, then finely chop the spinach.
2 Preheat the oven to 400°F/200°C (Gas Mark 6).
3 Heat the oil and sauté the onion and garlic together in it for 5 minutes. Drain and mash the tofu and add it to the onion and garlic, together with the nutmeg and season to taste. Then stir in the spinach.
4 Stuff the cannelloni tubes with the tofu and spinach mixture and divide them between 4 small, lightly greased ovenproof dishes or ramekins. Cover the tubes evenly with the Tomato Sauce and bake them in the preheated oven for 20 minutes. Serve at once.

Note: You can use small foil dishes when preparing individual portions of cannelloni in this way, though they do not look as attractive as ramekins. They can, of course, be cooked together and then separated when you are serving.

For variety, use Ricotta or another soft cheese instead of the tofu. You can also mix the spinach into a thick white sauce and use this mixture to fill the tubes. Instead of the ready-made cannelloni, try making your own pasta (see Walnut Cannelloni, page 66).

Spaghetti with Red Pesto Sauce

Sauce

55g (2 oz)	*fresh basil leaves, chopped*	*2 oz*
1 tbsp	*red wine vinegar*	*1 tbsp*
1 small	*red pepper, chopped*	*1 small*
1	*clove garlic, peeled and crushed*	*1*
1 small	*stick celery, chopped*	*1 small*
1 medium	*carrot, chopped*	*1 medium*
1 tbsp	*fresh parsley, chopped*	*1 tbsp*
30g (1 oz)	*pine nuts*	*¼ cup*
30g (1 oz)	*cashew nut pieces*	*¼ cup*
140ml (¼ pt)	*olive oil*	*⅔ cup*
30g (1 oz)	*Parmesan cheese, grated*	*¼ cup*
	seasoning to taste	
1 tbsp	*tomato purée (paste) (optional)*	*1 tbsp*
225g (8 oz)	*spaghetti*	*8 oz*
30g (1 oz)	*butter* or *margarine*	*2½ tbsp*
55g (2 oz)	*Parmesan cheese, grated*	*½ cup*

1 In a blender, combine all the sauce ingredients to make a purée, preferably not too smooth as some texture adds interest. The sauce should be fairly moist, too, so add a little more oil if it seems dry. Adjust the seasoning to taste and stir in the tomato purée, if using (it gives the sauce a richer colour).
2 Drop the spaghetti into a large pan of boiling salted water and cook it until it is *al dente*. Drain it well, then return it to the pan and stir in at least 4 tablespoons of the sauce. Taste it and add more sauce if you wish. Pile the spaghetti onto a serving dish at once and dot with the butter or margarine, sprinkling the ½ cup of Parmesan over the top. Take the dish straight to the table.

Note: This is an unusual pesto sauce. Serve it with a small portion of pasta as a starter at your next dinner party and you'll have your guests guessing (the classic pesto is green in colour because it is made with basil, pine nuts, Parmesan cheese and garlic).

The sauce keeps in the refrigerator for a couple of weeks if stored in an airtight container.

Ravioli with Ricotta and Watercress

225g (8 oz)	pasta dough (see page 153)	8 oz

Filling

225g (8 oz)	Ricotta cheese	1 cup
55g (2 oz)	Parmesan cheese, grated	½ cup
2	free-range eggs	2
½-1 bunch	watercress, washed and coarsely chopped seasoning to taste	½-1 bunch
1	free-range egg white	1
285ml (½ pt)	Tomato Sauce (see page 156), hot	1⅓ cups

1 Divide the dough in half, then roll each half out thinly to make rectangles. Mark one into ravioli-sized squares.
2 Now make the filling. Mash together the Ricotta and Parmesan cheeses, add the 2 eggs and watercress and season to taste. Brush the lines on the marked dough with the egg white. Place a spoonful of the cheese mixture in the middle of each of the squares, then carefully lay the second sheet of dough on top of the first. Press it down gently but firmly along the lines on the lower sheet and, using a sharp knife or serrated dough cutter, cut it into squares. Press the edges again to make sure each square is sealed.
3 Drop the ravioli, a few at a time, into a large pan of boiling salted water, stirring once so that they do not stick. Continue cooking them for 8 to 10 minutes or until they rise to the surface. Drain each batch well. Serve them with the hot Tomato Sauce.

Note: If you find the dough difficult to handle, divide it into quarters rather than half and follow the same method with the smaller sheets of dough. Spinach is the more usual filling, but watercress is an excellent alternative and makes a refreshing change.

Sweet and Sour Pasta Shells

225g (8 oz)	wholemeal (whole wheat) pasta shells	4 cups
2 tbsp	vegetable oil	2 tbsp
1 small	onion, sliced	1 small
30g (1 oz)	wholemeal (whole wheat) flour	¼ cup
425ml (¾ pt)	vegetable stock or water	2 cups
1 tbsp	cider vinegar	1 tbsp
1 tbsp	runny (liquid) honey	1 tbsp
1 tbsp	soy sauce	1 tbsp
¼ tsp	mustard powder	¼ tsp
3 slices	pineapple, fresh or tinned (canned) seasoning to taste	3 slices
55g (2 oz)	flaked almonds, slivered parsley sprigs, to garnish	½ cup

1 Drop the pasta into a large pan of boiling salted water and cook it until it is al dente.
2 Heat the oil and sauté the onion in it for a few minutes until it has softened. Stir in the flour and cook it, stirring, for a minute. Gradually add the vegetable stock or water, stirring continually and bring it to a gentle boil. Add the cider vinegar, honey, soy sauce and mustard. Coarsely chop or crush the pineapple, stir this into the sauce, season to taste and simmer gently for 5 more minutes.
3 Drain the pasta and divide it between 4 plates, topping each portion with some of the sweet and sour sauce and a sprinkling of the nuts. Garnish with the parsley and serve.

Note: This is a surprisingly easy dish to prepare. For a special occasion, top each serving with pine nuts instead of the almonds. It is a good idea to make up extra sauce and keep it in the refrigerator to use in a day or two's time or in a different recipe.

Tagliatelle with Aubergine and Mozzarella

1 medium	aubergine (eggplant), diced sea salt, as required	1 medium
2 tbsp	olive oil	2 tbsp
1	clove garlic, peeled and crushed	1
1 large	green pepper, thickly sliced	1 large
1 tbsp	fresh basil, coarsely chopped, plus extra to garnish	1 tbsp
2 medium	tomatoes, coarsely chopped seasoning to taste	2 medium
225g (8 oz)	wholemeal (whole wheat) tagliatelle	8 oz
170g (6 oz)	Mozzarella cheese, coarsely chopped	2 cups
1 tbsp	capers	1 tbsp
12	black olives, chopped	12

1 Spread the aubergine (eggplant) out on a plate and sprinkle sea salt over it. Leave it for 30 minutes or until the bitter juices have oozed out, then rinse it in cold water, drain it well and pat it dry. To make sure the aubergine (eggplant) is as dry as possible, press the cubes gently.
2 Heat the oil and sauté the garlic and green pepper in it until they have softened. Add the aubergine

(eggplant) and cook it for 10 minutes, stirring frequently. Add the basil and tomato and season to taste.

3 Meanwhile, cook the tagliatelle in plenty of boiling salted water. When it is almost *al dente*, stir the cheese into the aubergine (eggplant) and pepper mixture, together with the capers and olives. Then drain the pasta, pile it onto a serving dish, pour the sauce over the top and sprinkle the remaining basil over the top. Serve at once.

Note: If you want to avoid dairy produce, replace the cheese with cooked chick peas as they work especially well in this recipe.

Vegetable Chow Mein

225g (8 oz)	wholemeal (whole wheat) noodles	8 oz
2 tbsp	vegetable oil	2 tbsp
1 tsp	ground ginger	1 tsp
1 medium	onion, sliced	1 medium
2 medium	carrots, sliced	2 medium
½ small	head cauliflower, broken into florets	½ small
2	sticks celery, sliced	2
55g (2 oz)	beansprouts	1 cup
	soy sauce to taste	
	seasoning to taste	
30g (1 oz)	sesame seeds	¼ cup
	watercress sprigs, to garnish	

1 Bring a saucepan of water to the boil, drop in the noodles and bring it back to the boil. Then cover the saucepan, remove it from the heat and set it to one side.

2 In a wok or large frying pan (skillet), heat the oil and cook the ginger for 1 minute. Add the onion, carrot, cauliflower and celery and stir fry them over a high heat for 5 to 10 minutes or until they have softened slightly (but they should still be crisp). Stir in the beansprouts, flavour with the soy sauce and seasoning to taste.

3 Drain the noodles and stir them into the vegetables, cooking them briefly to heat through. Add the sesame seeds then serve the chow mein at once, garnished with the watercress.

Note: This is a quick and easy recipe – and it makes a change from serving stir-fried vegetables with rice. If you feel the need for more protein add cubes of tofu or a handful of cashew nuts.

Broccoli, Chick Peas and Pasta

455g (1 lb)	broccoli, trimmed and broken into florets	1 lb
225g (8 oz)	pasta shells	4 cups
55g (2 oz)	margarine	¼ cup
2 tbsp	vegetable oil	2 tbsp
1-2	cloves garlic, peeled and crushed	1-2
4	spring onions (scallions), chopped	4
225g (8 oz)	cooked (canned) chick peas (see page 9)	8 oz
170g (6 oz)	tofu, drained and crumbled	¾ cup
	seasoning to taste	
55g (2 oz)	wholemeal (whole wheat) breadcrumbs	1 cup

1 Steam the broccoli for 8 to 10 minutes or until it is just tender, then drain it and set it to one side.

2 Drop the pasta into a pan of boiling, salted water and cook it until it is *al dente*. Drain it well.

3 Meanwhile, heat half the margarine together with the oil and sauté the garlic in them for a few minutes. Then add the spring onions (scallions) and cook them for a few minutes. Stir in the chick peas (garbanzos), broccoli and tofu and continue cooking over a low heat, stirring continually, so that all the ingredients are piping hot. Add the pasta and cook the mixture for a minute more and season to taste.

4 In another pan, melt the remaining margarine and fry the breadcrumbs until they are crisp and golden brown. Transfer the vegetable and pasta mixture to a serving dish and sprinkle the fried breadcrumbs over the top.

Note: You can use other vegetables or cooked beans instead of those given. Try, too, stirring sour (soured) cream, curd or cottage cheese into the cooked vegetables instead of the tofu or add some scrambled eggs.

Creamed Macaroni with Mushrooms

225g (8 oz)	wholemeal (whole wheat) macaroni	8 oz
55g (2 oz)	margarine	¼ cup
225g (8 oz)	mushrooms, thickly sliced	4 cups
140g (5 oz)	garlic and herb cream cheese	⅔ cup
2 tbsp	fresh parsley, chopped freshly ground black pepper to taste	2 tbsp
4	tomatoes, quartered, to garnish	4

1 Cook the macaroni in a pan of boiling salted water until it is *al dente*, then drain it well.
2 Meanwhile, melt the margarine and gently fry the mushrooms in it, turning them so that both sides are lightly browned, then drain well.
3 Return the macaroni to its pan, add the mushrooms and stir in the cheese. Continue cooking for just a few minutes (the cheese melts to form a creamy sauce). Add the parsley and plenty of freshly ground black pepper. Divide the mixture between 4 plates and garnish with the tomato quarters before serving.

Note: A really quick recipe, it makes a satisfying and tasty lunch dish. There is quite a range of full- or low-fat cheeses flavoured with garlic and herbs, so experiment to find your personal favourite.

Walnut Cannelloni

225g (8 oz)	pasta dough (see page 153)	8 oz
Filling		
2 tbsp	vegetable oil	2 tbsp
1 large	onion, sliced	1 large
2 medium	courgettes (zucchini), finely chopped	2 medium
55g (2 oz)	wholemeal (whole wheat) breadcrumbs	1 cup
55g (2 oz)	walnuts (English walnuts), chopped	½ cup
55g (2 oz)	sweetcorn, cooked	⅓ cup
½ tsp	dried marjoram	½ tsp
1 large	free-range egg, lightly beaten seasoning to taste	1 large
285ml (½ pt)	White Sauce (see page 156)	1⅓ cups
30g (1 oz)	Cheddar cheese, grated fresh parsley, to garnish	¼ cup

1 Roll out the pasta dough and cut it into even-sized rectangles. Drop them into a pan of boiling salted water and, when they are *al dente* remove them from the pan and rinse with cold water. Drain them well, and lay them side by side on a clean tea towel (dish towel).
2 Preheat the oven to 400°F/200°C (Gas Mark 6).
3 Heat the oil and sauté the onion in it for a few minutes before adding the courgettes (zucchini). Cook them until they begin to soften. Then stir in the breadcrumbs, nuts, sweetcorn, marjoram and egg and season to taste.
4 Put a couple of spoonfuls of the mixture onto each of the pasta rectangles, roll them up carefully and lay them close together, join side downwards, in a lightly greased ovenproof dish. Pour the White Sauce over the cannelloni so that they are evenly covered and sprinkle the cheese over the top. Bake them in the preheated oven for 20 minutes. Serve at once, garnished with the parsley for a splash of colour.

Note: Cannelloni *is* fiddly to prepare, so it is worth making extra and freezing it. Do try other filling mixtures, too. For speed, use dried cannelloni tubes which just need to be stuffed and baked (see Cannelloni Florentine with Tofu, page 63).

Buckwheat Noodles with Miso Sauce

Noodles		
170g (6 oz)	buckwheat flour	1½ cups
55g (2 oz)	wholemeal (whole wheat) flour	½ cup
good pinch	salt	good pinch
1 large	free-range egg	1 extra large
3 tbsp	milk warm water, to mix	3 tbsp
Sauce		
2 tbsp	vegetable oil	2 tbsp
1	clove garlic, peeled and crushed	1
1 large	leek, cleaned and sliced	1 large
455g (1 lb)	tomatoes, chopped	2⅔ cups
1 tbsp	fresh parsley, chopped	1 tbsp
1 tbsp	miso	1 tbsp
30g (1 oz)	sunflower seeds	¼ cup

1 Start by making the noodles. Sift together the 2 flours and the salt. Beat the egg with the milk and add the mixture to the dry ingredients together with just enough warm water to make a firm but pliable dough. Knead it for a few minutes, then cover the bowl and leave it on one side for at least 30 minutes.
2 Then divide the dough in half and roll each out into long thin rectangles. Roll them up loosely and use a sharp knife to cut them into thin strips. Unroll them carefully.

3 Now make the sauce. Heat the oil and sauté the garlic in it for a few minutes. Then add the leek and cook it gently until it begins to soften. Stir in the tomato and parsley. Dissolve the miso in a small amount of hot water and add this to the pan. Cook the mixture briefly over a low heat.

4 Meanwhile, drop the noodles into a saucepan of boiling salted water (home-made noodles should take only minutes to cook). Drain them, divide them between 4 plates, top each portion with the sauce and sprinkle the sunflower seeds over the top, then serve at once.

Note: Although miso is said to be highly nutritious, you can replace it with yeast extract, if you prefer, or even vegetable stock flavoured with soy sauce.

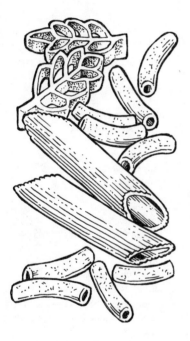

Tagliatelle with Nut Balls

225g (8 oz)	tagliatelle verde	8 oz
Nut balls		
225g (8 oz)	cashew nuts, ground	2 cups
55g (2 oz)	wholemeal (whole wheat) breadcrumbs	1 cup
1 tbsp	fresh chives, snipped	1 tbsp
	seasoning to taste	
	vegetable stock or milk, to bind	
	vegetable oil, for frying	
285ml (½ pt)	Tomato Sauce (see page 156)	1⅓ cups
	watercress sprigs, to garnish	

1 Cook the pasta in a large pan of boiling salted water until it is *al dente*.

2 Meanwhile, make the nut balls. Mix together the nuts, breadcrumbs and chives and season to taste, making sure that all the ingredients are well blended together. Add just enough stock or milk to bind the mixture together, then divide it into small, equal portions and roll them into balls.

3 Heat enough oil to shallow fry the balls, tipping the pan, until they have browned nicely all over. Drain them well. At the same time, heat the Tomato Sauce through.

4 Drain the pasta and top it with the Tomato Sauce and then place the nut balls on top. Garnish with the watercress and serve at once.

Note: To make the nut balls firmer, add 1 large (extra large), free-range egg to the mixture. Other nut or bean combinations can be used to make balls to serve with pasta, or try preparing some of the dry mixes on sale in wholefood shops in this way.

9
Grain Dishes

Cheese and Rice Balls

170g (6 oz)	raw brown rice	¾ cup
570ml (1 pt)	vegetable stock	2½ cups
2	tomatoes, peeled and chopped	2
2	free-range eggs, beaten	2
	seasoning to taste	
115g (4 oz)	diced Mozzarella cheese	generous cup
55g (2 oz)	fine wholemeal (whole wheat) breadcrumbs, or as required	1 cup
	vegetable oil, for frying	

1 Put the rice and stock into a pan, bring it to the boil, then cover the pan and simmer for 20 to 30 minutes or until the rice is tender. Drain it well, leave it to cool, then mix in the tomato and eggs and season to taste.
2 Flour your hands, put a spoonful of the rice mixture onto one palm, top it with a cube of cheese and carefully mould the rice around it to make a ball. Roll this very gently in the breadcrumbs until it is lightly and evenly coated. Repeat this method until all the rice mixture and cheese have been used up (you may find that you need more breadcrumbs).
3 Heat enough vegetable oil in a pan to deep fry the balls a few at a time, turning them frequently, but gently, to make sure that they brown evenly. Drain each batch and serve the Cheese and Rice Balls hot (the outside is crisp, while the cheese inside melts to a soft thick cream).

Note: These little balls make a delicious snack served with a salad. If you make the balls small, they are excellent buffet fare. Other cheeses can be used, too – Feta or blue cheese, for example, make an interesting contrast to the more bland rice.

Spicy Quinoa Salad

225g (8 oz)	raw quinoa	1 cup
	cold water, to cover	
1 small	orange pepper, finely chopped	1 small
4	spring onions (scallions), chopped	4
2	cloves garlic, peeled and crushed	2
2	sticks celery, finely chopped	2
55g (2 oz)	raisins	⅓ cup
2 tbsp	lemon juice	2 tbsp
2 tbsp	vegetable oil	2 tbsp
½ tsp	ground allspice	½ tsp
¼ tsp	chilli powder, or to taste	¼ tsp
	seasoning to taste	
55g (2 oz)	alfalfa sprouts	1 cup

1 Put the quinoa into a saucepan, cover it with cold water, bring it to the boil, then simmer for 10 minutes or until it is tender. Drain well.
2 Mix the cooked quinoa with the orange pepper, spring onions (scallions), garlic, celery and raisins.
3 Whisk together the lemon juice, oil, allspice and chilli powder and season to taste (or put the ingredients into a screw top jar and shake it well). Pour the mixture over the salad and toss it to coat the grains. Chill the salad, preferably overnight. Serve topped with the alfalfa sprouts.

Note: Quinoa is a tiny, golden grain with a mild flavour, lots of nutrients and comes originally from Peru. Use it in salads, for stuffing vegetables, or in place of rice to accompany curries and stir-fries. If you cannot find it in your local shops, you can still make this recipe, just substitute bulgar or rice.

Kasha-stuffed Lemons

4 medium	lemons	4 medium
85g (3 oz)	buckwheat (kasha)	⅓ cup
1 tbsp	lemon juice	1 tbsp
1 tbsp	capers, chopped	1 tbsp
3-4 tbsp	sour (soured) cream	3-4 tbsp
55g (2 oz)	pecan nuts, coarsely chopped	½ cup
1 tbsp	fresh chives, snipped	1 tbsp
	seasoning to taste	
	salad, to garnish	

1 Use a sharp knife to cut a thin slice from the base of the lemons, so that they will stand firmly. Then slice off the tops and scoop out as much of the flesh as you can.

2 Boil the buckwheat (kasha) in water for 20 to 30 minutes or until it is just tender (take care not to overcook it). Drain it well, leave it to cool, then mix the grains with the lemon juice, capers, cream, nuts and chives and season the mixture generously (if the mixture seems too dry, add more cream and/or lemon juice).

3 Spoon mixture into the prepared lemons and chill them briefly. Serve them on small plates with a colourful salad garnish (crisp, shredded red cabbage and green pepper rings, for example).

Note: This unusual starter is perfect for a special dinner as it is quick and easy to prepare, inexpensive and looks really attractive. You could use mayonnaise or a soft white cheese flavoured with garlic and herbs instead of the sour (soured) cream, if you like. Do use the scooped out lemon flesh for another recipe.

Millet and Sesame Croquettes

115g (4 oz)	millet	½ cup
½ small	onion, finely chopped	½ small
55g (2 oz)	mushrooms, finely chopped	1 cup
1 small	carrot (shredded)	1 small
2 tbsp	tahini	2 tbsp
1 tbsp	fresh parsley, chopped	1 tbsp
	seasoning to taste	
55g (2 oz)	sesame seeds	⅓ cup
4 tbsp	wholemeal (whole wheat) flour, or as required	4 tbsp
	vegetable oil, for frying	
285ml (½ pt)	Tomato Sauce (see page 156)	1⅓ cups
3-4 tbsp	natural (unsweetened) yogurt	3-4 tbsp

1 Put the millet into a pan and dry roast it for a few minutes, shaking the pan to heat it evenly, then cover it generously with water. Bring it to the boil, then lower the heat and simmer the millet for about 10 minutes or until it is soft. Drain it well.

2 Mix in the vegetables, tahini and parsley and season to taste. Add in most of the sesame seeds and enough flour to make the mixture fairly stiff. Break it into small, even-sized pieces and shape them into croquettes. Roll them in flour and the reserved sesame seeds, then chill them briefly.

3 Heat enough oil to deep fry the croquettes. Handle them gently and fry them until they are crisp and browned. Drain them well. Meanwhile, heat the Tomato Sauce, stir in the yogurt, then transfer the sauce to a jug so people can help themselves when you serve the croquettes.

Note: An inexpensive and filling grain, millet is ideal for snacks such as these croquettes. You can use any vegetables in place of those suggested, though do be sure to chop them finely. Ring the changes by adding an egg or two instead of the tahini (which will also make the croquettes firmer in texture), some grated (shredded) cheese, other nuts instead of the seeds.

Barley and Broccoli Salad

170g (6 oz)	pot barley	¾ cup
425ml (¾ pt)	water	2 cups
455g (1 lb)	broccoli, trimmed and broken into florets	1 lb
6	radishes, sliced	6
115g (4 oz)	cottage cheese	½ cup
	seasoning to taste	
55g (2 oz)	walnuts (English walnuts) coarsely chopped	½ cup
½ bunch	watercress, to garnish	½ bunch

1 Dry roast the barley in a pan for a few minutes, shaking the pan occasionally, then add the water and bring it to the boil. Cook the barley covered for about 45 minutes or until it is tender, adding more water if necessary. Drain it well and put it to one side to cool.

2 Meanwhile, plunge the broccoli florets into boiling water and cook them for 3 minutes, then drain them, rinse them in cold water and drain again.

4 In a salad bowl, stir together the barley, broccoli and radish slices. Pile the cottage cheese into the middle, season to taste, then sprinkle the nuts over the top. Garnish with watercress.

Note: This is an original and filling salad. Use pot barley rather than pearl barley. Although it takes longer to cook, it is far superior to pot barley both in terms of nutrition and taste.

Creamy Vegetable Crumble with Wheat Berry Topping

170g (6 oz)	green beans, trimmed and sliced	scant ½ cup
1 small	red pepper, sliced	1 small
1 large	stick celery, sliced	1 large
115g (4 oz)	sweetcorn, fresh or frozen	⅔ cup
285ml (½ pt)	White Sauce (see page 156)	1⅓ cups
2 tbsp	single (light) or sour (soured) cream	2 tbsp
¼ tsp	ground nutmeg, or to taste	¼ tsp
	seasoning to taste	

Topping

115g (4 oz)	wheat berries, cooked	1 cup
1 large	free-range egg, beaten	1 extra large
	seasoning to taste	

1 Preheat the oven to 400°F/200°C (Gas Mark 6).
2 Put the beans, red pepper, celery and sweetcorn into a pan, cover them with boiling water and cook them for about 10 minutes or until the vegetables are just tender, then drain them well. Combine them with the White Sauce, cream and nutmeg and season generously. Transfer the mixture to a small, ovenproof dish.
3 Next, make the topping. Stir together the drained wheat berries and egg and season to taste. Spread this mixture evenly over the vegetables.
4 Bake the crumble in the preheated oven for 20 minutes or until the top is cooked, then serve it at once.

Note: Ideal for lunch, this dish is also a good way of using up leftover grains. Any grains can be used in place of the whole wheat berries, but their lovely nutty texture make them an especially satisfying contrast to the creamy vegetable mixture.

Brown Rice Timbales

225g (8 oz)	raw brown rice	1 cup
570ml (1 pt)	water	2½ cups
2 tbsp	French Dressing or to taste	2 tbsp
55g (2 oz)	flaked (slivered) almonds, roasted and coarsely ground	½ cup
½ small	fennel bulb, finely chopped	½ small
½ bunch	watercress, washed and chopped	½ bunch
3	tomatoes, peeled and chopped	3
	seasoning to taste	
	extra watercress, to garnish	
	tomato slices, to garnish	
	mayonnaise (dairy or soya) to serve	

1 Cook the rice in the water until it is tender (about 25 to 30 minutes). Drain it well and put it into a bowl. Stir in the French Dressing, then add the almonds, fennel, watercress and tomatoes, mixing them together well. Season to taste.
2 Lightly grease 4 small moulds and divide the mixture between them, pressing it down firmly into them. Cover each one with foil and chill for at least 1 hour. When the timbales are ready, remove the foil, cover each mould with a small plate, invert it carefully and gently lift off the mould so that they hold their shape. Decorate them with the tomato slices and watercress and then serve them accompanied with fresh mayonnaise.

Note: Serve the timbales as a starter or as an accompaniment to a main dish. They are also good with a tahini or yogurt sauce.

Couscous in Courgette Boats

4 medium	courgettes (zucchini), wiped	4 medium
115g (4 oz)	couscous	⅔ cup
425ml (¾ pt)	vegetable stock or water	2 cups
1 tbsp	vegetable oil	1 tbsp
½ small	onion, sliced	½ small
½ tsp	dried dill	½ tsp
	seasoning to taste	
2	tomatoes, chopped	2
115g (4 oz)	Red Leicester cheese, grated	1 cup
	soya 'bacon' bits (optional)	

1 Drop the courgettes (zucchini) into a pan of boiling water and cook them for just a few minutes, then remove them and drain them well. Cut each one in half lengthways and scoop out as much of the flesh as possible without breaking the skin, leaving 8 shells. Chop the scooped out flesh and reserve it.
2 Put the couscous into a pan with the stock or water, bring it to the boil, then cook it for 10 minutes or until it is just tender (take care not to overcook it as it will then become soggy).
3 Preheat the oven to 375°F/190°C (Gas Mark 5).
4 In a clean pan, heat the oil and sauté the onion until it begins to soften. Add the reserved courgette (zucchini) flesh, stir and cook it for a few more minutes. Add the dill and tomato and season to taste. Continue

cooking until everything is tender. Mix this with the couscous and half the cheese.

5 Place the courgette (zucchini) shells side by side in a lightly greased ovenproof dish or tin (pan). Fill each one with some of the couscous mixture, piling it high. Sprinkle the remaining cheese over the top and bake them in the preheated oven for 15 minutes or until the filling has heated through. Garnish with the 'bacon' bits, if using.

Note: This same filling can be used with marrow rings, peppers or aubergine (eggplant). Or use it to fill tomatoes and serve cold as part of a buffet.

Fruity Millet Pilaff

30g (1 oz)	margarine	2½ tbsp
1 small	onion, sliced	1 small
225g (8 oz)	millet	1 cup
425ml (¾ pt)	vegetable stock	2 cups
1	stick celery, sliced	1
1 medium	green pepper, sliced	1 medium
55g (2 oz)	raisins	⅓ cup
1 medium	red apple, diced	1 medium
55g (2 oz)	brazil nuts, chopped	½ cup

1 Melt the margarine and sauté the onion in it for 5 minutes. Stir in the millet and cook it briefly. Add the stock, bring it to the boil, cover the pan and simmer the mixture for 10 minutes. Stir in the celery and green pepper, adding a little more liquid at this point if the mixture is becoming dry, and cook it for 10 minutes more or until the millet is just tender.

Drain the millet mixture and stir in the raisins and apple. Divide the pilaf between 4 small plates, sprinkle the nuts over the top, then serve.

Note: This is good just as it is for a quick lunch snack or served as a side dish with, for example, a nut roast or soufflé. You can use half millet, half rice or any other grain if you like.

Red and Green Risotto

55g (2 oz)	chick peas, soaked overnight	½ cup
30g (1 oz)	margarine	2½ tbsp
2	cloves garlic, peeled and crushed	2
1 small	onion, sliced	1 small
2 small	red peppers, diced	2 small
2 small	green peppers, diced	2 small
225g (8 oz)	brown rice	1 cup
1 tsp	dried basil seasoning to taste	1 tsp
285ml (½ pt)	vegetable stock	1⅓ cups
200ml (⅓ pt)	white wine fresh parsley, chopped, to garnish	¾ cup

1 Drain the chick peas, put into a saucepan with fresh water, and bring to a boil. Continue boiling for 10 minutes, then lower the heat and cook for 30 minutes or until just tender. Drain and set aside.

2 Meanwhile melt the margarine and sauté the garlic, onion and red and green peppers in it for a few minutes, then cover the pan and cook them gently for 5 more minutes. Stir in the rice and basil and season to taste. Add the stock and wine and cook the mixture gently for 20 minutes. Add the chick peas and cook for 5 more minutes or until the rice is tender and most, if not all, of the liquid has been absorbed (you can, of course, add more during the cooking process if the rice seems too dry). Fluff up the risotto with a fork, sprinkle the parsley over it to garnish, then serve.

Note: In Italy, risotto is often served as a starter. If you follow this tradition, choose a light main course, such as an omelette and salad. Alternatively, serve it for lunch. For a change, replace the chick peas with cooked and coarsely chopped fresh chestnuts.

Three-cheese Buckwheat Bake

225g (8 oz)	buckwheat (kasha)	1 cup
425ml (¾ pt)	vegetable stock	2 cups
2 medium	leeks, cleaned and sliced	2 medium
115g (4 oz)	peas, fresh or frozen	⅔ cup
395-g (14-oz)	can tomatoes, chopped seasoning to taste	14-oz
2 tbsp	vegetable oil	2 tbsp
115g (4 oz)	Ricotta cheese	½ cup
55g (2 oz)	Cheddar cheese, grated	½ cup
55g (2 oz)	Parmesan cheese, grated watercress, to garnish	½ cup

1 Dry roast the buckwheat (kasha) for 3 minutes, shaking the pan continually, then add the vegetable stock and cook for 20 minutes. Stir in the leeks and peas and cook for 10 minutes more or until the buckwheat (kasha) is just tender, then drain the mixture well. Add the tomatoes and season to taste.

2 Preheat the oven to 350°F/180°C (Gas Mark 4).

3 Lightly grease a small, ovenproof dish. Spread a third of the buckwheat (kasha) and vegetable mixture over the bottom, top with the Ricotta cheese, add another layer of the buckwheat (kasha) and vegetable mixture, then the Cheddar cheese. Top this with the remaining buckwheat (kasha) and vegetable mixture, then the Parmesan cheese.

4 Bake in the preheated oven for 20 minutes or until piping hot, then serve garnished with the watercress.

Note: This is a very filling snack for those with big appetites. Use other grains if you like.

Aubergine with Feta and Wheat Berries

170g (6 oz)	wheat berries	¾ cup
2 small	aubergines (eggplants), diced	2 small
	sea salt, as required	
1 tbsp	vegetable oil	1 tbsp
1 small	onion, chopped	1 small
1	clove garlic, peeled and crushed	1
1 tsp	ground allspice	1 tsp
2 tbsp	tomato purée (paste)	2 tbsp
115g (4 oz)	peas, cooked	⅔ cup
1 tbsp	fresh oregano, chopped	1 tbsp
170g (6 oz)	Feta cheese, diced	2 cups

1 Dry roast the wheat berries, shaking the pan continually, until they begin to pop. Add enough water to the pan to cover them, bring it to the boil, then lower the heat and simmer them for 45 minutes or until they are tender, checking that there is sufficient water every now and again. Drain them well.
2 Meanwhile, spread the aubergine (eggplant) out, sprinkle salt over it and leave it for 30 minutes or until the bitter juices have oozed out. Rinse it with cold water, drain it and then pat it dry.
3 Preheat the oven to 350°F/180°C (Gas Mark 4).
4 Heat the oil and sauté the onion and garlic in it for 5 minutes. Stir in the allspice, cooking it briefly. Add the aubergine (eggplant) together with the tomato purée and a spoonful or two of water, stir, cover the pan and cook the mixture gently for 10 minutes. Then add the peas and oregano.
5 Transfer the wheat berries to 4 lightly greased ramekins, top them with the aubergine (eggplant) mix, sprinkle the Feta cheese over the top, cover them with foil and bake in the preheated oven for 20 to 30 minutes to heat through.

Note: Use dried oregano if you prefer. For speed, simply put the hot wheat berries onto 4 small plates and top with the aubergine (eggplant) and cheese mixture. Although the flavours do not get the chance to blend as well as when the ingredients are baked in the oven, the resulting combination is still very tasty.

Home-made Tacos with Tofu

225g (8 oz)	maize flour (cornmeal)	1½ cups
6 tbsp	boiling water	6 tbsp
225g (8 oz)	wholemeal (whole wheat) flour	2 cups
2 tbsp	baking powder	2 tbsp
scant 140ml (¼ pt)	milk	⅔ cup
	vegetable oil, for frying	

Topping

1 tbsp	vegetable oil	1 tbsp
2 medium	carrots, cut into sticks	2 medium
1 tbsp	aniseed, or to taste	1 tbsp
170g (6 oz)	tofu, drained	¾ cup
	seasoning to taste	
	fresh parsley, chopped, to garnish	

1 Soak the maize flour (cornmeal) in the boiling water for 10 minutes. Sift together the flour and baking powder, then add the mixture to the maize flour (cornmeal). Stir in just enough of the milk to make a fairly firm dough. Transfer the dough to a floured board and knead it for 5 minutes, then cover it with polythene and chill it for 30 minutes.
2 Next, make the topping. Heat the oil and sauté the carrot with the aniseed for 5 minutes. Mash the tofu and add it to the pan and season to taste. Cover the pan and cook the mixture gently for 5 more minutes or until the carrots are tender.
3 Meanwhile, break the dough into 8 equal pieces, dust them with flour and roll out each one into a small circle. Heat enough oil to shallow fry them for a few minutes each side. As soon as they are cooked, hang them over a rolling pin and leave them to cool, when they will have set and become crisp.
4 Fill these tacos with the carrot and tofu mixture, garnish with the parsley and serve at once.

Note: These corn tacos can be filled with any vegetable/nut/cheese mixture and make a perfect snack.

Egg-fried Mixed Grains

55g (2 oz)	brown rice	¼ cup
55g (2 oz)	pot barley, soaked overnight	¼ cup
55g (2 oz)	wheat berries, soaked overnight	¼ cup
55g (2 oz)	rye grains, cracked using a rolling pin	¼ cup
570ml (1 pt)	vegetable stock	2½ cups
2 tbsp	vegetable oil	2 tbsp
½ tsp	ground cumin	½ tsp
½ tsp	ground coriander	½ tsp
¼ tsp	ground ginger	¼ tsp
2 tbsp	sesame seeds	2 tbsp
2	free-range eggs, beaten	2
55g (2 oz)	mung beansprouts	1 cup
	soy sauce to taste	

1 Drain the pot barley and wheat berries. Put all the grains into a saucepan together with the stock, bring it to the boil, cover and cook for 30 to 45 minutes or until the grains are just tender, then drain them well.
2 Heat the oil and add the spices. Stir the mixture and

cook it for a few minutes. Add the sesame seeds and beaten eggs together with the cooked grains. Stir until the eggs cook. Add the mung beansprouts, flavour to taste with soy sauce, then serve at once.

Note: Any grains can be used in this recipe, providing you take care to adjust the cooking time if necessary (it is possible to buy them ready mixed). Serve with Chinese Vegetable Rolls (see page 127) for a delicious light lunch.

Bulgar with Avocado

2 tbsp	vegetable oil	2 tbsp
1 medium	onion, chopped	1 medium
1 small	red or green chilli pepper, finely chopped	1 small
225g (8 oz)	bulgar	1⅓ cups
425ml (¾ pt)	vegetable stock	2 cups
115g (4 oz)	sweetcorn seasoning to taste	⅔ cup
1 large	avocado, peeled and stone (pit) removed raw onion rings, to garnish	1 large

1 Heat the oil and sauté the onion and chilli pepper in it for 5 minutes. Stir in the bulgar, cook it briefly, then add the stock and sweetcorn and season to taste. Bring the mixture to the boil, then lower the heat and cook it for 10 minutes or until the bulgar is just tender (if any liquid remains, drain the bulgar so that it is dry and fluffy).
2 Cut the avocado flesh into cubes, stir them into the other ingredients and serve at once, topped with the onion rings.

Note: Bulgar is cracked wheat. It cooks very quickly so is ideal for those times when you want a filling snack in a hurry.

Wild Rice with Oyster Mushrooms

85g (3 oz)	wild rice	¾ cup
85g (3 oz)	white rice	¾ cup
570ml (1 pt)	vegetable stock	2½ cups
30g (2 oz)	butter	2½ tbsp
340g (12 oz)	oyster mushrooms, thickly sliced	6 cups
1 tbsp	fresh chives, snipped freshly ground black pepper to taste Raddichio leaves, to serve	1 tbsp
85g (3 oz)	Parmesan cheese, grated	¾ cup

1 Rinse both types of rice. Put them into a pan, together with the vegetable stock. Bring it to the boil, then cook it gently for 20 minutes or until the rice is tender.
2 Meanwhile, melt the butter and gently sauté the mushrooms in it, turning them occasionally until they just begin to colour. Do not let them shrivel.
3 Drain the rice well (the grains should be separate). Stir in the mushrooms, chives and freshly ground black pepper to taste. Make small nests of the Raddichio leaves on 4 small plates and spoon some of the mixture onto each. Sprinkle the Parmesan over each portion and serve at once.

Note: Serve this as a starter at a dinner party. Though it is simplicity itself to prepare, this recipe relies on its unusual ingredients to turn it into something special. Wild rice (not strictly a rice, but a kind of grass seed) is exotic and expensive, but it blends well with white rice. Oyster mushrooms have a unique taste, the Raddichio leaves add colour and a contrasting bitterness. If possible, use fresh Parmesan cheese and grate (shred) it at the last moment for maximum flavour.

Vegetable Oat Slices

1 small	courgette (zucchini), finely chopped	1 small
1 small	red pepper, finely chopped	1 small
1 tsp	vegetable oil	1 tsp
55g (2 oz)	mushrooms, finely chopped	1 cup
115g (4 oz)	Cheddar cheese, grated	1 cup
2	free-range eggs, lightly beaten	2
115g (4 oz)	rolled oats	1 cup
½ tsp	dried oregano seasoning to taste	½ tsp
30g (1 oz)	sesame seeds	2 tbsp

1 Drop the prepared courgette (zucchini) and red pepper into hot water and cook them for just 2 minutes, then drain them well.
2 Preheat the oven to 350°F/180°C (Gas Mark 4).
3 Heat the oil and sauté the mushrooms until they are soft. Drain them and mix them with the courgette (zucchini) and red pepper mixture. cheese, egg, oats and oregano and season to taste.
4 Grease a shallow tin (pan) and press the mixture into it, smoothing the top before sprinkling the sesame seeds over and pressing them gently down into the mixture. Bake in the preheated oven for 20 minutes or until it is just firm. Mark it into slices at once and serve it either hot or cold.

Note: A spicy tomato sauce goes well with these slices, which are really like a savoury flapjack. For a change, try using breadcrumbs instead of the oats.

Fried Rice with Vegetables and Coconut

225g (8 oz)	brown rice	1 cup
55g (2 oz)	margarine	¼ cup
1	clove garlic, peeled and crushed	1
1 small	green pepper, sliced	1 small
½ small	cauliflower, broken into florets	½ small
2	sticks celery, sliced	2
1 tbsp	lemon juice	1 tbsp
2 tbsp	soy sauce	2 tbsp
4	slices pineapple, fresh or tinned (canned)	4
55g (2 oz)	coconut flakes, roasted seasoning to taste	⅔ cup

1 Cook the rice in plenty of water until it is tender (about 20 to 30 minutes). Drain well.
2 Melt the margarine and sauté the garlic, green pepper, cauliflower and celery in it for 5 minutes, stirring them frequently. Add the lemon juice and soy sauce, cover the pan, and cook for 10 more minutes or until the vegetables are just tender, taking care they do not burn.
3 Cut the pineapple into cubes.
4 Add the rice, pineapple cubes and coconut flakes to the vegetables and cook the mixture over a low heat, stirring continually, for 5 minutes or until it has heated through. Season it to taste, then serve at once.

Note: Frying rice is an excellent way to heat up any that has been left over from a previous meal. Add other vegetables, nuts, chopped hard-boiled (hard-cooked) eggs or grated (shredded) cheese when you feel like a change.

10
Pizzas

Smoked Tofu and Pepper Pizzas

225g (8 oz)	pizza dough of your choice (see pages 155-156)	8 oz

Topping

285ml (½ pt)	Tomato Sauce (see page 156)	1⅓ cups
2 medium	green peppers, sliced	2 medium
115g (4 oz)	mushrooms, sliced	2 cups
285g (10 oz)	smoked tofu, drained seasoning to taste	2½ cups
2 tbsp	vegetable oil	2 tbsp

1 Make up the pizza dough according to the instructions.
2 Preheat the oven to 400°F/200°C (Gas Mark 6).
3 Divide the dough into quarters and roll each out into a small circle (round). Put them on a lightly greased baking sheet.
4 Now for the topping. Spread the Tomato Sauce over the pizza bases, then arrange the green pepper and mushroom slices decoratively on top. Coarsely chop the smoked tofu, scatter it over the pizzas, and season them generously. Trickle the oil over the vegetables.
5 Bake the pizzas in the preheated oven for 20 minutes or until the bases are cooked. Cut them into slices and serve at once.

Note: As an alternative to the smoked tofu, try adding sliced Quorn, which has a 'chicken'-like texture and taste – ideal when you're sharing your snack meal with meat-eaters!

Garlic French Bread Pizzas

2 small	sticks French bread	2 small

Topping

4 tbsp	vegetable oil	4 tbsp
1 tbsp	olive oil	1 tbsp
6	cloves garlic, peeled and chopped	6
1 tbsp	fresh parsley, chopped	1 tbsp
½ tbsp	oregano, chopped	½ tbsp
½ tbsp	marjoram, chopped seasoning to taste	½ tbsp
140g (5 oz)	Mozzarella cheese, sliced	5 oz

1 Preheat the oven to 400°F/200°C (Gas Mark 6).
2 Cut the sticks of bread in half, then cut each piece in half lengthways.
3 Now make the topping. Combine the oils, garlic and herbs in a blender and season to taste. Adjust the consistency by adding more oil if necessary (you can also give the sauce a richer flavour by using more garlic).
4 Spread each piece of bread with some of the garlic sauce (any extra can be stored in a jar in the refrigerator for another time or recipe). Top with the slices of Mozzarella cheese.
5 Bake the French bread pizzas in the preheated oven for 10 minutes or until the base is crisp and the cheese has melted (Alternatively, cook them under a hot grill/broiler.)

Note: When time is limited, use one of the excellent ready-made garlic spreads. For a change, spread the bread with tomato sauce and top with Bel Paese cheese and a sprinkling of Parmesan.

Broccoli Amandine Pizzettes

225g (8 oz)	pizza dough of your choice (see pages 155-156)	8 oz

Topping		
1 tbsp	vegetable oil	1 tbsp
1 small	onion, sliced	1 small
1	clove garlic, peeled and crushed	1
200-g (7-oz)	can tomatoes, chopped	7-oz
455g (1 lb)	broccoli, fresh or frozen	1 lb
30g (1 oz)	margarine	2½ tbsp
85g (3 oz)	flaked (slivered) almonds	¾ cup
1 tbsp	lemon juice seasoning to taste	1 tbsp

1 Preheat the oven to 400°F/200°C (Gas Mark 6).
2 Make up the pizza dough according to the instructions. When it is ready, divide it into 8 small, evenly sized pieces and roll them out into circles (rounds). Put them on a lightly greased baking sheet and bake in the preheated oven for 10 to 15 minutes, or until they are just cooked.
3 Meanwhile, make the topping. Heat the oil and sauté the onion and garlic together in it for 5 minutes, then add the tomatoes. Trim the broccoli, break into florets and stir it into the mixture. Cook it for a few minutes, then cover the pan and steam it gently for a further 5 minutes or until the broccoli is tender.
4 Melt the margarine in another pan and fry the almonds for a few minutes, shaking the pan from time to time, until they are golden brown.
5 Spoon the broccoli mixture onto the pizzettes, press it down slightly, then sprinkle the almonds over the top. Either serve at once or return them to the oven for a few minutes more to heat through.

Note: These are tasty served either hot or cold and are excellent for parties. To make sure the topping stays put, you can spread the cooked bases with a Tomato or White Sauce. You could also top them with some grated (shredded) cheese and bake them in the oven long enough for it to melt. Mini pizzas can also, of course, be topped with a variety of other ingredients – just experiment.

Ricotta, Spinach and Sweetcorn Pizzas

225g (8 oz)	pizza dough of your choice (see pages 155-156)	8 oz

Topping		
2 tbsp	vegetable oil	1 tbsp
1-2	cloves garlic, peeled and crushed	1-2
395-g (14-oz)	tin (can) tomatoes, chopped	14-oz
680g (1½ lb)	spinach, well washed and shredded	15 cups
170g (6 oz)	cooked sweetcorn	1 cup
225g (8 oz)	Ricotta cheese	1 cup
115g (4 oz)	Cheddar cheese, grated seasoning to taste	1 cup

1 Make up the pizza dough according to the instructions.
2 When it is ready, divide the dough in half, roll each out into a medium-sized circle (round) and lay these on a lightly greased baking sheet.
3 Preheat the oven to 400°F/200°C (Gas Mark 6).
4 Now make the topping. Heat the oil and sauté the garlic briefly in it, then add the tomato and cook the mixture over a medium heat until most of the liquid has evaporated and you have a thick sauce. Cook the spinach in a covered pan in just the water that remains on its leaves, then drain it well. Drain the sweetcorn. Divide the tomato sauce between the pizzas, spreading it out to the edges. Top it with the Ricotta, then the spinach, then the sweetcorn and, lastly, the Cheddar. Season to taste.
5 Bake the pizzas in the preheated oven for 20 to 30 minutes or until the bases are crisp and the cheese is bubbling and starting to brown, then cut them into slices and serve.

Note: These are an ideal midsummer pizza, especially if they are made using a crisper dough. Replace the sweetcorn with cooked peas if you prefer, or with nuts such as walnuts (English walnuts).

Leek and Tahini Pizzas

225g (8 oz)	pizza dough of your choice (see pages 155-156)	8 oz

Topping		
455g (1 lb)	leeks, cleaned and trimmed	1, lb
1 tbsp	vegetable oil	1 tbsp
30g (1 oz)	wholemeal (whole wheat) flour	¼ cup
200ml (⅓ pt)	cold water	¾ cup
3-4 tbsp	tahini soy sauce to taste seasoning to taste	3-4 tbsp
2 tbsp	sesame seeds	2 tbsp
2 large	tomatoes, sliced, to garnish	2 large

1 Preheat the oven to 400°F/200°C (Gas Mark 6).
2 Make up the pizza dough according to the instructions. When it is ready, divide the dough into quarters and shape each piece into a small circle (round). Put the pizza bases onto a lightly greased baking sheet and bake them in the preheated oven for 20 minutes or until they are just cooked.
3 Meanwhile, prepare the topping. Slice the leeks and steam them until they are tender, then drain them well.
4 At the same time, heat the oil in another pan and add the flour. Cook it briefly then gradually stir in the water and continue cooking and stirring until you have a thick sauce. Add the tahini, stirring until it dissolves completely, then add some soy sauce and season to taste. Stir in the leeks.
5 Pile the mixture onto the cooked pizzas, sprinkle the sesame seeds over the top and garnish with the tomato slices. If all the ingredients are still hot, serve the pizzas at once, but if they have cooled too much in the process, pop them back in the oven for 5 minutes to heat through.

Note: Leeks are also good in a creamy yogurt sauce or one made with cheese. Also, try replacing them with cauliflower and decorating with rings of red pepper instead of the slices of tomato.

Ratatouille Pizzas

225g (8 oz)	pizza dough of your choice (see pages 155-156)	8 oz

Topping		
2 tbsp	vegetable oil	2 tbsp
2	cloves garlic, peeled and chopped	2
1 medium	aubergine (eggplant), diced	1 medium
1 medium	red pepper, diced	1 medium
1 medium	green pepper, diced	1 medium
1 small	courgette (zucchini), sliced	1 medium
285g (10 oz)	tofu, drained and crumbled	1¼ cups
2 tsp	fresh basil, chopped seasoning to taste parsley sprigs, to garnish	2 tsp

1 Make up the pizza dough according to the instructions.
2 Now make the topping. Heat the oil and sauté the garlic in it for 5 minutes, then stir in all the vegetables and fry them for a few minutes, stirring continually. Add a little water and simmer for 10 minutes or until everything is tender. Add the tofu and cook it for a few more minutes.

3 Preheat the oven to 400°F/200°C (Gas Mark 6).
4 Leave the mixture to cool for a few minutes, then drain off any excess liquid and process the vegetables and tofu briefly in a blender to make a chunky purée. Add the basil and season to taste.
5 Divide the dough in half or into quarters and roll the pieces out to make 2 medium-sized or 4 small circles (rounds). Put them on a lightly greased baking sheet and bake them in the preheated oven for 20 minutes. Leave the oven on.
6 Drain the purée again and then spread it over the cooked pizza bases. Return the pizzas to the oven for 5 minutes to heat through and serve them generously garnished with the sprigs of parsley.

Note: The ratatouille can, of course, be added to the pizza without being blended – just stir the crumbled tofu into the mixture. Take care not to make it too moist or the liquid will soak into the base and make it soggy. Sprinkle chopped walnuts (English walnuts) over the top for a tasty crunch.

Pitta Pizzas with Feta Cheese

4 medium	wholemeal (whole wheat) pitta breads	4 medium
4 tbsp	tomato purée (paste)	4 tbsp
170g (6 oz)	Feta cheese, crumbled	2 scant cups
4 medium	tomatoes, sliced	4 medium
½ tsp	dried oregano	½ tsp
10	pimiento stuffed green olives, sliced	10

1 Preheat the oven to 400°F/200°C (Gas Mark 6).
2 Arrange the pitta breads side by side on a baking sheet. For each one, spread some of the tomato purée over the top, sprinkle some of the cheese over that, arrange some of the tomato slices on top, then scatter some of the oregano and sliced olives over that.
3 Bake the pitta pizzas in the preheated oven for 10 minutes or until the bread is hot through and the cheese has melted, then serve at once.

Note: Using pitta breads as a base for mini pizzas means you can throw a snack together in minutes. Try other toppings, too, such as cooked spinach in a creamy sauce, hummus with a generous amount of parsley scattered over it or garlic spread topped with flaked (slivered) almonds.

Cooked-in-the-pan Egg and Tomato Pizzas

Dough

225g (8 oz)	self-raising wholemeal (self-rising whole wheat) flour	2 cups
	sea salt to taste	
115g (4 oz)	vegetable suet	1 cup
140ml (¼ pt)	water	⅔ cup
	vegetable oil, for cooking	

Topping

285ml (½ pt)	Tomato Sauce (see page 156)	1⅓ cups
2 tbsp	sour (soured) cream or fromage frais	2 tbsp
	seasoning to taste	
6	free-range eggs, hard-boiled, peeled and chopped	6
	fresh parsley, chopped, to garnish	

1 First, make the dough. Sift together the flour and salt. Use your fingertips to rub the vegetable suet into the flour until the mixture resembles breadcrumbs. Add the water to make a soft dough. Roll it out to make 2 medium-sized circles (rounds).

2 Heat some oil in a frying pan (skillet) and cook the pizza bases for about 5 minutes on each side or until they are golden brown.

3 Meanwhile, make the topping. Gently heat the Tomato Sauce, then stir in the cream or fromage frais and season to taste.

4 Spread the creamy Tomato Sauce over the pizza bases, top this with the chopped egg and plenty of parsley. Serve at once.

Note: To make these pizzas even more special, put 8 small artichoke hearts (fresh or tinned) on top of the sauce with the egg, heating them through first.

Sage Derby and Walnut Pizzas

225g (8 oz)	pizza dough of your choice (see pages 155-156)	8 oz

Topping

115g (4 oz)	Sage Derby cheese	generous cup
115g (4 oz)	margarine	½ cup
55g (2 oz)	walnut (English walnut) pieces, chopped	½ cup

1 Preheat the oven to 400°F/200°C (Gas Mark 6).

2 Make up the pizza dough according to the instructions. When it is ready, divide it in half and roll out each piece into a medium-sized circle (round). Put them on a lightly greased baking sheet and bake them in the preheated oven for 20 minutes or until they are just cooked.

3 Meanwhile, make the topping. Mash together the cheese and margarine. Spread this over the hot pizza bases and sprinkle the nuts over the top. Cook the pizzas under a hot grill (broiler) for a few minutes only until the cheese has melted. Serve them at once, cut into wedges.

Note: This is an especially simple topping, yet it is very tasty. Garnish the pizzas with rings of red pepper and lots of parsley for occasions when appearance is as important as taste. Alternatively, use this topping on the cooked-in-the-pan pizza bases (see previous recipe) or even on wedges of French bread, when unexpected guests are also hungry ones!

Pizzas with 'Sausage'

225g (8 oz)	pizza dough of your choice (see pages 155-156)	8 oz
2 tbsp	vegetable oil	2 tbsp

Topping

4 large	tomatoes, sliced	4 large
1 large	green pepper	1 large
4 medium	vegetarian 'sausages'	4 medium
1 tsp	dried oregano	1 tsp
	seasoning to taste	

1 Make up the pizza dough according to the instructions. When it is ready, divide it into quarters and roll each piece out into a small circle (round). Put them on a lightly greased baking sheet. Brush the tops with a little of the oil.

2 Preheat the oven to 400°F/200°C (Gas Mark 6).

3 Now add the topping: Arrange the sliced tomatoes on the prepared bases. Drop the pepper into boiling water and cook it for just a couple of minutes, then remove it from the pan and drain it well. Slice it into rings and lay these on top of the tomatoes. Slice the 'sausages' and arrange these decoratively on the bases, sprinkling the oregano over the top and seasoning to taste. Trickle some vegetable oil over the topping.

4 Bake the pizzas in the preheated oven for 20 to 30 minutes or until the bases and topping are cooked. Serve hot.

Note: You can now buy many different varieties of vegetarian 'sausages': they come in tins (cans), vacuum packed, frozen or in a dry mix form. Alternatively, make up your own using lentils and nuts (see page 141).

Chilli Aduki Pizzas

225g (8 oz)	pizza dough of your choice (see pages 155-156)	8 oz
Topping		
1 tbsp	vegetable oil	1 tbsp
1 small	leek, cleaned and chopped	1 small
1	clove garlic, peeled and crushed	1
1 small	green chilli pepper, deseeded and finely chopped	1 small
200-g (7-oz)	can tomatoes, chopped	7-oz
2 tbsp	tomato purée (paste)	2 tbsp
225g (8 oz)	aduki beans, cooked (see page 9)	½ cup
½ tsp	dried basil seasoning to taste	½ tsp
4 medium	tomatoes, sliced, to garnish	4 medium
8	black olives, stoned (pitted) and chopped, to garnish fresh parsley, chopped, to garnish	8

1 Make up the pizza dough according to the instructions.
2 Preheat the oven to 400°F/200°C (Gas Mark 6).
3 Now make the topping. Heat the oil and sauté the leek, garlic and chilli pepper in it for a few minutes. Stir in the tomato and tomato purée and continue cooking until they break down into a sauce. Coarsely mash the aduki beans and add them to the sauce, together with the basil, and seasoning to taste.
4 Divide the pizza dough into quarters and roll out each piece into a small circle (round). Put them on a lightly greased baking sheet and bake them in the preheated oven for 10 minutes. Leave the oven on.
5 Spread the chilli aduki mixture over the pizza bases, decorate with the tomato and olives, and return the pizzas to the oven for another 10 minutes or until the topping has cooked and heated through. Serve them straight away, topped with a generous sprinkling of the parsley.

Note: Chilli peppers vary enormously in the intensity of their flavour, so use more or less pepper as required. Keep in mind too that green ones are likely to be milder than the red. You can use chilli powder instead, or sprinkle chilli flakes over your pizzas before cooking them, rather than adding the chilli flavour to the sauce.

Deep Pan Pizza with Courgettes

Dough		
170g (6 oz)	wholemeal (whole wheat) flour sea salt to taste	1½ cups
85g (3 oz)	margarine	⅓ cup
2 tbsp	cold water, to mix	2 tbsp
Filling		
2 medium	courgettes (zucchini), sliced	2 medium
1 tbsp	vegetable oil	1 tbsp
30g (1 oz)	wholemeal (whole wheat) flour	¼ cup
140ml (¼ pt)	milk	⅔ cup
140ml (¼ pt)	thick set, natural (unsweetened) yogurt	⅔ cup
½ tsp	dried marjoram seasoning to taste	½ tsp
4 medium	tomatoes, sliced, to garnish parsley sprigs, to garnish	4 medium

1 Preheat the oven to 400°F/200°C (Gas Mark 6).
2 First make the dough. Sift together the flour and salt. Use your fingertips to rub the margarine into the flour until the mixture resembles breadcrumbs, then add the cold water and mix to make a smooth dough (you may find you need more water, just add it as necessary). Roll the dough out and line the base and sides of a small ring (ring from a loose-bottomed tart pan) standing on a baking sheet or a flan dish (tart pan). Bake the pizza base in the preheated oven for 15 minutes. Leave the oven on.
3 Meanwhile, make the filling. Steam the courgettes (zucchini) for just a few minutes, then drain it well.
4 In a small pan, heat the oil and stir in the flour, cooking it briefly. Gradually add the milk and bring the sauce slowly to a boil, stirring continually. Take the pan off the heat and beat in the yogurt and marjoram and season to taste. Then, carefully stir in the courgette (zucchini).
5 Spoon the mixture into the pizza case, smooth the top, garnish with the tomato slices and bake it in the oven for 10 more minutes. Cut the pizza into wedges, garnish them with the sprigs of parsley and serve.

Note: You can use grated Cheddar cheese instead of the yogurt. You could also make a thick sauce by puréeing tofu and flavouring it with herbs, plus a pinch or two of chilli powder or garlic salt for extra flavour.

Welsh Rarebit Pizzas

225g (8 oz)	pizza dough of your choice (see pages 155-156)	8 oz

Topping

55g (2 oz)	margarine	¼ cup
30g (1 oz)	wholemeal (whole wheat) flour	¼ cup
140ml (¼ pt)	milk	⅔ cup
285g (10 oz)	Cheddar cheese, grated	2½ cups
2	free-range egg yolks	2
1 tsp	vegetarian Worcestershire sauce	1 tsp
1 tsp	mustard powder seasoning to taste alfalfa sprouts	1 tsp

1 Preheat the oven to 400°F/200°C (Gas Mark 6).
2 Make up the pizza dough according to the instructions. Divide the dough into quarters and roll out each piece into a small circle (round). Put them on a lightly greased baking sheet and bake them in the preheated oven for 20 minutes or until they are just cooked.
3 Meanwhile, make the topping. Melt the margarine and stir in the flour. Cook it for 2 minutes before gradually adding the milk. Continue cooking, stirring continually, until the sauce thickens. Then add the cheese, egg yolks, Worcestershire sauce and mustard and season to taste. Cook these last ingredients briefly, still stirring.
4 Spread the mixture over the cooked pizza bases, then grill (broil) them for a few minutes until the topping is golden brown. Serve the pizzas at once, garnished with a generous helping of alfalfa sprouts.

Note: Any extra sauce can be stored in a screwtop jar in the refrigerator for a few days.

To ring the changes, add herbs to the sauce or vary the cheeses (Cheshire and Edam are both good alternatives). Try, too, replacing the milk with beer for a more traditional sauce or sprinkling the top with chopped peanuts or soya 'bacon' bits for more crunch.

Fennel and Cottage Cheese Pizzas

225g (8 oz)	pizza dough of your choice (see pages 155-156)	8 oz

Topping

2 small	fennel bulbs	2 small
115g (4 oz)	margarine	½ cup
1 tbsp	vegetable oil	1 tbsp
1 small	onion, sliced	1 small
4 large	tomatoes, peeled	4 large
1 tbsp	lemon juice seasoning to taste	1 tbsp
225g (8 oz)	cottage cheese	1 cup
1 tsp	fresh oregano, chopped	1 tsp
1 tsp	fresh basil, chopped	1 tsp
55g (2 oz)	Parmesan cheese, grated	½ cup

1 Preheat the oven to 400°F/200°C (Gas Mark 6).
2 Make up the pizza dough according to the instructions. Divide the dough in half and roll out each piece into a medium-sized circle (round). Put them on a lightly greased baking sheet and bake them in the preheated oven for 10 minutes. Leave the oven on.
3 Meanwhile, make the topping. Remove the stems and outer leaves of the fennel, wash the bulbs, dry them well and slice them. Heat half the margarine together with the oil and cook the fennel slices briefly, then add a few spoonfuls of water, cover the pan and simmer them for 10 minutes or until they are tender.
4 Meanwhile, melt the remaining margarine in another pan and sauté the onion for a few minutes. Add the tomato and lemon juice and season to taste, then simmer the mixture until the vegetables have broken down to form a thick sauce.
5 Spread the tomato sauce over the pizza bases, top with the fennel slices, cottage cheese, herbs, and Parmesan and season to taste. Bake the pizzas in the oven for 15 to 20 minutes or until the base is crisp and the cheese has melted, then cut into slices and serve.

Note: For an even more unusual pizza, replace the fennel with pineapple chunks and maybe a few walnuts.

Potato Pizzas

Base

225g (8 oz)	potatoes, peeled and chopped	1⅓ cups
55g (2 oz)	margarine	¼ cup
115g (4 oz)	self-raising wholemeal flour (self-rising whole wheat flour) seasoning to taste	1 cup

Topping

2 tbsp	vegetable oil	2 tbsp
1 medium	onion, sliced	1 medium
1 medium	yellow pepper, sliced	1 medium
1 medium	courgette (zucchini), coarsely chopped seasoning to taste	1 medium
140g (5 oz)	Bel Paese cheese, sliced	5 oz

1 First, make the bases. Steam the potatoes until they are cooked, then drain them very well and mash them. Add

the margarine and flour and season to taste, then knead the mixture briefly to make a soft dough. Divide it in half and roll each piece out to make a medium-sized circle (round) and arrange them on a lightly greased baking sheet.

2 Preheat the oven to 400°F/200°C (Gas Mark 6).

3 Now make the topping. Heat the oil and sauté the onion and yellow pepper together in it for 5 minutes, then add the courgettes (zucchini) and continue cooking until all the vegetables are tender. Season to taste.

4 Spread the vegetable mixture over the pizza bases and put the cheese slices over the top. Bake them in the preheated oven for 30 minutes or until the base is cooked and the cheese has melted, then cut them into wedges and serve.

Note: This base is much quicker to make than the more traditional base. It is also an excellent way to use up leftover potatoes! Vary the toppings by using different vegetables scattered with other cheeses or beans, nuts – whatever you have to hand.

Nutty Vegetable Pizza Squares

225g (8 oz)	pizza dough of your choice (see pages 155-156)	8 oz

Topping

285ml (½ pt)	Tomato Sauce (see page 156)	¾ cup
1 medium	leek, cleaned and sliced	1 medium
1 large	stick celery, chopped	1 large
½ small	cauliflower, broken into florets	½ small
1 medium	carrot, sliced seasoning to taste	1 medium
115g (4 oz)	Edam cheese, grated	1 cup
55g (2 oz)	hazelnuts, coarsely ground	½ cup

1 Make up the pizza dough according to the instructions.

2 When it is ready, roll it out to fit the base of a shallow tin (a Swiss roll tin/jelly roll pan is ideal).

3 Now make the topping. Spread the Tomato Sauce evenly over the pizza base.

4 Preheat the oven to 400°F/200°C (Gas Mark 6).

5 Steam the vegetables together for just a few minutes to soften them, then drain them well. Spread them across the pizza base, season well, then scatter the cheese and nuts over the top.

6 Bake the pizza in the preheated oven for 20 minutes or until the dough is cooked. Cut it into squares and serve.

Note: Pizza squares are easy to pack, making them ideal for lunch boxes or picnics. You can also let them get cold then cut them into small fingers to serve with drinks. If you don't want to use dairy products, try using soya cheese instead of the Edam.

Creamy Mushroom Pizzas

225g (8 oz)	pizza dough of your choice (see pages 155-156)	8 oz

Topping

55g (2 oz)	margarine	¼ cup
340g (12 oz)	mushrooms, thickly sliced	6 cups
2 tbsp	vegetable oil	2 tbsp
1 large	onion, sliced	1 large
½-1	clove garlic, peeled and crushed	½-1
30g (1 oz)	wholemeal (whole wheat) flour	¼ cup
285ml (½ pt)	milk, dairy or soya	1⅓ cups
1 tsp	ground coriander seasoning to taste	1 tsp
55g (2 oz)	peas, cooked and drained chives, snipped, to garnish garlic croûtons, lightly crushed, to garnish	4 tbsp

1 Preheat the oven to 400°F/200°C (Gas Mark 6).

2 Make the pizza dough according to the instructions.

3 When it is ready, divide it into quarters and roll each piece out into a small circle (round). Put them on a lightly greased baking sheet and bake them in the preheated oven for 15 minutes. Leave the oven on.

4 Meanwhile, make the topping. Melt the margarine and very gently fry the mushrooms just long enough for them to begin to colour (they should still retain their shape), then drain them and set them to one side.

5 In another pan, heat the oil and sauté the onion and garlic together for 5 minutes. Stir in the flour, cook it briefly, then gradually add the milk, stirring, and bring it gently to the boil. Continue stirring until the sauce thickens, then flavour it with the coriander and season it to taste. Stir in the mushrooms and drained peas, spread the mixture over the pizza bases, and return them to the oven for 10 minutes or until the bases are cooked. Cut the pizzas into wedges and serve, garnished with the chives and croûtons.

Note: Herbs can be used instead of the coriander. Tarragon, for example, goes especially well. Instead of the garlic croûtons you can add a contrast to the creamy texture of the topping by sprinkling it with soya 'bacon' bits or salted peanuts.

Crispy-topped Garlic Pizzas

225g (8 oz)	pizza dough of your choice (see pages 155-156)	8 oz

Topping

2 tbsp	vegetable oil	2 tbsp
4	cloves garlic, peeled and crushed	4
2 large	onions, sliced	2 large
30g (1 oz)	wholemeal (whole wheat) flour	¼ cup
200ml (⅓ pt)	vegetable stock	¾ cup
2 tbsp	fresh parsley, chopped seasoning to taste	2 tbsp
2 tbsp	capers	2 tbsp
30g (1 oz)	margarine	2½ tbsp
55g (2 oz)	wholemeal (whole wheat) breadcrumbs parsley sprigs, to garnish	1 cup

1 Preheat the oven to 400°F/200°C (Gas Mark 6).
2 Make up the dough according to the instructions. When it is ready, divide it into quarters and roll each piece out into a small circle (round). Put them on a lightly greased baking sheet and bake them in the preheated oven for 10 minutes. Leave the oven on.
3 Meanwhile, heat the oil and lightly fry the garlic and onion together in it for 5 minutes. Then sprinkle in the flour and cook it briefly. Gradually add the vegetable stock, stirring continually, then the parsley and seasoning to taste. Bring the sauce to the boil, stirring continually still, until it thickens. Continue to cook it for 5 more minutes, then stir in the capers.
4 Melt the margarine and fry the breadcrumbs until they are crisp.
5 Spread the onion and garlic sauce over the pizza bases, sprinkle the breadcrumbs over the top, then return them to the oven for a further 10 minutes or until the bases are cooked. Cut them into wedges, garnish with the sprigs of parsley and serve.

Note: Try using dairy or soya milk instead of the stock for a creamier sauce. If you eat cheese you might like to add a layer of curd (cottage cheese, mashed) or Ricotta cheese under the sauce and/or to top the pizzas with a generous sprinkling of Parmesan cheese. Alternatively, top them with slices of hard-boiled (hard-cooked) egg.

11

Pancakes

Brussels Sprouts Creole Pancakes

285ml (½ pt)	batter of your choice (see pages 154-155) vegetable oil, for frying	1⅓ cups

Filling

455g (1 lb)	Brussels sprouts, trimmed	1 lb
55g (2 oz)	margarine	¼ cup
1 medium	onion, sliced	1 medium
1 small	red pepper, sliced	1 small
1	clove garlic, peeled and crushed	1
4 medium	tomatoes, chopped	4 medium
1 tbsp	tomato purée (paste)	1 tbsp
1 tsp	mixed dried herbs seasoning to taste parsley sprigs, to garnish	1 tsp

1 Make up the pancake batter and chill it.
2 Meanwhile, make the filling. Halve the Brussels sprouts.
3 Melt the margarine and sauté the onion, red pepper and garlic in it for 5 minutes to soften them, then stir in the Brussels sprouts, tomato, tomato purée and herbs and season to taste. Cover the pan and cook the mixture gently for about 10 minutes or until the Brussels sprouts are just tender (you might need to add a little water if the mixture starts to dry out and, if you do, stir a little extra tomato purée into it).
4 While the filling is cooking, make the pancakes. Fill them with the vegetable mixture, fold them, and serve garnished with the fresh parsley sprigs.

Note: To make this a more filling snack, an obvious addition to the filling would be chestnuts. Cooked chick peas (garbanzos), which have a similar texture would also work well with these ingredients. For something completely different, stir in cubes of raw or lightly fried tofu.

Tahini Onion Pancakes

285ml (½ pt)	batter of your choice (see pages 154-155) vegetable oil, for frying	1⅓ cups

Filling

455g (1 lb)	onions, thickly sliced	1 lb
1 large	red pepper, sliced	1 large
2-4 tbsp	light tahini	2-4 tbsp
1-2 tbsp	lemon juice	1-2 tbsp
½ tsp	garlic salt, or to taste	½ tsp
1 tbsp	fresh chives, snipped seasoning to taste lemon wedges, to serve	1 tbsp

1 Make up the batter and chill it.
2 Meanwhile, make the filling. Cook the onion and red pepper gently in a saucepan in a light covering of water for 10 minutes or until they are just tender, then drain them well. Stir in the tahini, lemon juice, garlic salt and chives and season to taste (the onions should be evenly coated with the mixture, but not be too sticky – add a little water if necessary).
3 Meanwhile, make the pancakes in the usual way. Spread each one thinly with the tahini onion mixture, roll them up and serve them topped with a wedge of lemon.

Note: A delicious alternative can be made using peanut butter instead of tahini or sour (soured) cream. A celery salad goes well with these pancakes.

Avocado Pancakes

285ml (½ pt)	batter of your choice (see pages 154-155) vegetable oil, for frying	1⅔ cups
Filling		
2 large	ripe avocados	2 large ripe
2 medium	spring onions (scallions), finely chopped	2 medium
½-1	clove garlic, peeled and crushed	½-1
2 tbsp	lemon juice	2 tbsp
2 tbsp	vegetable oil seasoning to taste	2 tbsp
55g (2 oz)	brazil nuts, coarsely chopped	½ cup
1 tbsp	fresh chives, snipped alfalfa sprouts, to garnish	1 tbsp
4 medium	tomatoes, sliced, to garnish	4 medium

1 Make up the pancake batter and chill it.
2 Meanwhile, make the filling. Halve the avocados and remove the stones (pits) and peel. Mash the flesh together with the spring onions (scallions), garlic, lemon juice and oil and season to taste. Stir in the nuts.
3 Cook the pancakes in the usual way, then divide the avocado mixture between them and pile some alfalfa sprouts on top, roll them up, and garnish with the slices of tomato. Serve hot.

Note: Sour cream or natural (unsweetened) yogurt can be stirred into the avocado mixture. Instead of the chives, you could add spices, such as chilli powder or just a little curry paste. For an even quicker filling, just wrap the pancakes around slices of avocado sprinkled with chopped spring onions (scallions) and add nuts or slices of Mozzarella cheese.

Sweet and Sour Pancakes

285ml (½ pt)	batter of your choice (see pages 154-155) vegetable oil, for frying	1⅓ cups
Filling		
1 medium	carrot, sliced	1 medium
½ small	white cabbage, sliced	½ small
2 tbsp	vegetable oil	2 tbsp
1	clove garlic, peeled and crushed	1
1 tbsp	raw cane sugar	1 tbsp
2 tbsp	lemon juice	2 tbsp
2 tbsp	chopped pineapple, fresh or canned	2 tbsp
55g (2 oz)	aduki beans, cooked (see page 9) parsley sprigs, to garnish	¼ cup

1 Make up the pancake batter and chill it.
2 Meanwhile, make the filling. Steam the carrot and cabbage very briefly, then drain them well.
3 Heat the oil and cook the garlic in it for 2 minutes, then stir in the sugar and continue cooking until it begins to caramelize. Stir in the carrot and cabbage, lemon juice and pineapple. Cover the pan, lower the heat and simmer the mixture for 5 minutes or until the vegetables are just tender, taking care not to overcook them. Stir in the drained beans and heat them through briefly.
4 Meanwhile, make the pancakes. Fill each one with a spoonful or two of the sweet and sour mixture, roll them up and serve them garnished with some sprigs of parsley.

Note: To thicken the sauce, stir 1 to 2 teaspoons arrowroot into a little pineapple or orange juice, add to the mixture and bring it gently to the boil.
   Any leftover beans can be used instead of the aduki beans, or you could use peas or sunflower seeds.

Creamed Spinach Pancakes

Soufflé batter

115g (4 oz)	wholemeal (whole wheat) flour	1 cup
pinch	sea salt	pinch
2	free-range eggs, separated	2
285ml (½ pt)	milk vegetable oil, for frying	1⅓ cups
Filling		
680g (1½ lb)	fresh spinach, well washed	1 lb
30g (1 oz)	raisins	2 tbsp
good pinch	ground nutmeg	good pinch
140ml (¼ pt)	double (heavy) cream	⅔ cup
30g (1 oz)	margarine	2½ tbsp
55g (2 oz)	wholemeal (whole wheat) breadcrumbs	1 cup

1 First, make the soufflé batter.
2 Sift together the flour and salt, then add the egg yolks and stir the mixture lightly. Still stirring, gradually add the milk, then beat it in well. In another bowl, whisk the egg whites until just becoming stiff, then fold them very gently into the batter using a metal spoon. Make the pancakes immediately in the usual way.
3 Meanwhile make the filling. Cook the spinach gently in a covered saucepan in just the water that remains on the leaves (it should have softened within about 5 minutes). Take the pan off the heat, drain the spinach well, chop it coarsely, then return it to the pan and stir in the raisins, nutmeg and cream and heat through very gently.
4 Divide the spinach mixture between the pancakes, roll

them up, dot them with the margarine and sprinkle the breadcrumbs over the top. Put them under the grill (broiler) for a minute or two to brown.

Note: The egg whites make this batter lighter than usual. With the mild, creamy filling it is a particularly delicate dish, making it good as a starter to a special meal. Though the double (heavy) cream *is* delicious, you could use lower fat alternatives such as curd (cottage cheese, mashed) or Ricotta cheese or fromage frais.

Tofu Pancakes with Courgettes

285ml (½ pt)	batter of your choice (see pages 154-155) vegetable oil, for frying	1⅓ cups
Filling		
3 tbsp	vegetable oil	3 tbsp
285g (10 oz)	tofu, drained and finely diced	1¼ cups
2 medium	courgettes (zucchini), chopped	2 medium
30g (1 oz)	sunflower seeds soy sauce to taste seasoning to taste	¼ cup
285ml (½ pt)	Tomato Sauce (see page 156)	1⅓ cups

1 Prepare the batter and chill it.
2 Meanwhile, make the filling. Heat 1 tablespoon of the oil and fry the tofu, stirring it frequently, until it is all lightly browned. Remove it from the pan and keep it warm. Add the rest of the oil to the pan and sauté the courgettes (zucchini) until they begin to soften. Return the tofu to the pan, together with the sunflower seeds and soy sauce and seasoning to taste. Stir them all together and heat the mixture gently for just a few more minutes.
3 Preheat the oven to 350°F/180°C (Gas Mark 4).
4 Meanwhile, make the pancakes in the usual way. Spoon some of the tofu mixture onto each pancake, roll them up and put them side by side into an ovenproof dish. Pour the Tomato Sauce over them and bake them in the preheated oven for 15 minutes.

Note: If you are short of time, just heat the Tomato Sauce through and pour it over the individual pancakes or omit the sauce altogether and top them with slices of fresh tomato.

Mushroom, Almond and Beansprout Pancakes

285ml (½ pt)	batter of your choice (see pages 154-155) vegetable oil, for frying	1⅓ cups
Filling		
2 tbsp	vegetable oil	2 tbsp
2	spring onions (scallions), chopped	2
170g (6 oz)	mushrooms, thickly sliced	3 cups
2 tbsp	soy sauce	2 tbsp
a little	cold water seasoning to taste	a little
1 generous tbsp	margarine	1 heaped tbsp
55g (2 oz)	almonds, coarsely chopped	½ cup
115g (4 oz)	beansprouts watercress, to garnish	4 oz

1 Prepare the batter and chill it.
2 Meanwhile, make the filling. Heat the oil and lightly sauté the spring onions (scallions) for 5 minutes. Add the mushrooms, stir them in and cook until they just begin to soften (they should still be firm). Sprinkle with soy sauce, turn the mushrooms, and continue cooking until they are glazed with the sauce. Add the water, season to taste and cook the mixture for a minute more.
3 In a separate pan melt the margarine and fry the almonds until they are crisp and golden brown. Stir them and the beansprouts into the mushroom mixture.
4 Meanwhile, make the pancakes in the usual way. Fill each one with some of the mushroom mixture, roll them up and garnish them generously with the watercress before serving.

Note: To make these extra special, top them with a cheese sauce, some grated (shredded) Parmesan and grill (broil) them to melt the Parmesan.

Succotash Pancakes

285ml (½ pt)	batter of your choice (see pages 154-155)	1⅓ cups
	vegetable oil, for frying	

Filling

170g (6 oz)	peas, fresh or frozen	1 cup
170g (6 oz)	sweetcorn, fresh or frozen	1 cup
70ml (⅛ pt)	single, double or sour (light, heavy or soured) cream, plus extra single (light) cream, to serve	¼ cup
1 tbsp	fresh parsley, chopped	1 tbsp
	seasoning to taste	
	fresh chives, snipped, to garnish	

1 Make up the batter and chill it.
2 Meanwhile, make the filling. Cook the peas and sweetcorn until they are just tender, then drain them well. Stir in the cream and parsley and season to taste, then keep the mixture warm, taking care not to let it boil.
3 Meanwhile, make the pancakes in the usual way. Roll each one around a few spoonfuls of the mixture and serve them with a trickle of single (light) cream over the top and garnished with plenty of the fresh chives.

Note: This is a really quick filling to make for when time is limited. Add plain or garlic croûtons to the peas and sweetcorn for a more filling snack. Succotash can also be made using broad (fava) beans and, for a vegan version make it with a small amount of concentrated soya milk instead of the cream.

Broccoli au Gratin Pancakes

Batter

85g (3 oz)	buckwheat flour	⅔ cup
55g (2 oz)	wholemeal (whole wheat) flour	½ cup
pinch	sea salt	pinch
1	free-range egg, lightly beaten	1
285ml (½ pt)	water	1⅓ cups
	vegetable oil, for frying	

Filling

680g (1½ lb)	fresh broccoli, trimmed and broken into florets or frozen	1½ lb
30g (1 oz)	margarine	2½ tbsp
½ small	onion, chopped	½ small
30g (1 oz)	wholemeal (whole wheat) flour	¼ cup
285ml (½ pt)	milk	1⅓ cups
good pinch	ground nutmeg	good pinch
140g (5 oz)	Gruyère cheese, grated	1¼ cups
	seasoning to taste	
4	tomatoes, sliced	4

1 First make the batter. Sift together the flours and salt. Add the lightly beaten egg, then gradually add the water, stirring each addition in well so that the batter is smooth and lump free. Beat it well to lighten, then chill it for at least 30 minutes.
2 Meanwhile, make the filling. Cook the broccoli for 10 to 15 minutes or until just cooked (if possible, stand the broccoli so that the stalks only are in water, while the more fragile heads are being steamed). Drain it well.
3 While the broccoli is cooking, make a sauce. Melt the margarine and sauté the onion in it, then stir in the flour and cook it for a minute more before adding the milk gradually, stirring all the time. Simmer the sauce until it thickens. Add the nutmeg and most of the cheese and season to taste. Carefully stir the broccoli into the sauce.
4 Heat the oil and make the pancakes in the usual way. Fill each one with some of the broccoli mixture and roll them up. Put the filled pancakes side by side in a heatproof dish, sprinkle the remaining cheese over the top and lay the tomato slices neatly on top, then cook them under a grill (broiler) for a minute or two.

Note: Try other vegetables such as celery or cauliflower in place of the broccoli or a combination, such as leeks with diced parsnip. If liked, you can wrap the vegetables in the pancakes, top them with the cheese sauce mixed with an egg and bake them in the oven.

Pancakes with Scrambled Tofu

285ml (½ pt)	batter of your choice (see pages 154-155)	1⅓ cups
	vegetable oil, for frying	

Filling

55g (2 oz)	margarine	¼ cup
1 small	carrot, grated	1 small
1 small	onion, grated	1 small
395g (14 oz)	smoked tofu, drained	1¾ cups
1 tsp	fresh parsley, chopped	1 tsp
1 tsp	fresh marjoram, chopped	1 tsp
	seasoning to taste	
30g (1 oz)	sesame seeds, roasted	¼ cup
	parsley sprigs, to garnish	

1 Make the batter and chill it.
2 Meanwhile, make the filling. Melt the margarine and

gently sauté the carrot and onion in it for 5 minutes. Crumble the tofu and add it to the pan, then continue cooking and stirring until it begins to colour. Add the herbs and season to taste, then stir in the sesame seeds.
3 While it is heating through, make the pancakes. Fold each one over a spoonful or two of the scrambled tofu and serve at once, garnished with a few sprigs of parsley.

Note: Instead of using herbs with the tofu, try using plain tofu and adding spices such as turmeric and cumin. You can make it with scrambled eggs, too, following the same method.

Chinese Pancake Rolls

285ml (½ pt)	batter of your choice (see pages 154-155) vegetable oil, for frying	1⅓ cups

Filling

4 tbsp	vegetable oil	4 tbsp
1 small	onion, sliced	1 small
1 small	red pepper, sliced	1 small
55g (2 oz)	mange-tout (snow peas)	2 oz
55g (2 oz)	mushrooms, sliced	1 cup
55g (2 oz)	cashew nuts, coarsely chopped	½ cup
1 tsp	cornflour (cornstarch)	1 tsp
2 tbsp	soy sauce	2 tbsp
1 tbsp	medium sherry (sherry wine)	1 tbsp
55g (2 oz)	beansprouts	1 cup

1 Make the batter and chill it for 30 minutes, then make 8 small pancakes, drain them well and set them to one side.
2 Now, make the filling. Heat 2 tablespoons of the oil and sauté the onion in it for a few minutes. Then add the red pepper, mange-tout (snow peas) and mushrooms and cook them for 5 to 10 minutes or until they are just tender, then stir in the cashews. Whisk together the cornflour (cornstarch), soy sauce and sherry (sherry wine) and pour this over the mixture. Heat it until it is boiling, then stir in the beansprouts.
3 Put a spoonful of the filling onto a cooked pancake, fold in the sides, then roll it up to form a small parcel. Repeat this for the rest of the pancakes and filling. Heat the remaining oil and deep fry them carefully, a couple at a time, until they are golden. Drain them very well and serve at once.

Note: Although not absolutely necessary, you could seal the ends of the rolls with a mixture of cornflour and water before frying.
  Any vegetables can be used in place of those given for the filling, and try using mashed tofu instead of the nuts.

Broad Bean Pancakes with Parsley Sauce

285ml (½ pt)	batter of your choice (see pages 154-155) vegetable oil, for frying	1⅓ cups

Filling

455g (1 lb)	young broad (fava) beans	1 lb
1 medium	onion, sliced	1 medium

Sauce

30g (1 oz)	margarine	2½ tbsp
30g (1 oz)	wholemeal (whole wheat) flour	¼ cup
200ml (⅓ pt)	vegetable stock	¾ cup
1	free-range egg yolk	1
3 tbsp	single (light) cream	3 tbsp
2 tbsp	fresh parsley, chopped, plus extra to garnish	2 tbsp
2 tbsp	lemon juice seasoning to taste	2 tbsp

1 Make the batter and chill it for at least 30 minutes.
2 Meanwhile, make the filling. Remove the beans from the pods and cook them, with the onion, in boiling water for 20 minutes or until they are tender. Drain them and set to one side.
3 Next, make the sauce. Melt the margarine in a clean pan and add the flour, cooking it briefly before gradually stirring in the stock. Continue to simmer the sauce for a few minutes. In a small bowl, beat together the egg yolk and cream and add a few spoonfuls of the hot sauce, mix them together well. Return this mixture to the sauce in the pan and, over a low heat, stir the sauce continuously until it thickens. Add the parsley and lemon juice and season to taste.
4 Make the pancakes in the usual way, then fill each one with some of the beans and onions, roll them up and spread a few spoonfuls of the sauce over the top. Garnish with the extra parsley and serve at once.

Note: The broad (fava) beans are also very good with a garlic-flavoured tomato sauce.

Nutty Lentil Pancakes

285ml (½ pt)	batter of your choice (see pages 154-155)	1⅓ cups
	vegetable oil, for frying	

Filling

30g (1 oz)	margarine	2½ tbsp
1	clove garlic, peeled and crushed	1
½ small	red pepper, chopped	½ small
1	stick celery, chopped	1
115g (4 oz)	split red lentils	½ cup
	water or vegetable stock	
85g (3 oz)	hazelnuts, coarsely chopped	⅔ cup
½ tsp	dried sage, or to taste	½ tsp
	seasoning to taste	
	extra margarine	
	watercress, to garnish	

1 Make the batter and chill it.
2 Meanwhile, make the filling. Melt the margarine and sauté the garlic, red pepper and celery in it for 10 minutes until they have softened. Stir in the lentils, cover them with the water or stock, bring it to the boil, lower the heat, cover the pan and simmer the lentils for 20 minutes or until they are very soft.
3 Mash the lentil mixture to a thick, moist purée (adding extra liquid if it is a bit dry). Stir in the hazelnuts and sage and season to taste.
4 Towards the end of the lentils' cooking time, make the pancakes. Fill each one with some of the hot lentil purée, roll it up and dot the top with some of the margarine. Grill (broil) them for a few minutes, if liked, then garnish them with the watercress sprigs and serve.

Note: This purée should be smooth and creamy, so beat it well. You could also stir in some cream, yogurt, cream cheese or even just some butter. Any nuts can be used instead of the hazelnuts.

Curried Pancakes with Cucumber Raita

Batter

115g (4 oz)	wholemeal (whole wheat) flour	1 cup
2	free-range eggs	2
285ml (½ pt)	half milk, half water mixed	1⅓ cups
1 tbsp	vegetable oil	1 tbsp
2 tbsp	natural (unsweetened) yogurt	2 tbsp
2 tsp	curry powder	2 tsps
	vegetable oil, for frying	

Filling

200ml (⅓ pt)	thick, natural (unsweetened), set yogurt	¾ cup
1 large	cucumber, coarsely chopped and well drained	1 large
1 tbsp	fresh mint, chopped	1 tbsp
pinch	chilli powder	pinch
small piece	cucumber, sliced, to garnish	small piece
2 tsp	cumin seeds, to garnish	2 tsp

1 First, make the batter. Sift the flour, add the eggs and gradually stir in the milk and water to make a smooth batter. Add the oil, yogurt and curry powder and beat the mixture well to incorporate some air to lighten it, then chill it for 30 minutes.
2 Meanwhile make the filling. Combine the yogurt with the cucumber, then add the mint and chilli powder.
3 Make the pancakes in the usual way. Fill each one with some of the cucumber raita, fold it and serve it at once garnished with a few slices of cucumber and a sprinkling of cumin seeds.

Note: As this filling is especially moist, you could put the pancakes on individual plates before filling them. Alternatively, fill the pancakes with chopped cucumber (maybe mixed with other salad ingredients, such as celery, red pepper and tomatoes), then spoon the cucumber raita over the folded pancakes. Whichever way you serve them, they make a delightful, quick, light lunch.

Egg and Walnut Pancakes

285ml (½ pt)	batter of your choice (see pages 154-155)	1⅓ cups
	vegetable oil, for frying	

Filling

30g (1 oz)	margarine	2½ tbsp
30g (1 oz)	wholemeal (whole wheat) flour	¼ cup
200ml (⅓ pt)	milk	¾ cup
85g (3 oz)	walnuts, coarsely chopped	⅔ cup
4	free-range eggs, hard-boiled, mashed or chopped	4
good pinch	ground nutmeg	good pinch
	seasoning to taste	
	extra margarine, for topping	
30g (1 oz)	wholemeal (whole wheat) breadcrumbs, for sprinkling	½ cup

1 Make the pancake batter and chill it.
2 Meanwhile, make the filling. Melt the margarine and sprinkle in the flour, cooking it briefly. Gradually stir in the milk and continue cooking and stirring until you have a thick sauce. Add the nuts and nutmeg and season to taste (if the mixture is too dry, add a little more milk).
3 Now make the pancakes in the usual way. Wrap each one around a spoonful of the filling, dot them with margarine, sprinkle the breadcrumbs over them and cook them under a grill (broiler) for just a minute. Serve them at once.

Note: Instead of the walnuts, you could mix the eggs with lightly cooked vegetables, such as carrots, tomatoes, broccoli or whatever else you happen to have. For a special occasion starter try adding asparagus tips. You can boost the protein content, if you like, by sprinkling nuts over the folded pancakes.

Aubergine Provençale Pancakes

285ml	batter of your choice	1⅓ cups
(½ pt)	(see pages 154-155)	
	vegetable oil, for frying	

Filling

1 medium	aubergine (eggplant)	1 medium
	sea salt, as necessary	
2 tbsp	olive oil	2 tbsp
1	clove garlic, peeled and crushed	1
1 small	onion, chopped	1 small
225g (8 oz)	tomatoes, chopped	8 oz
1 tbsp	fresh parsley, chopped	1 tbsp
1 tbsp	fresh basil or chervil, chopped	1 tbsp
	seasoning to taste	
225g (8 oz)	cooked chick peas (garbanzos) (see page 9)	8 oz
	parsley sprigs, to garnish	
	wedges of lemon, to garnish	

1 Make the batter and chill it for 30 minutes.
2 Meanwhile, make the filling. Dice the aubergine (eggplant), spread it on a plate, sprinkle salt over it and leave it for 30 minutes or until the bitter juices have oozed out. Rinse it with cold water, drain well and pat dry.
3 Heat the oil and sauté the garlic and onion in it for a few minutes. Add the aubergine (eggplant) and cook it for 5 to 10 minutes, stirring frequently. Add the tomato and herbs and season to taste. Cook the mixture for 5 more minutes, then stir in the chick peas (garbanzos).

Continue cooking the mixture just long enough to heat them through.
4 Make the pancakes in the usual way and fill each one with some of the aubergine (eggplant) provençale mixture. Serve them rolled up and garnished with sprigs of parsley and wedges of lemon.

Note: To turn this into an even more satisfying snack, arrange the pancakes in an ovenproof dish, top them with a white or cheese sauce and a generous sprinkling of breadcrumbs and bake them in a 425°F/220°C (Gas Mark 7) oven for 10 minutes. The chick peas add protein as well as interest (use leftovers or tinned/canned ones when in a hurry) or substitute other pulses (legumes) such as kidney beans or peas.

Quick, Creamy Leek Pancakes

285ml (½ pt)	batter of your choice	1⅓ cups
	(see pages 154-155)	
	vegetable oil, for frying	

Filling

4 medium	leeks, washed, trimmed and chopped into small chunks	4 medium
170g (6 oz)	herb and garlic cream cheese	¾ cup
	freshly ground black pepper to taste	
2 medium	tomatoes, sliced	2 medium
	fresh chives, snipped, to garnish	

1 Make the batter and chill it for 30 minutes.
2 Meanwhile, make the filling. Steam the leeks gently until they are tender. Drain them well, then return them to the saucepan and stir in the cheese until it melts completely, adding freshly ground black pepper to taste.
3 At the same time, make the pancakes in the usual way. Fill each one with some of the leek mixture, roll it up and top it with slices of tomato and garnish it with chives.

Note: Any vegetables can be used instead of the leeks. For a more subtle taste, try stirring in curd (cottage cheese, mashed), cream or Ricotta cheese.

Asparagus Pancakes with Mock Hollandaise Sauce

285ml (½ pt)	batter of your choice (see pages 154-155) vegetable oil, for frying	1⅓ cups

Filling

455g (1 lb)	young asparagus spears, trimmed	1 lb
55g (2 oz)	margarine or butter	¼ cup
30g (1 oz7	wholemeal (whole wheat) flour	¼ cup
285ml (½ pt)	milk	1⅓ cups
1 small	free-range egg yolk	1 small
good squeeze	lemon juice	good squeeze
	seasoning to taste	
	fresh tarragon, chopped, to garnish	

1 Make the batter and chill it for 30 minutes.
2 Meanwhile, make the filling. Tie the asparagus in a bunch and stand it in a deep pan of boiling water, then cover, so that the tougher stems are boiled, but the tender tips are steamed. Cook them for 10 minutes, drain them well, then trim off any tough ends of stalks.
3 Melt half the margarine or butter and add the flour. Sauté it for a minute, then gradually stir in the milk and bring the sauce to the boil, stirring continually until it thickens. Remove the pan from the heat and leave it to cool for a few minutes. Then beat in the remaining margarine or butter, egg yolk and lemon juice and season to taste. Keep the sauce warm while you make the pancakes.
4 Make the pancakes in the usual way, then fill each one with a few spears of asparagus, roll it up and serve it with a few spoonfuls of sauce spread over the top and garnished generously with the fresh tarragon.

Note: Fresh asparagus is available for only a short time and is usually expensive, so this is a recipe for those occasions when you want to serve something indulgent. Asparagus should be cooked in a special pan, but you can adapt a normal one by making a lid of foil. Alternatively, use frozen or tinned (canned) asparagus. Real Hollandaise sauce can, of course, be served instead, but it is not just richer in fat and calories, it takes longer to make!

12

Breads, Spreads and Other Fillings

Breads

Double Gloucester Bread

455g (1 lb)	self-raising wholemeal flour (self-rising whole wheat flour)	4 cups
pinch	sea salt	pinch
55g (2 oz)	margarine	¼ cup
170g (6 oz)	Double Gloucester cheese, grated	1½ cups
1 large	free-range egg	1 large
200ml (⅓ pt)	milk	¾ cup

1 Sift the flour into a bowl with the salt, then use your fingertips to rub in the margarine until the mixture resembles fine breadcrumbs. Stir in most of the cheese.
2 Preheat the oven to 425°F/220°C (Gas Mark 7).
3 Whisk together the egg and milk and add it to the flour and cheese, mixing well until you have a soft dough (add a little more milk if it is too dry). Turn the dough out onto a floured board and knead it lightly for a few minutes.
4 Grease a small loaf tin (pan), shape the dough into a loaf and drop it into the tin, pressing it down gently. Bake it in the preheated oven for 45 to 50 minutes or until a knife when inserted into the loaf comes out clean. Transfer it to a wire rack to cool.

Note: Try using Gruyère or Red Leicester cheese for a change or add finely chopped onion, garlic or celery. Add seeds – caraway goes especially well. Served with soup or salad, this delicious loaf adds protein, making a nutritionally balanced snack. One of my favourite combinations is a sandwich made from 2 slices of this loaf, puréed avocado and a generous helping of alfalfa sprouts.

Cornbread

85g (3 oz)	maize flour (cornmeal)	⅔ cup
85g (3 oz)	wholemeal (whole wheat) flour	¾ cup
1½ tsp	baking powder	1½ tsp
pinch	sea salt	pinch
1	free-range egg	1
140ml (¼ pt)	milk	⅔ cup
2 tbsp	honey	2 tbsp
1 tbsp	vegetable oil	1 tbsp

1 Preheat the oven to 400°F/200°C (Gas Mark 6).
2 Sift together the cornmeal, flour, baking powder and salt.
3 Beat the egg and add the milk, honey and oil. Combine this mixture with the dry ingredients and beat it to make a soft batter, adding a little extra milk if it is too dry or more flour if it seems too moist.
4 Lightly grease a small, square tin (pan), pour in the batter and bake in the preheated oven for 20 minutes or until the cornbread is well risen and firm to the touch. Leave it covered with a tea towel (dish towel) for a few minutes, then carefully remove it from the tin (pan) and cut into squares. It can be served hot, or left to cool on a wire rack.

Note: Traditionally eaten in the southern States of the USA, cornbread is good with sweet toppings such as jam or maple syrup but is also surprisingly good with such savoury dishes as scrambled eggs, bean stews and vegetable soups. Remember it next time you run out of bread!

Oatmeal Bread

455g (1 lb)	unbleached white flour	4 cups
170g (6 oz)	wholemeal (whole wheat) flour	1½ cups
115g (4 oz)	rolled oats	1 cup
2 good tsp	easy blend dried yeast	2 good tsp
1 tbsp	molasses	1 tbsp
3 tbsp	vegetable oil	3 tbsp
570ml (1 pt)	warm water	2½ cups
1-2 tbsp	milk	1-2 tbsp

1 Stir together the two flours, half the oats and all of the yeast. Lightly whisk together the molasses, oil and water and add this mixture at once to the dry mixture, beating it in well.
2 Preheat the oven to 400°F/200°C (Gas Mark 6).
3 Put the dough in a warm, floured bowl, cover it with polythene or a damp cloth and leave in a warm place for 1 hour or until it has doubled in size.
4 Meanwhile, soak the rest of the oats in the milk.
5 Grease 2 medium-sized loaf tins (pans). Knock back (punch down) the dough, divide it in half, shape each into a loaf and put one in each of the tins (pans). Gently squeeze the soaked oats to remove the excess milk, then scatter them over the tops of the loaves. Cover them, as before, and leave them in a warm spot to rise to the top of the tins (pans).
6 Bake them in the preheated oven for 30 to 40 minutes. To test whether or not they are cooked, slip them out of the tins (pans) and tap the base with your knuckles. If they sound hollow, they are done. Transfer them to wire racks to cool.

Note: You can use sugar or honey as a sweetener, although the molasses does give the loaves a slightly richer taste. The oats give an unusual texture. This is an excellent bread for sandwiches.

Soda Bread

455g (1 lb)	wholemeal (whole wheat) flour	4 cups
pinch	sea salt	pinch
1 tsp	bicarbonate of soda (baking soda)	1 tsp
about 285ml (½ pt)	sour (soured) milk (see note)	about 1⅓ cups

1 Preheat the oven to 400°F/200°C (Gas Mark 6).
2 Sift together the flour, salt and bicarbonate of soda (baking soda). Stir in enough of the sour (soured) milk to make a soft but not sticky dough. Turn it out onto a floured board, dust your hands with flour and knead it briefly. Divide it in half and shape each one into a round loaf. Put them onto a lightly greased baking sheet, flatten them slightly, then use the back of a knife to mark the top of each loaf with a cross.
3 Bake them in the preheated oven for 30 to 40 minutes or until firm to the touch. The loaves should also sound hollow when tapped on the base with your knuckles. Cool them on a wire rack (they are best eaten while they are still warm, broken into chunks).

Note: Soda bread is an excellent way to use up milk that has gone sour. You can also encourage fresh milk to turn by adding a few drops of lemon juice and then leaving it for a few hours. Alternatively, buy sour (soured) milk in the shops or use buttermilk instead.

Wholemeal Baps with Poppy Seeds

15g (½ oz)	dried yeast	1 tbsp
1 tsp	raw cane sugar	1 tsp
425ml (¾ pt)	warm water	2 cups
680g (1½ lb)	wholemeal (whole wheat) flour	6 cups
pinch	sea salt	pinch
85g (3 oz)	poppy seeds	½ cup
3 tbsp	sunflower seeds	3 tbsp
3 tbsp	pumpkin seeds	3 tbsp

1 Put the yeast into a small bowl, add the sugar and about a third of the water, stirring so that the yeast dissolves. Cover the bowl and leave it in a warm, draught-free spot until the liquid becomes frothy.
2 In a large, warmed bowl, sift together the flour, salt and most of the poppy seeds. Make a well in the centre, pour in the yeast mixture and the rest of the water and mix them together well. Transfer the dough to a floured surface and knead it until it is smooth and elastic. Return it to the bowl, cover with polythene or a damp cloth and leave it in a warm spot until it has doubled in size.
3 Preheat the oven to 425°F/220°C (Gas Mark 7).
4 Knock the dough back (punch it down), then divide it into 12 small or 8 larger pieces and shape them into baps (burger buns). Put them on lightly greased baking sheets, sprinkle the remaining poppy seeds, sunflower and pumpkin seeds over the tops, cover them carefully and leave them to rise again.
5 Bake them in the preheated oven for 10 to 15 minutes or until they are cooked on the outside. Leave them to cool with a cloth over them so that the middles stay soft.

Note: Plain baps (burger buns) can be made by omitting the seeds.

Onion and Herb Loaf

15g (½ oz)	dried yeast	1 tbsp
1 tsp	raw cane sugar	1 tsp
200ml (⅓ pt)	half warm milk, half warm water mixed	¾ cup
225g (8 oz)	wholemeal (whole wheat) flour	2 cups
55g (2 oz)	soya flour	½ cup
1 small	onion, chopped	1 small
1 tsp	fresh oregano, chopped	1 tsp
1 tsp	fresh marjoram, chopped	1 tsp
1 tsp	fresh sage, chopped	1 tsp
30g (1 oz)	margarine	2½ tbsp

1 Mix the yeast and sugar with half the warm milk and water, stir well, then set the mixture aside in a warm spot and cover the bowl. Leave it until it is frothy.

2 Meanwhile, in a warmed bowl sift together the flours, stir in the onion (first draining off any excess liquid) and the herbs. Melt the margarine in the remaining milk and water and add this to the bowl, together with the yeast, using a wooden spoon to mix them together thoroughly. Cover the bowl with polythene or a damp cloth and leave it in a warm, draught-free spot until the dough has tripled in size. Knock it back (punch it down) and knead it briefly again before transferring it to a greased loaf tin (pan). Leave it to rise.

3 Meanwhile, preheat the oven to 350°F/180°C (Gas Mark 4).

4 Bake the loaf in the preheated oven for 50 minutes to an hour (it is done when you rap the base with your knuckles and it sounds hollow). Cool it briefly in the tin (pan), then transfer it to a wire rack to cool completely.

Note: This bread is perfect for sandwiches with a difference. Alternatively, serve it at a buffet, cut into squares and topped with cheese (soft white ones make an especially good combination), nut butters or hummus. You can, of course, use dried herbs, although the flavour will not be quite as good. If you do so, halve the quantities given in the ingredients.

Pitta Breads

340g (12 oz)	wholemeal (whole wheat) flour	3 cups
good pinch	sea salt	good pinch
1 rounded tsp	easy blend dried yeast	1 rounded tsp
1 tsp	vegetable oil	1 tsp
200ml (⅓ pt)	warm water	¾ cup

1 Preheat the oven to 450°F/230°C (Gas Mark 8).

2 Stir together the flour, salt and yeast. Whisk the oil into the water, then add it to the flour mixture, mixing it in well to make a smooth dough. Turn it out onto a floured board and knead for 5 minutes. Return it to a clean, oiled bowl, cover it with polythene or a tea towel (dish towel) and leave it in a warm spot until doubled in size.

3 Knead the dough briefly again, then divide it into 8 evenly sized pieces. Shape each piece into an oval and roll it out gently to about 1 cm (½ in) thickness. Dust them with flour, put them on ungreased baking sheets and leave them, covered, for 15 to 20 minutes or until they have risen.

4 Bake the breads for 8 to 10 minutes in the preheated oven or until they have puffed up, then cover them with a tea towel (dish towel) until they are needed. (The oven needs to be very hot before you put the breads in to bake as it is the full heat that makes the pockets form.)

Note: To eat pitta breads, break them in half across their width, then push the sides together to open out the pockets. You can then fill these with whatever you like. Pitta bread is also tasty with dips (either tear them into pieces or cut them into strips), particularly warmed and served with hummus.

Spreads

Miso Avocado Spread

85g (3 oz)	split red lentils	good ⅓ cup
1 large	avocado	1 large
1 tsp	lemon juice	1 tsp
½-1 tsp	miso, or to taste	½-1 tsp
1 tbsp	fresh parsley, chopped	1 tbsp

1 Cook the lentils in boiling water until they are tender.

2 Peel the avocado, remove the stone (pit) then mash the flesh together with the lemon juice.

3 Drain the lentils, reserving 1 tablespoon of the cooking liquid. Dissolve the miso in the reserved water. Mash the lentils, add the miso mixture and then combine it with the avocado and parsley (if necessary, drain off any excess liquid). Chill the spread for a while before using it.

Note: This is an unusual and rather sophisticated spread. Use it on biscuits and serve them as something to nibble with drinks, sprinkled, maybe, with chopped nuts. You can use any cooked pulses (legumes) instead of the lentils. Leftover hummus is also good. Alternatively, ring the changes by replacing the lentils with a low-fat soft cheese such as cottage or Ricotta.

Hazelnut and Carob Spread

170g (6 oz)	hazelnuts, roasted (see note)	1½ cups
2-4 tbsp	carob spread vegetable oil	2-4 tbsp
1 tsp	vanilla essence (extract) (optional)	1 tsp

1 Finely grind the hazelnuts, then mix the resulting powder with the carob spread, adding a spoonful or two of oil. The spread should be thick and smooth. Then stir in the vanilla essence (extract), if using.
2 Store the spread in a screw top jar in the refrigerator and it should keep for some time, though the flavour will deteriorate if it is kept too long.

Note: This is a popular spread with children and delicious in sandwiches with slices of fresh pear.

To roast the hazelnuts, put them in a 300°F/150°C (Gas Mark 2) oven and cook them on a baking sheet, shaking it occasionally, until they begin to colour (the darker they are, the stronger they will taste). Leave the nuts to cool and then rub off the skins.

Carob spread is available in most wholefood shops, but if you cannot find it, mix some carob powder with oil, sweeten it with honey or syrup, and use that instead.

Blue Cheese and Watercress Spread

115g (4 oz)	blue cheese	4 oz
115g (4 oz)	curd cheese (cottage cheese, mashed)	½ cup
	milk, if necessary	
½-1 bunch	watercress, washed and coarsely chopped	½-1 bunch
3	gherkins, chopped	3
	freshly ground black pepper	

1 Mash the two cheeses together, adding a little milk if the spread seems too dry. Mix in the watercress and gherkins, making sure that they are evenly distributed, and season it to taste with the freshly ground black pepper. Chill the spread until it is needed.

Note: This is a fairly delicately flavoured blue cheese spread, so, if you like a stronger flavour, use more blue cheese and less curd cheese (cottage cheese, mashed). Other soft cheeses can be used instead of the curd cheese (cottage cheese, mashed) and, for a completely different taste, use Feta cheese instead of the blue and fresh herbs, such as parsley and/or chives, instead of the watercress.

Apple Butter

1.15 k (2 lb)	cooking (tart) apples, peeled and cored	2 lb
140ml (¼ pt)	cider or water	⅔ cup
170g (6 oz)	raw cane sugar	1 cup
1 tsp	ground cinnamon	1 tsp
1 tsp	ground ginger	1 tsp
1 tsp	ground allspice	1 tsp

1 Slice the apples and put them into a heavy-based pan with the cider or water. Cook the apples very gently and, using a wooden spoon, stir them frequently until they cook down to a soft mush (add a little more liquid, if necessary, but do not make the apples too wet).
2 Add the sugar and spices and continue to cook the mixture gently, still stirring frequently, until the purée is a rich brown colour and thick in texture. Cool it briefly, then transfer it to sterilized jars, seal them and store them in a cool place.

Note: Apple Butter is great in sandwiches with slices of strong or blue cheese or a sprinkling of nuts. It can also be used as a topping for yogurt or ice-cream, stirred into your breakfast porridge or as a filling for sponge (layer) cakes. As it takes time to cook, it is worth making extra, and keeping it ready to use when it is needed.

Crunchy Lemon Carrot Spread

3 large	carrots, grated	3 large
	mayonnaise (dairy or soya), as required	
1-2 tsp	lemon juice	1-2 tsp
1 tsp	lemon peel, finely grated	1 tsp
55g (2 oz)	walnuts (English walnuts) chopped	½ cup
	seasoning to taste	

1 Put the grated carrot into a bowl and stir in just enough mayonnaise to moisten it. Add the lemon juice, peel and walnuts and season to taste. Use it at once.

Note: Mayonnaise flavoured with lemon is also delicious with salads or it can be used as a sauce to serve with vegetables such as asparagus. If you find you like it, add the juice and peel to a small jar of mayonnaise a few days before you use it, which will give the flavour a chance to ripen.

Curried Chick Pea Spread

115g (4 oz)	dried chick peas (garbanzos), soaked overnight (see page 9)	½ cup
1 tbsp	vegetable oil	1 tbsp
1	clove garlic, peeled and crushed	1
1 small	onion, finely sliced	1 small
1 tbsp	curry powder	1 tbsp
1 tsp	lemon juice	1 tsp
	garam masala to taste (optional)	

1 Cook and drain the chick peas (garbanzos), then either blend them in a liquidizer or food processor or mash them by hand. Set them aside.
2 Heat the oil and sauté the garlic and onion in it until they have softened. Add the curry powder and cook the mixture for a few more minutes. Add the lemon juice, then stir in the chick peas (garbanzos) and mix everything together well. Add garam masala for a more strongly flavoured spread. If possible chill before using.

Note: This spread is good in sandwiches with crispy lettuce and cucumber slices. For a smoother spread, cook the garlic and onion with the curry powder, then add a drop more liquid with the chick peas (garbanzos) and put everything into a blender. This is, of course, an excellent way to use up any cooked pulses (legumes), or use tinned (canned) ones when you are in a rush. For a creamier spread, blend in some low-fat cream cheese or curd cheese (cottage cheese, mashed).

Vegetable Sandwich Spread

115g (4 oz)	peanuts, coarsely chopped	¾ cup
1	stick celery, very finely chopped	1
1 small	onion, very finely chopped	1 small
¼	cucumber, very finely chopped	¼
1 medium	carrot, very finely chopped	1 medium
1-2 tbsp	vegetable oil	1-2 tbsp
1-2 tbsp	cider vinegar	1-2 tbsp
	seasoning to taste	

1 Put the peanuts and all the vegetables into a bowl and mix them together. Add enough oil and cider vinegar to moisten the ingredients, then season them well.
2 Press the mixture down into a screw-top jar and keep the spread in a cool place until needed.

Note: This recipe was devised by a vegan friend and is very similar to the classic vegetable spread. A nice variation is made by replacing some of the peanuts with sesame seeds. The spread also makes a tasty topping for jacket potatoes.

Sandwich fillings

American Club Sandwiches

12	slices wholemeal (whole wheat) bread	12
	margarine or butter, as required	
115g (4 oz)	Red Leicester cheese, sliced or grated	4 oz
4	spring onions (scallions), chopped	4
¼ small	cucumber, sliced	¼ small
	mayonnaise, as required	
55g (2 oz)	alfalfa sprouts	1 cup
55g (2 oz)	almonds, coarsely chopped	½ cup
4	tomatoes, quartered, to garnish	4

1 Spread the slices of bread with margarine or butter. Lay 4 of the slices side by side and put the cheese slices, spring onions (scallions) and cucumber on them. Top each one with a slice of bread and spread mayonnaise, alfalfa and almonds over them. Top with the final slices, margarine or butter side down. Press the club sandwiches gently so that they hold together.
2 Serve the sandwiches garnished with the tomatoes.

Note: These towering sandwiches make an excellent snack for anyone with a big appetite. They can be filled with whatever you wish, but make sure the flavours of the ingredients will go well together.

Spinach Sandwiches

225g (8 oz)	fresh spinach, well washed	8 oz
8	slices unbleached white bread	8
	margarine or butter, as required	
pinch	ground nutmeg	pinch
115g (4 oz)	Mozzarella cheese, sliced	4 oz

1 Shred the spinach coarsely, then put it into a pan with just the water that remains on the leaves, cover the pan and cook the spinach for a few minutes until it has softened. Drain the spinach very well (do not chop it up).
2 Spread the bread with margarine or butter, then lay the spinach across 4 of the slices and sprinkle with the nutmeg. Lay the Mozzarella slices over the spinach, then top each with 1 of the remaining slices of bread.

Note: When making sandwiches it is more usual to use spinach raw, as a salad ingredient, but cooked spinach is often used in Italy and makes an unusual sandwich filling. Instead of Mozzarella, try it with Ricotta cheese sprinkled with grated (shredded) Parmesan. Unbleached white bread has a softer texture than wholemeal (whole wheat), which works better with the filling.

Tahini Banana Sandwiches

8	slices wholemeal (whole wheat) bread	8
	margarine or butter, as required	
140ml (¼ pt)	tahini	⅔ cup
2-4 tbsp	honey or maple syrup	2-4 tbsp
2 small	bananas, sliced	2 small
	ground cinnamon, to taste (optional)	

1 Spread the bread with margarine or butter.
2 Stir together the tahini and honey or maple syrup, then taste it and adjust the sweetness to suit. Spread some of the mixture over the 4 slices of bread, top with the slices of banana and, if using, sprinkle some cinnamon over the banana, then add the remaining slices of bread.

Note: For a more savoury spread, mix tahini with a nut butter, add some finely chopped spring onions (scallions) and radishes and season it with soy sauce or garlic salt.

Greek-style Stuffed Pitta Breads

4	wholemeal (whole wheat) pitta breads	4
½ small	cucumber, diced	½ small
2 medium	tomatoes, chopped	2 medium
¼ medium	crisp lettuce, shredded	¼ medium
85g (3 oz)	Feta cheese, crumbled	scant cup
12	stuffed green olives, sliced	12
	seasoning to taste	

1 Halve and split open the pitta breads to make 8 pockets.
2 In a bowl mix together the cucumber, tomato, lettuce, cheese and olives and season the mixture generously. Stuff the mixture into the pitta pockets and then serve them at once.

Note: This same mixture can also be used to fill sandwiches. For a change, substitute coarsely chopped cooked chick peas (garbanzos) for the cheese.

Fried Tofu Sandwiches

	wholemeal (whole wheat) flour, as required	
	seasoning to taste	
285g (10 oz)	tofu, drained and thinly sliced	10 oz
	vegetable oil, for frying	
1	French bread	1
1 small	head Chinese leaves, shredded	1 small
1 small	yellow pepper, cut into rings	1 small
	gomasio, as required	

1 Put some flour into a shallow dish and season it well, then dip the tofu slices into the flour, shaking them to remove any excess.
2 Heat some oil and shallow fry the tofu slices, turning them once, until they are golden brown on the outside and hot right through.
3 Cut the loaf diagonally to make 4 chunks and cut these in half. For each, put some of the Chinese leaves on the bottom, top this with some of the yellow pepper rings, then the fried tofu and a fine sprinkling of gomasio. Cover with the other half of the bread. Serve the sandwiches at once.

Note: This is a really filling snack. If liked, you can flavour the tofu by first marinating it in soy sauce, maybe adding some ginger and garlic salt (you can also now buy ready-marinated tofu, which is excellent when time is limited). Gomasio is a highly nutritious seasoning made by lightly roasting sesame seeds, mixing them with sea or rock salt, then grinding the two together to make a coarse brown powder. To make your own, use approximately 4 parts sesame to 1 part salt (the darker the seeds are, the more bitter the taste will be).

Date and Walnut Sandwiches

225g (8 oz)	*dates, stoned (pitted)*	*1¾ cups*
1 tbsp	*orange juice*	*1 tbsp*
140ml (¼ pt)	*water*	*⅔ cup*
55g (2 oz)	*walnuts (English walnuts), coarsely chopped*	*½ cup*
8	*slices wholemeal (whole wheat) bread margarine or butter, as required*	*8*

1 Chop the dates and put them into a pan together with the orange juice and water. Cook them gently, stirring continually with a wooden spoon. Gradually they will soften so that you can easily mash them to form a thick purée (if necessary, drain off any excess liquid). Stir in the walnuts.
2 Spread the bread slices with margarine or butter, then spread 4 of them generously with the date and walnut mix and top with the remaining slices.

Note: To make these sandwiches even more delicious, spread the second slice of bread with a full or low-fat cream cheese. These are great for a buffet – simply cut off the crusts, then cut each sandwich diagonally to make four small triangles.

Egg, Mushroom and Beansprout Sandwiches

55g (2 oz)	*margarine*	*¼ cup*
85g (3 oz)	*mushrooms, chopped*	*1½ cups*
4	*free-range eggs, beaten seasoning to taste*	*4*
1 tsp	*fresh mint, chopped*	*1 tsp*
8	*slices granary (multi grain) bread margarine or butter, as required*	*8*
55g (2 oz)	*mung beansprouts*	*1 cup*

1 Melt half the margarine and lightly sauté the mushrooms in it until they have softened. In another pan, melt the remaining margarine and add the beaten eggs. Cook the mixture gently, stirring, until it has set, then season to taste. Drain the mushrooms and add them, with the mint, then set the pan aside to cool briefly.
2 Spread the bread with margarine or butter. Top 4 of the slices with the egg and mushroom mixture, sprinkle with beansprouts and cover with the remaining bread.

Note: This is a good lunch-time sandwich. If you serve them while the filling is still warm, eat them with a knife and fork.

Instead of scrambling the eggs, you could hard-boil (hard-cook) and chop them, then stir them into the mushrooms.

13
Salads and Dressings

Mushroom and Fennel Salad

170g (6 oz)	button mushrooms, wiped and thickly sliced	3 cups
1 small	fennel bulb, chopped	1 small
2 tsp	lemon juice	2 tsp
3 tbsp	olive oil	3 tbsp
	seasoning to taste	
2	heads chicory (endive)	2
55g (2 oz)	walnut (English walnut) pieces	½ cup
	parsley sprigs, to garnish	

1 In a bowl, combine the mushroom and fennel with the lemon juice and oil and season to taste.
2 Line a small bowl with the chicory (endive) leaves, then spoon the mushroom and fennel mixture into the middle. Sprinkle the walnuts over the salad and garnish it with the sprigs of parsley.

Note: Artichoke hearts, fresh or from a tin (can), make this into a special-occasion salad that is good as a starter. Also, try it with a creamy garlic dressing instead of the lemon juice and oil for a different flavour and texture.

Pasta Salad with Mozzarella Cheese

115g (4 oz)	wholemeal (whole wheat) pasta shells	2 cups
½ small	cauliflower, broken into florets	½ small
1 medium	green pepper, sliced	1 medium
3 medium	tomatoes, quartered	3 medium
115g (4 oz)	Mozzarella cheese, diced	heaped cup

Dressing

2 tbsp	lemon juice	2 tbsp
2 tsp	olive oil	2 tsp
1 tbsp	fresh basil, chopped	1 tbsp
	seasoning to taste	
	fresh basil leaves, to garnish	

1 Cook the pasta shells in plenty of boiling water for 10 minutes or until they are *al dente*. Drain them, rinse them in cold water, drain them well again and set them to one side.
2 In a bowl, gently stir together the pasta, cauliflower (either use it raw or steam it for a few minutes to soften it slightly), pepper, tomato and cheese.
3 Now, make the dressing. Put the lemon juice, oil, chopped basil and seasoning into a bowl or screw top jar and whisk or shake to blend them together. Stir the dressing into the salad, then serve it garnished with the basil leaves.

Note: This is a filling snack in itself and any vegetables can be used with pasta in this way. Instead of the cheese you could try cooked beans, nuts, diced tofu or tempeh to add protein.

Minted Beetroot Salad

2 small	young beetroots (beets)	2 small
2	sticks celery, finely chopped	2
½ small	onion, finely chopped	½ small
55g (2 oz)	raisins	⅓ cup

Dressing

4 tbsp	vegetable oil	4 tbsp
1 tbsp	lemon juice	1 tbsp
1-2 tbsp	fresh mint, chopped	1-2 tbsp
	seasoning to taste	
	crisp lettuce, shredded, to serve	
2 tbsp	walnut (English walnut) pieces, chopped (optional)	2 tbsp

1 Peel the raw beetroots (beet) and either grate (shred) them coarsely or chop them into thin sticks. Put them into a bowl and mix with the celery, onion and raisins.

2 Now, make the dressing. Whisk the ingredients together or put them into a screw top jar and shake them together well. Pour the dressing over the salad, stir, cover it, then chill briefly. When you are ready to serve, make a nest of the shredded lettuce and pile the salad into the middle. Sprinkle the nuts over the top, if using.

Note: Young beetroots (beets) are delicious raw and the smaller they are, the sweeter and crisper their flesh is likely to be. When they are unavailable, cooked ones can be used in a similar way. Instead of mint, you can try using caraway seeds to flavour the dressing. Alternatively, serve the beetroot with natural (unsweetened) yogurt or sour (soured) cream.

Fruity Salad with Cottage Cheese Dressing

2 medium	carrots, coarsely grated	2 medium
2	sticks celery, chopped	2
115g (4 oz)	dates, chopped	2/3 cup
115g (4 oz)	seedless grapes	3/4 cup
1 large	pear, peeled, cored and chopped	1 large
good squeeze	lemon juice	good squeeze
1/2 bunch	watercress, washed	1/2 bunch

Dressing

115g (4 oz)	cottage cheese	1/2 cup
140ml (1/4 pt)	natural (unsweetened) yogurt	2/3 cup
1 tbsp	honey	1 tbsp
1 tsp	lemon juice	1 tsp
	freshly ground black pepper to taste (optional)	
30g (1 oz)	flaked (slivered) almonds, roasted (see note)	1/4 cup

1 In a bowl, combine the carrot, celery, dates and grapes. Mix the pear with the lemon juice to prevent it discolouring, then add it to the bowl together with the watercress.

2 Next, make the dressing. Either sieve (strain) or mash the cottage cheese, then blend it with the yogurt, honey and lemon juice. Freshly ground black pepper makes an unusual addition to this sweet dressing. Add it at this point, if using.

3 Pile the fruity salad into a serving dish, spoon the dressing over the top and sprinkle the almonds over the dressing.

Note: To make a completely balanced meal, simply serve this salad with a few slices of wholemeal (whole wheat) or rye bread.

The nuts can be used raw, but have more flavour if they are dry roasted first. Do this by spreading them across the base of a heavy pan and cooking them over a medium heat, shaking the pan frequently, until they begin to colour. Nuts roasted this way can be stored in an airtight container and used as they are needed.

Spinach and Avocado Salad

2 medium	ripe avocados	2 medium
1 tbsp	lemon juice	1 tbsp
2 tbsp	vegetable oil	2 tbsp
4	free-range eggs, hard-boiled	4
	seasoning to taste	
225g (8 oz)	young fresh spinach leaves	8 oz
	soya 'bacon' bits to taste	

1 Peel the avocados, remove the stones (pits) and then carefully dice the flesh. Mix it gently with the lemon juice and oil. Chop the eggs and add them, together with the seasoning.

2 Wash the spinach leaves, pat them dry, remove any tough stalks, then shred the leaves and put them into a bowl. Spoon the avocado mixture into the middle, sprinkle the soya 'bacon' bits over the top, and serve.

Note: As an alternative to the 'bacon' bits, try garlic croûtons. To make these, first sauté 1 or 2 crushed (minced) garlic cloves in oil, then remove the garlic and fry small cubes of wholemeal (whole wheat) bread in the flavoured oil. When they are crisp and brown, drain them well and sprinkle them over the salad.

Cucumber, Pepper and Coconut Salad

1 large	cucumber, diced	1 large
1 small	red pepper, diced	1 small
1 small	green pepper, diced	1 small

Dressing		
55g (2 oz)	creamed coconut, grated	2 oz
½-1	green chilli pepper, deseeded and chopped	½-1
2-3 tbsp	water	2-3 tbsp
200ml (⅓ pt)	natural (unsweetened) yogurt, or as required	¾ cup
	seasoning to taste	
	lettuce, shredded, to serve	
	coconut flakes, roasted	

1 Stir together the cucumber and red and green pepper.
2 Now, make the dressing. Use a blender to combine the coconut, chilli and water. Mix in the yogurt and season to taste. Check the flavour is to your taste (if it is too hot, add a little more yogurt).
3 Make a bed of the shredded lettuce, pile the cucumber and pepper mixture into the middle, spoon some of the dressing over it and sprinkle the coconut flakes over the top. Any leftover dressing can be handed around at the table.

Note: Though green chillies are less hot than the red ones, they can still be very fiery and, as different kinds will vary considerably in strength, it is a good idea to go carefully when using them in this or any recipe.

For a completely different salad based on the same ingredients, omit the chilli altogether and add some fresh strawberries to the cucumber and peppers.

Tabbouleh (Bulgar Salad) with Seeds

170g (6 oz)	bulgar	¾ cup
3	spring onions (scallions), chopped	3
3 medium	tomatoes, chopped	3 medium
2 tbsp	olive oil	2 tbsp
2 tbsp	lemon juice	2 tbsp
3 tbsp	fresh parsley, chopped	3 tbsp
3 tbsp	fresh mint, chopped	3 tbsp
55g (2 oz)	sunflower seeds	½ cup
55g (2 oz)	sesame seeds	½ cup
	crisp lettuce, shredded, to serve	
10	black olives, chopped, to garnish	10

1 Soak the bulgar in cold water for an hour (the grains should then be plump and tender). Drain the bulgar well, then tip it into the middle of a clean tea towel (dish towel), bring up the corners and twist them together to force out any remaining water.
2 Put the bulgar into a bowl, then stir in the onion, tomato, oil, lemon juice and herbs. The two most prominent flavours should be lemon and mint, so taste the Tabbouleh and, if necessary, add more of these ingredients.
3 Briefly dry-roast the sunflower seeds, then stir into the bulgar with the sesame seeds.
4 Line individual bowls with the lettuce, divide the mixture between them and garnish with the olives.

Note: An unusual starter, or make it up in larger amounts to serve as part of a buffet meal. Adapt it by using various nuts instead of the seeds - pistachios go especially well. Or add some lightly fried chopped tofu, or hard boiled eggs.

Apricot Coleslaw with Cheese

1 small	white cabbage, grated	1 small
1 medium	carrot, grated	1 medium
¼ small	onion, grated	¼ small
85g (3 oz)	dried apricots, chopped	½ cup
2 tbsp	lemon juice	2 tbsp
2 tbsp	vegetable oil	2 tbsp
115g (4 oz)	Edam cheese, diced	1 cup
1 tbsp	caraway seeds	1 tbsp
	seasoning to taste	

1 Simply combine all the ingredients, using more lemon juice and oil if necessary. Season the salad generously and chill it briefly before serving.

Note: Any cheese can be used in this coleslaw, but try blue cheese for an interesting contrast. Alternatively, replace the cheese with nuts. Other dried or fresh fruits could be used.

Three Bean Salad

225g (8 oz)	green beans, fresh or frozen	½ cup
55g (2 oz)	black beans, cooked (see page 9)	⅓ cup
55g (2 oz)	chick peas (garbanzos), cooked (see page 9)	⅓ cup
2	sticks celery, chopped	2
2-4	radishes, sliced	2-4

Dressing		
4 tbsp	vegetable oil	4 tbsp
1 tbsp	lemon juice	1 tbsp

1-2 tbsp	vegetarian	1-2 tbsp
	Worcestershire sauce	
	seasoning to taste	
	fresh parsley, chopped,	
	to garnish	

1 Cook the green beans until they are just tender, then rinse them in cold water and drain them well.
2 Mix them with the drained black beans and chick peas (garbanzos) and stir in the celery and radishes.
3 Now make the dressing. Whisk together the oil, lemon juice and Worcestershire sauce and season to taste (or put the ingredients into a screw top jar and shake it well). Pour the dressing over the beans and sprinkle the parsley over the salad to garnish.

Note: The black beans make an unusual addition to this salad, but you can use any other pulses (legumes) you have to hand – try broad (fava) beans, kidney beans or haricot (navy) beans. This is an excellent way to use up any leftover beans, which can be kept frozen until needed. In emergencies, use tinned (canned) beans.

Oriental Salad with Mange-Tout

115g (4 oz)	mange-tout (snow peas)	4 oz
1 medium	carrot, sliced	1 medium
1 medium	red pepper, sliced	1 medium
2	sticks celery, chopped	2
55g (2 oz)	mushrooms, sliced	1 cup
115g (4 oz)	beansprouts	2 cups
225-g (8-oz)	can water chestnuts,	8-oz
	sliced (optional)	

Dressing

2 tbsp	lemon juice	2 tbsp
4 tbsp	vegetable oil	4 tbsp
1-2 tsp	soy sauce	1-2 tsp
¼ tsp	ground ginger, or to	¼ tsp
	taste	
85g (3 oz)	cashew nuts	⅔ cup
	Chinese leaves,	
	shredded, to serve	

1 Wash and trim the mange-tout (snow peas). If these are very young and fresh they can be eaten raw, but if they are older, blanch them in boiling water for literally a minute or two, then rinse in cold water and drain them well.
2 In a bowl, stir together the mange-tout (snow peas), carrot, red pepper, celery, mushrooms, beansprouts and water chestnuts.
3 Now make the dressing. Whisk the dressing ingredients together or shake them in a screw top jar. Pour it over the vegetables and toss the salad gently. Line the base

of a serving bowl with the Chinese leaves, pile in the salad mixture and sprinkle the cashews over the top.

Note: Mange-tout (snow peas) are very young peas that are eaten whole and need only to be trimmed at the ends.
To turn this light, crisp salad into a more filling snack, stir some cooked brown rice in with the vegetables.

New Potato Salad

455g (1 lb)	small new potatoes,	1 lb
	scrubbed	
225g (8 oz)	tomatoes, chopped	1½ cups
1 small	fennel bulb, chopped	1 small
12	black olives, stoned	12
	(pitted) and chopped	

Dressing

4 tbsp	mayonnaise	4 tbsp
2 tbsp	milk	2 tbsp
	seasoning to taste	
	fresh chives, snipped, to	
	garnish	

1 Steam the potatoes until they are just cooked, leave them to cool briefly, then halve or quarter them, depending on the size, leaving very small potatoes whole.
2 In a bowl, combine the potato with the tomato, fennel and olives.
3 Now make the dressing. Stir together the mayonnaise and milk and season to taste. Stir it into the potatoes gently and chill the salad before serving, garnished with a generous sprinkling of the chives.

Note: This salad is also delicious made with sour (soured) cream instead of the mayonnaise and milk. Anyone avoiding animal products can replace them with tofu mayonnaise diluted with a drop of water. Alternatively, make a dressing with oil and lemon juice, then whisk in some light tahini.

Curried Flageolet Salad

115g (4 oz)	dried flageolet beans, soaked overnight (see page 9)	⅔ cup
1 small	crown broccoli, broken into florets	1 small
1 small	red pepper, sliced	1 small
2	spring onions (scallions), chopped	2

Dressing

2 tbsp	vegetable oil	2 tbsp
2 tbsp	white wine vinegar	2 tbsp
1 tsp	curry powder, or to taste	1 tsp
2-4 tbsp	fromage frais	2-4 tbsp
	seasoning to taste	

1 Cook and drain the beans. Rinse them with cold water, drain well, then set them to one side.
2 Meanwhile, steam the broccoli for just a few minutes, then drain it and leave it to cool. Mix together the broccoli, flageolets, red pepper and spring onion (scallion).
3 Now make the dressing. Combine all the ingredients, adjusting the flavour to taste, and chill it briefly. Stir the dressing into the beans and vegetables and serve.

Note: Omit the fromage frais if you like a less creamy dressing. Other vegetables and pulses (legumes) can be used in much the same way. Mix a few spoonfuls of Sweet and Sour Sauce (see page 157) into an oil and wine vinegar dressing for a complete change.

Radish and Cauliflower Salad with Yogurt Mayonnaise

Dressing

140ml (¼ pt)	natural (unsweetened) yogurt	⅔ cup
140ml (¼ pt)	mayonnaise	⅔ cup
1	spring onion (scallion), chopped	1
1 tbsp	fresh chives, snipped	1 tbsp
¼ tsp	dried basil	¼ tsp
¼ tsp	dried dill	¼ tsp
¼ tsp	paprika	¼ tsp
good squeeze	lemon juice	good squeeze
	seasoning to taste	
1 small	cauliflower	1 small
8	radishes, quartered	8
	crisp lettuce, shredded	
	watercress sprigs, to garnish	

1 First, make the dressing. Mix together the ingredients and chill them for an hour.
2 Steam the cauliflower for 5 minutes, then rinse it with cold water, drain it well and set it to one side. When it is cool, break it into large florets. Line a small salad bowl with the lettuce and top it with the cauliflower and quartered radishes.
3 Spoon some of the dressing over the salad and garnish it with the watercress sprigs. Any extra dressing can be put into a jug and brought to the table for people to help themselves to more.

Note: Instead of adding herbs to the yogurt mayonnaise, try stirring in some tomato purée (paste) or curry paste. For extra protein, add chopped hard-boiled (hard-cooked) eggs or a sprinkling of nuts.

Bread Salad

1 small	cucumber, sliced	1 small
1 small	crisp lettuce, shredded	1 small
3	tomatoes, chopped	3
1 small	leek, cleaned and finely chopped	1 small
½	green pepper, chopped	½
4 thin	slices wholemeal (whole wheat) bread	4 thin

Tofu dressing

170g (6 oz)	silken tofu, drained	¾ cup
2 tbsp	cider vinegar	2 tbsp
2 tbsp	vegetable oil	2 tbsp
good pinch	garlic salt	good pinch
	seasoning to taste	

1 Mix all the vegetables together in a bowl. Toast the bread, leave it to cool, then cut it into small cubes and set these to one side.
2 Now make the dressing. Mash the tofu and then blend it with the other ingredients to make a smooth, creamy sauce and chill it briefly. Adjust the seasoning to taste.
3 Spoon some of the dressing over the salad, mix it in lightly, sprinkle the bread cubes over the top and mix again. Any extra dressing can be served at the table for anyone who wants more.

Note: A crunchy, tasty salad, ideal for lunch on a hot day. Young leeks are delicious raw, but if they are unavailable, replace them with spring onions (scallions) or a sprinkling of snipped chives. In the Middle East a similar salad is made using pitta bread that is first toasted, then cut into strips – an idea worth trying for a change.

Red Cabbage Salad

½ medium	red cabbage, shredded	½ medium
1 large	orange, peeled and sliced	1 large
115g (4 oz)	sweetcorn, cooked	⅔ cup
½	cucumber, diced	½
30g (1 oz)	hazelnuts, roasted and coarsely chopped	3 tbsp

Dressing

4 tbsp	vegetable oil	4 tbsp
2 tbsp	cider vinegar	2 tbsp
good pinch	mustard powder	good pinch
good pinch	ground cumin	good pinch
	seasoning to taste	
	soft lettuce, to serve	

1 Mix the cabbage with the orange, sweetcorn, cucumber and hazelnuts.
2 Now make the dressing. Whisk the ingredients together or shake them in a screw top jar. Pour the dressing over the salad, then mix it in gently. Make a bed of lettuce leaves and spoon the salad into the middle.

Note: Add raisins if you like a sweeter salad. Ground ginger can be used in place of the cumin, as can other spices.

Egg Salad with Spicy Dressing

6	free-range eggs, hard-boiled (hard-cooked)	6
1 small	cucumber, diced	1 small
55g (2 oz)	mushrooms, sliced	1 cup
1 tbsp	capers	1 tbsp
10	pimiento stuffed green olives, sliced	10

Dressing

3 tbsp	vegetable oil	3 tbsp
3 tbsp	cider vinegar	3 tbsp
¼ tsp	paprika	¼ tsp
¼ tsp	chilli powder, or to taste	¼ tsp
¼ tsp	mustard powder	¼ tsp
good pinch	raw cane sugar	good pinch
1 head	chicory (endive), chopped	1 head
	fresh chives, snipped, to garnish	

1 Peel the eggs, cut them into quarters, then mix them gently with the cucumber, mushrooms, capers and olives.
2 Now make the dressing. Combine the salad dressing ingredients, either by whisking them together in a bowl or by putting them into a screw top jar and shaking it well. Stir it into the egg mixture and chill briefly.
3 Line a shallow dish with the chicory (endive), pile the egg salad into the middle, garnish it with the chives and serve.

Note: An alternative way to serve this salad is to replace the eggs with Quorn, which is a vegetarian meat substitute. Shallow fry cubes of Quorn, then toss them with the salad ingredients.

Winter Rice Salad

170g (6 oz)	brown rice	¾ cup
1 small	parsnip, peeled	1 small
4 small	Brussels sprouts, trimmed	4 small
1 medium	carrot, chopped	1 medium
2	sticks celery, chopped	2
55g (2 oz)	dates, chopped	½ cup

Dressing

2 tbsp	vegetable oil	2 tbsp
2 tbsp	cider vinegar	2 tbsp
1 tbsp	apple juice	1 tbsp
55g (6 oz)	salted peanuts, to garnish	½ cup

1 Cook the rice in water for 30 minutes or until it is just beginning to soften (the exact cooking time will vary depending on the rice you use). Rinse it with cold water and drain it well.
2 If the parsnip and Brussels sprouts are young and fresh, they can be used raw. Simply slice or grate (shred) them. If they are a little older, slice them and then cook them very briefly before rinsing them in cold water and draining them.
3 In a bowl combine the parsnip, Brussels sprouts, carrot, celery and dates. Add the rice to this mixture.
4 Next, make the dressing. Mix together the ingredients and stir the dressing into the salad. Sprinkle the nuts over the salad to garnish and serve.

Note: The salted peanuts make an interesting contrast to the other ingredients in this salad. If, however, you prefer to avoid salt, use plain peanuts or any other kind of nuts (chopped Brazil nuts are good). Any vegetables can be used instead of those given.

Italian Salad Bowl with Smoked Tofu

1 medium	chicory (endive)	1 medium
1 bunch	watercress	1 bunch
1 small	Lollo Rosso lettuce	1 small
1 medium	yellow pepper	1 medium
12	green olives	12
2 tbsp	olive oil	2 tbsp
good squeeze	lemon juice	good squeeze
	seasoning to taste	
225g (8 oz)	smoked tofu, drained	1 cup
3 medium	tomatoes, quartered	3 medium

1 Break the chicory (endive) into separate leaves, wash and trim the watercress, and wash and coarsely shred the lettuce. Slice the yellow pepper and olives. Combine all the ingredients in a bowl, trickle the oil and lemon juice over them and toss the salad gently to coat the vegetables evenly.
2 Dry the tofu, cut into thin, rectangular slices and grill (broil) them, turning them occasionally, until they are crisp and lightly browned. Cool them, then scatter them over the prepared salad. Put the bowl on a plate and arrange the tomatoes around the base of the bowl as a garnish.

Note: This light, rather bitter salad makes an excellent starter. Accompany it with warm, wholemeal (whole wheat) garlic bread. For an authentic Italian version, replace the tofu with fresh Parmesan or Pecorino cheese, using a potato (vegetable) peeler to slice the cheese into curly strips. If you cannot get Lollo Rosso lettuce, use Raddichio.

Celeriac Salad

2 small	celeriacs (knob celerys)	2 small
2 tbsp	lemon juice	2 tbsp
1 medium	apple, coarsely grated	1 medium
55g (2 oz)	sultanas (golden seedless raisins)	⅓ cup

Dressing

2 tbsp	mayonnaise	2 tbsp
140ml (¼ pt)	natural (unsweetened) yogurt	⅔ cup
½ tbsp	medium strength mustard	½ tbsp
	seasoning to taste	

1 Peel the celeriacs (knob celerys), then coarsely grate (shred) the flesh or cut them into thin sticks. Put these into a bowl, cover them with water, add the lemon juice and leave them for 10 minutes, then drain them well.
2 Mix the celeriac with the apple and sultanas (golden seedless raisins).
3 Next, make the dressing. Stir the ingredients together. Add it to the salad and chill it briefly before serving.

Note: Celeriac (knob celery) is the swollen root of a plant that has a flavour reminiscent of celery. Choose roots that are firm and heavy.

Celeriac prepared this way also tastes good with just fruit juice instead of the dressing, adding a spoonful or two of yogurt if liked.

Salad with 'Sausage'

455g (1 lb)	potatoes, scrubbed and cooked	1 lb
6	vegetarian 'sausages', sliced	6
2	sticks celery, chopped	2
55g (2 oz)	peas, cooked	⅓ cup
3 tbsp	mayonnaise (dairy or soya)	3 tbsp
	seasoning to taste	
	watercress sprigs, to garnish	

1 Dice the potatoes and put them into a bowl with the sliced 'sausages', celery and peas. Stir in just enough mayonnaise to moisten the ingredients, then season the salad well.
2 Spoon the salad into a serving bowl and top it with plenty of watercress to garnish.

Note: This German-style salad is a hearty snack in itself. Meatless sausages can be purchased in many varieties – tinned, frozen, vacuum-packed or in a mix form all ready to be shaped and cooked.

14
Egg and Cheese Dishes

Herb and Pistachio Nut Omelettes

55g (2 oz)	margarine	¼ cup
55g (2 oz)	unsalted pistachio nuts, shelled	⅓ cup
8	free-range eggs	8
1 tbsp	fresh parsley, chopped	1 tbsp
1 tbsp	fresh chives, snipped	1 tbsp
¼ tsp	fresh rosemary, finely chopped	¼ tsp
140ml (¼ pt)	natural (unsweetened) yogurt seasoning to taste parsley sprigs, to garnish	⅔ cup

1 Melt half the margarine and gently fry half the nuts for a few minutes.
2 Beat together the eggs and herbs, add the yogurt, and season to taste. Pour half this mixture into the pan. Cook it gently, lifting the sides of the omelette with a spatula to allow the uncooked mixture to run underneath. When it is just set, fold the omelette, cut it in half and serve it at once, garnished with sprigs of parsley.
3 Cook the remaining mixture in the same way.

Note: This is a quick-to-make snack that, because of the nuts, is also rather special. A more everyday version can be made using other nuts, such as raw peanuts or chopped hazelnuts.

Piperade

55g (2 oz)	margarine	¼ cup
1 small	onion, chopped	1 small
1	clove garlic, peeled and crushed	1
1 small	red pepper, sliced	1 small
1 small	green pepper, sliced	1 small
6	free-range eggs, beaten	6
2 tbsp	water or milk	2 tbsp
1 tbsp	fresh basil, chopped, plus extra to garnish seasoning to taste	1 tbsp
225g (8 oz)	tomatoes, chopped	1½ cups

1 Melt the margarine, add the onion and garlic and cook them in it for a few minutes. Stir in the red and green peppers and cook them for 5 minutes.
2 Mix the eggs with the water or milk and basil and season to taste. Pour the mixture over the vegetables, stir and cook it for a few minutes. Add the tomatoes. Continue cooking, tilting the pan to allow the uncooked mixture to run under the omelette as it sets. Then, pop it under a hot grill (broiler) for a few minutes more so that the top sets firm.
3 Cut it into thick wedges, scatter the extra basil over the top and serve at once.

Note: A traditional vegetable omelette that really is full of flavour. Of course you can break with tradition and use any vegetables you fancy. Add some leftover chopped potatoes and you will have a completely balanced meal in minutes.

Italian Cheese Omelettes

55g (2 oz)	spaghetti (optional)	2 oz
8	free-range eggs, beaten	8
55g (2 oz)	Parmesan cheese, grated	½ cup
3 tbsp	margarine	3 tbsp
	seasoning to taste	
55g (2 oz)	margarine	¼ cup
115g (4 oz)	Mozzarella cheese, thinly sliced	4 oz
2	tomatoes, sliced, to garnish	2

1 Break the spaghetti into smaller pieces, if using, and then cook it in a pan of boiling water until just tender. Drain well.
2 Mix together the eggs, Parmesan cheese, spaghetti and water and season to taste. Heat a little of the margarine in an omelette pan and pour in about a quarter of the egg mixture (if preferred, mix each up individually as you go along, whisking 2 eggs with 1 tablespoon of the Parmesan). Cook it gently until it is just beginning to set, tipping the pan and lifting the sides so that any uncooked egg goes under the omelette. Lay some of the slices of the Mozzarella in the middle, fold the omelette in half, garnish it with tomato slices and serve at once.
3 Repeat until all the ingredients have been used up.

Note: Ricotta or cottage cheese make a subtly flavoured, creamier omelette; try them instead of the Mozzarella for a change. For a complete contrast, use Feta or blue cheese.

Red Pepper Omelettes with Croûtons

115g (4 oz)	margarine	½ cup
¼ tsp	ground nutmeg	¼ tsp
¼ tsp	ground cinnamon	¼ tsp
4	slices wholemeal (whole wheat) bread, diced	4
1 large	red pepper, sliced	1 large
8	free-range eggs, separated	8
115ml (4 fl oz)	creamy milk	½ cup
	seasoning to taste	
	parsley sprigs, to garnish	

1 Heat 30g (1 oz/2 tbsp) of the margarine, add the spices and fry the bread, stirring frequently, until it is evenly browned and crisp in texture.
2 Melt another 30g (1 oz/2 tbsp) of the margarine in a clean pan, add the red pepper slices and cook them gently until they soften. Remove them from the pan with a slotted spoon.

3 Beat together the egg yolks and the milk and season them to taste. Whisk the egg whites until they are stiff, then use a metal spoon to fold this mixture into the egg yolks and milk mixture.
4 Heat half of the remaining margarine in an omelette pan and carefully pour in half of the mixture. Cook it gently until it is beginning to set, then put the pan under the grill (broiler) and cook the omelette until the top also sets. Arrange half of the pepper slices over the top and sprinkle with half the croûtons, then fold it, cut it in half and serve it garnished with the parsley sprigs. Make another omelette in the same way with the remaining ingredients.

Note: You can flavour the croûtons with garlic instead of the spices if you like. Also, cook twice as much as you need and keep the extra in an airtight container for use with soup or salad another day.

Deep-fried Cheese Cubes

225g (8 oz)	Mozzarella cheese	8 oz
	wholemeal (whole wheat) flour, as required	
	sea salt to taste	
2 large	free-range eggs, beaten	2 extra large
115g (4 oz)	wholemeal (whole wheat) breadcrumbs	2 cups
	vegetable oil, for frying	

1 Dry the Mozzarella and cut it into 2.5-cm (1-in) cubes. Sift together a little flour and some sea salt. Coat the cheese cubes in the flour, then dip them into the egg, then the breadcrumbs. Repeat this so that the coating is thick.
2 Heat a deep pan of vegetable oil and drop in the cubes, a couple at a time, and cook them for a few minutes until they are golden and crisp on the outside, creamy inside. Drain them well on paper towels, then serve them piping hot.

Note: Eaten with wholemeal (whole wheat) bread and a tomato salad, these make a simple but tasty snack. Serve at a buffet accompanied by a spicy tomato dip or creamy béchamel sauce with mushrooms added, and watch them disappear in a flash. Cheddar cheese can be used instead of Mozzarella.

Grilled Haloumi Cheese with Tomato Ketchup

340g (12 oz)	Haloumi cheese	12 oz

Tomato ketchup

285ml (½ pt)	tomato purée (paste)	1⅓ cups
3 tbsp	vegetable oil	3 tbsp
3 tbsp	white wine vinegar	3 tbsp
2 tbsp	honey	2 tbsp
1 tsp	ground cinnamon, or to taste	1 tsp
	seasoning to taste	

1 Dry the Haloumi cheese and cut it into thick, even slices.
2 Next, make the ketchup (catsup) by combining all the ingredients and mixing them well, adjust the flavouring to taste. Pour the sauce into a small saucepan and heat it gently.
3 Meanwhile, put the cheese slices under a hot grill (broiler) and cook them until they brown. Use a spatula to turn them and then grill (broil) the other side. Serve them with the ketchup (catsup).

Note: Haloumi is a white, firm goats' cheese with a salty taste. It comes from Cyprus. Ideal for cooking, it can also be baked or fried and is especially useful for instant snacks.

Oeufs en Cocotte

55g (2 oz)	margarine	¼ cup
4	free-range eggs	4
4 tbsp	single (light) cream	4 tbsp
1 tbsp	fresh chives, snipped	1 tbsp
	seasoning to taste	
	wholemeal (whole wheat) toast, as required	

1 Divide the margarine between 4 ramekins. Stand them in a shallow tin (pan), pour hot water into it around the ramekins until it comes half way up their sides, and heat the tin (pan) gently until the margarine has melted. Break an egg into each ramekin. Add chives and seasoning to the cream, then pour a spoonful over each egg.
2 Cover the pan with a lid and continue cooking for about 5 minutes or until the eggs have just set (do not overcook them). Serve them at once with triangles of warm, wholemeal (whole wheat) toast.

Note: This is a simple yet elegant and classic starter. To make the dish a little more special, put a few spoonfuls of vegetable purée under the eggs before you cook them. For example, aubergine (eggplant), fresh peas, leeks or spinach all work very well.

Fennel Soufflettes

2 small	fennel bulbs, trimmed	2 small
85g (3 oz)	margarine	⅓ cup
55g (2 oz)	wholemeal (whole wheat) flour	½ cup
285ml (½ pt)	milk	1⅓ cups
3	free-range eggs, separated	3
	seasoning to taste	
30g (1 oz)	flaked (slivered) almonds	¼ cup

1 Cook the fennel bulbs in boiling water for 10 minutes or until tender. Drain well, then either chop very finely or blend to make a purée.
2 Preheat the oven to 375°F/190°C (Gas Mark 5).
3 Melt the margarine and stir in the flour. Cook it for a minute, then gradually add the milk, stirring continuously, and continue cooking and stirring until the sauce thickens. Cool it briefly then stir in the egg yolks, seasoning to taste, and add the fennel purée. Whisk the egg whites until they are stiff, then, using a metal spoon, gently fold them into the fennel mixture.
4 Lightly grease 4 ramekins. Divide the egg sauce between them and bake in the preheated oven for 30 minutes or until they are firm and have lightly browned on top. The almonds can be added at the beginning, though they will be less likely to burn if added half way through the cooking time. Serve the soufflettes at once.

Note: These are an attractive starter. Other vegetable purées can be used to make these soufflettes, for example spinach or celery. Instead of topping them with nuts, you could stir some finely chopped nuts into the sauce with the purée.

Potato Cheese Soufflé

680g (1½ lb)	potatoes	1½ lb
3	free-range eggs, separated	3
115g (4 oz)	Double Gloucester cheese, grated	1 cup
55g (2 oz)	margarine seasoning to taste	¼ cup

1 Peel the potatoes, halve or quarter them, then steam them until they are tender. Drain them very well before mashing them to make a smooth purée (you can return the purée to a clean pan at this point and cook it very gently for a few minutes to ensure that no excess moisture remains).
2 Preheat the oven to 375°F/190°C (Gas Mark 5).
3 While the purée is still warm, stir in the egg yolks, cheese and margarine and season to taste. Whisk the egg whites until they are stiff then use a metal spoon to gently fold them into the potato mixture. Transfer the mixture to a greased soufflé dish and bake it in the preheated oven for 30 minutes or until it has puffed up and is golden brown on top. Serve it at once.

Note: This is an inexpensive and substantial soufflé – ideal for a family lunch.

Potted Cheese

225g (8 oz)	Cheddar cheese, grated	2 cups
55g (2 oz)	butter or margarine	¼ cup
1 tbsp	dry sherry (sherry wine)	1 tbsp
½ tsp	mixed dried herbs seasoning to taste	½ tsp

1 Using a heavy based pan or a double boiler stir together the cheese, most of the butter or margarine, the sherry (sherry wine) and herbs and season to taste. Heat the mixture gently, stirring continually until the cheese and butter or margarine have melted and are thoroughly blended. Divide the mixture between 4 ramekins, smoothing the tops. Melt the remaining butter or margarine and brush some over the top of the cheese mixture then chill the pots well.

Note: Serve your potted cheese with triangles of warm, wholemeal (whole wheat) toast, French bread or Cornish wafers (crackers). The Potted Cheese is good as a starter or a summer's day snack. Try other cheeses, too, such as Cheshire or Red Leicester. Though the butter is higher in saturated fats, it is always used in this traditional recipe and really does improve the flavour, but the choice is yours.

Scotch Eggs

170g (6 oz)	dried aduki beans, soaked overnight (see page 9)	¾ cup
4 large	free-range eggs, hard-boiled	4 extra large
6	spring onions, (scallions), chopped	6
1 tsp	dried mixed herbs seasoning to taste	1 tsp
2	free-range eggs, beaten wholemeal (whole wheat) flour, as required	2
55g (2 oz)	dried wholemeal (whole wheat) breadcrumbs, or more as required vegetable oil, for frying	½ cup

1 Cook and drain the beans.
2 Peel the eggs carefully.
3 Mash the beans to a thick smooth purée, stir in the spring onions (scallions) and herbs and season to taste. Add half the beaten egg and mix thoroughly.
4 Divide the bean mixture into quarters, flatten each into a circle (round), lay a boiled egg in the middle and use your hands to mould the mixture evenly around it, smoothing the paste as you work. Repeat this for the other eggs.
5 Gently roll each egg in the flour, dip it in the remaining beaten egg, then coat it thickly with breadcrumbs (you may find you need more).
6 Pour sufficient vegetable oil into a pan to deep fry the eggs and heat it until a cube of bread dropped into it browns in 30 seconds. Carefully lower the eggs into the oil and fry them for about 3 minutes or until they are golden brown. Remove them with a slotted spoon, drain them well, then leave them to cool.

Note: These Scotch Eggs are good with salad, served at buffet parties or in packed lunches. You can use any leftover or tinned (canned) beans instead of the aduki beans. Also, you can coat the eggs in one of the many excellent and versatile dry mixes available.

Tomato Cheese Fondue

1	clove garlic, halved	1
200ml (⅓ pt)	dry white wine	¾ cup
455g (1 lb)	Cheddar cheese, grated	4 cups
1 generous tbsp	cornflour (cornstarch)	1 generous tbsp
	seasoning to taste	
2 tbsp	fresh parsley, chopped	2 tbsp
140ml (¼ pt)	Tomato Sauce (see page 156)	⅔ cup

1 Grease a fondue pan, then rub the cut garlic around the sides and base to give a faint garlic flavour to the fondue.
2 Pour in the wine, reserving a spoonful, add the cheese and cook the mixture very gently, stirring it continually until the cheese melts. Stir the cornflour into the reserved wine to make a smooth paste, add this to the pan, and continue cooking and stirring until the sauce begins to bubble and thicken. Season it well, then add the parsley and Tomato Sauce, making sure they are thoroughly blended with the cheese mixture (the Tomato Sauce should be smooth, so blend it if necessary or use tomato purée).
3 Stand the fondue pan on a warming tray in the centre of the table. Serve it with a variety of ingredients to be dipped into the fondue. For example: cubes of wholemeal (whole wheat) or French bread, cauliflower florets, button mushrooms, radishes, chunks of celery and cucumber, or crisps (potato chips) and tortilla chips.

Note: Other fondues can be made in much the same way. For example, omit the tomato sauce or replace the wine with cider or light ale. You could add spices, too, such as nutmeg or mustard powder, or use other cheeses. Though fondue is best if stood over a warming tray at the table, it can also be made in a heavy-based pan and simply transferred to a hot dish just before being served.

Spinach Bake with Cheese and Yogurt

55g (2 oz)	margarine	¼ cup
1 small	onion, sliced	1 small
680g (1½ lb)	fresh spinach, well washed	1½ lb
2 large	free-range eggs, beaten	2 large
285ml (½ pt)	natural (unsweetened) yogurt	1⅓ cups
85g (3 oz)	Gruyère cheese, grated seasoning to taste	¾ cup
55g (2 oz)	wholemeal (whole wheat) breadcrumbs	1 cup

1 Preheat the oven to 375°F/190°C (Gas Mark 5).
2 Melt the margarine and sauté the onion in it for a few minutes. Coarsely shred the spinach, add it to the pan, stir, then cover the pan and cook over a low heat for 5 minutes or until the spinach is tender. Drain it well and put it into a small, greased ovenproof dish.
3 Mix together the eggs, yogurt and most of the cheese and season to taste. Pour the mixture over the spinach, smooth the top and sprinkle the remaining cheese and the breadcrumbs over the top.
4 Bake it in the preheated oven for 20 to 25 minutes or until the yogurt has set, then serve it at once.

Note: This is a simple yet tasty way to make a light meal out of spinach. You can, of course, use frozen spinach instead of fresh.

Mozzarella in 'Carrozza'

225g (8 oz)	Mozzarella cheese	8 oz
8 thin	slices wholemeal (whole wheat) bread	8 thin
2 large	free-range eggs seasoning to taste vegetable oil, for frying mustard and cress or parsley, to garnish	2 extra large

1 Pat the cheese dry and cut it into 8 thin slices. Trim the crusts off the bread and cut each piece in half diagonally. Sandwich the cheese between the bread triangles to make 8 small sandwiches.
2 Beat the eggs, season to taste, then soak the sandwiches in the mixture, turning them over after 5 minutes and leaving them there until all the egg has been absorbed. Press them together so that they keep their shape.
3 Heat some vegetable oil in a pan and shallow fry the cheese sandwiches over a moderate heat for a few minutes on each side. The bread should become golden and crisp, the cheese creamy.
4 Drain them on paper towels and serve them hot, garnished with the mustard and cress or parsley.

Note: This traditional Italian recipe is often served as a starter, though it makes a good snack, especially when accompanied by a crisp green salad. Other cheeses can be used instead of the Mozzarella.

Savoury Bread and Butter Pudding

2 tbsp	vegetable oil	2 tbsp
1 large	onion, sliced	1 large
2	sticks celery, finely chopped	2
6 small	slices wholemeal (whole wheat) bread	6 small
	butter, as required	
	yeast extract, as required (optional)	
4	free-range eggs	4
425ml (¾ pt)	hot milk (not boiling)	2 cups
½ tsp	dried oregano	½ tsp
	seasoning to taste	

1 Heat the oil and sauté the onion and celery in it for 5 to 10 minutes or until they have softened. Remove them from the pan with a slotted spoon and put them to one side.
2 Trim the crusts from the bread, cut the slices in half diagonally and spread each triangle with some butter and yeast extract, if using. Arrange them in a small, lightly greased ovenproof dish and spread the onion and celery over them.
3 Whisk together the eggs, milk and oregano and season to taste. Pour this over the bread and vegetables and leave them to soak for 30 minutes. Preheat the oven to 325°F/170°C (Gas Mark 3).
4 Bake the pudding in the preheated oven for about an hour or until the eggs have set. Take care that the top does not burn, if necessary, lowering the heat, then serve at once.

Note: Adapt this recipe to suit yourself, adding whatever vegetables come to hand, such as peas or beans, nuts or maybe grated (shredded) cheese in with the egg custard. This is a satisfying and inexpensive snack meal.

Nutty Baked Camembert

225-g (8-oz) round	Camembert cheese	8-oz round
30g (1 oz)	butter or margarine	2½ tbsp
30g (1 oz)	flaked (slivered) almonds	3 tbsp

1 Preheat the oven to 350°F/180°C (Gas Mark 4).
2 Put the cheese onto a heatproof plate and spread the butter or margarine lightly over the top and sides. Sprinkle with the almonds.
3 Bake the cheese in the preheated oven for 15 minutes, by which time it should be heated right through but not be too soft. Serve it at once.

Note: This is a really easy but impressive way to start a special meal. Cut the cooked cheese into small wedges and serve them with wholemeal (whole wheat) toast, Melba toast or crispbreads. Celery sticks make a nice addition. Try it, too, with other nuts, such as hazelnuts, which go very well. You can also prepare Brie in the same way.

Nutty Courgette Roulade

Roulade

55g (2 oz)	margarine	¼ cup
1	clove garlic, peeled and crushed	1
1 large	courgette (zucchini), finely chopped	1 large
45g (1½ oz)	wholemeal (whole wheat) flour	6 tbsp
200ml (⅓ pt)	milk	¾ cup
3 large	free-range eggs, separated	3 extra large
	seasoning to taste	

Filling

140ml (¼ pt)	sour (soured) cream	⅔ cup
170g (6 oz)	sweetcorn, cooked and drained	1 cup
55g (2 oz)	walnuts (English walnuts) chopped	½ cup
1 tbsp	fresh chives, snipped	1 tbsp
	seasoning to taste	
	parsley sprigs, to garnish	

1 Preheat the oven to 400°F/200°C (Gas Mark 6).
2 Melt the margarine and sauté the garlic in it for a few minutes. Add the courgette (zucchini), stir and cook for 5 minutes or until soft. Stir in the flour, cook it briefly, then gradually add the milk, stirring continually, until the sauce thickens. Add the egg yolks and season generously. Whisk the egg whites until they are stiff and use a metal spoon to fold them gently into the courgette (zucchini) mixture.
3 Line a Swiss roll tin (jelly roll pan) with greased greaseproof (waxed) paper, making it larger all round than the tin (pan). Pour in the mixture and bake it in the preheated oven for 30 minutes or until it has risen and springs back when lightly pressed.
4 Meanwhile, make the filling. Stir together the cream, sweetcorn, walnuts and chives and season to taste.
5 Use the paper to help lift the sponge from the tin. Spread the filling evenly over the top, then carefully roll it up along the long edge. Cut it into thick slices and serve it at once, garnishing each slice with a sprig of parsley.

Note: This makes a very elegant and original start to a meal. It can also be served with Tomato Sauce (see page 156), but be careful not to make it too strongly flavoured or it will mask the subtle flavours of the roulade. Other versions can be made using fresh herbs instead of the courgettes (zucchini), or adding cheese to the sponge mix. Try other fillings, too, such as fried onions and croûtons or spinach mixed with pine nuts and garlic. If necessary, bind the ingredients together with curd (cottage cheese, mashed) or Ricotta cheese or mayonnaise.

Indian Stuffed Eggs

6	free-range eggs, hard-boiled and peeled	6
3-4 tbsp	natural (unsweetened) yogurt	3-4 tbsp
1-2 tsp	mild curry paste	1-2 tsp
1 tbsp	mango chutney, chopped	1 tbsp
30g (1 oz)	salted peanuts, chopped crisp lettuce, shredded, to serve garam masala to taste (optional)	3 tbsp

1 Neatly halve the eggs and remove the yolks. In a bowl mash these together with the yogurt and curry paste, adjusting the taste to suit. Stir in the chutney and nuts, then pile the filling back into the egg whites and use a fork to swirl the tops.
2 On 4 small plates, make nests of shredded lettuce, arrange 3 egg halves on each one and top them with a sprinkling of garam masala, if using, then serve them at once.

Note: Use mayonnaise instead of the yogurt or a creamy soft cheese if you like. A spoonful or 2 of chopped red pepper makes the filling extra pretty, which is worthwhile if you are serving the eggs at a buffet.

Quick Cheese and Nut Whirls

225g (8 oz)	frozen puff pastry, thawed	8 oz
55g (2 oz)	blue cheese, crumbled	1 cup
55g (2 oz)	pecan nuts, chopped	½ cup
30g (1 oz)	curd cheese (cottage cheese, mashed)	2 tbsp
1 tbsp	watercress, chopped seasoning to taste watercress sprigs, to garnish	1 tbsp

1 Roll the pastry out into a rectangle about 20 by 30 cm (8 by 12 in).
2 Mix together the blue cheese, nuts, curd cheese (cottage cheese), watercress and seasoning to taste. Spread this mixture evenly over the pastry, then roll the pastry up from the long edge. Carefully wrap the roll in polythene or foil and chill it for 30 minutes. Preheat the oven to 425°F/220°C (Gas Mark 7). Using a sharp knife, cut the chilled dough into thin slices and put them on a baking sheet covered with foil.
3 Bake them in the preheated oven for 10 minutes or until they have browned nicely. Leave them to cool slightly on the baking sheet before transferring them to a wire rack. When they are cold, they can be stored in an airtight container for a few days, though they are best eaten fresh. To serve, arrange them on a plate and garnish with the sprigs of watercress.

Note: These are perfect for parties or to nibble with drinks. Try using Cheddar instead of the blue cheese and cream cheese instead of the curd (cottage) or any other cheeses you have to hand. Try, too, replacing the watercress with fresh herbs, such as sage, basil or chives.

Oeufs Mollets in Parsnip Nests

2 large	*parsnips, peeled and diced*	*2 large*
30g (1 oz)	*margarine*	*2½ tbsp*
2	*free-range eggs, beaten*	*2*
2 tbsp	*single (light) cream*	*2 tbsp*
¼ tsp	*ground allspice*	*¼ tsp*
285ml (½ pt)	*White Sauce (see page 156)*	*1⅓ cups*
3 tbsp	*fresh parsley, chopped*	*3 tbsp*
good squeeze	*lemon juice*	*good squeeze*
4	*free-range eggs*	*4*
2 large	*tomatoes, thinly sliced, to garnish*	*2 large*

1 Preheat the oven to 400°F/200°C (Gas Mark 6).
2 Steam the parsnips for about 10 minutes or until they are tender. Drain them well and then press them through a sieve or mash them very well to make a thick, smooth purée. Add the margarine, egg, cream and allspice.
3 Grease a baking sheet and, using a piping bag, make 4 rings with the purée. (Alternatively, simply divide the mixture into quarters and shape each piece with a spoon or your hands to make rougher but equally effective nests.) Bake them in the preheated oven for about 15 minutes or until they have set.
4 Meanwhile, heat the White Sauce and add the parsley and lemon juice to it.
5 Boil the eggs for exactly 3½ minutes so that the whites are firm but the yolks are still runny, then plunge them at once into cold water to stop them cooking any more and carefully peel off the shells.
6 Transfer the parsnip nests to small plates, put a whole egg in the centre of each, and cover with some of the sauce. Garnish with the slices of tomato. Serve at once.

Note: Though in fact *oeufs mollets* means simply 'boiled eggs', served like this they make an attractive starter to a special meal. You could use potatoes instead of parsnips, maybe adding some cheese to the mixture. Alternatively, half fill ramekins with vegetable purée and top them with the egg and then the sauce.

Small Gougères

140ml (¼ pt)	*water*	*⅔ cup*
55g (2 oz)	*margarine*	*¼ cup*
¼ tsp	*mustard powder*	*¼ tsp*
	seasoning to taste	
85g (3 oz)	*wholemeal (whole wheat) flour, well sifted*	*¾ cup*
2 large	*free-range eggs*	*2 extra large*
55g (2 oz)	*Gruyère cheese, grated, plus extra for sprinkling*	*½ cup*
	egg and water mixed, for brushing	

1 Preheat the oven to 400°F/200°C (Gas Mark 6).
2 In a saucepan bring the water to the boil and add the margarine and mustard and season to taste. Remove the pan from the heat and add all the well sifted flour at once, using a wooden spoon to stir it in. Return the pan to the heat and continue cooking very gently, stirring continually, until the mixture leaves the sides of the pan.
3 Off the heat, make a well in the middle of the mixture and add the eggs, beating them in thoroughly until the dough is smooth and glossy. Stir in the cheese.
4 Grease a baking sheet. Pipe or spoon 12 small balls of the mixture onto the sheet, leaving space between them. Brush the tops lightly with the egg and water mixture, then sprinkle a little cheese over them.
5 Bake them in the preheated oven for 20 to 30 minutes or until the gougères have puffed up and are crisp. Pierce the sides with a sharp knife and return them to the oven (leaving the door open) for 5 to 10 more minutes, then serve them at once.

Note: Individual gougères such as these are delicious served alongside vegetables. An alternative way to serve gougère is to pipe the mixture around the inside edge of a round, greased, ovenproof dish before baking. The ring can then be transferred to a serving dish and the centre filled with a mixture of vegetables in whatever sauce you choose. Either way gougères are perfect for a snack with a difference.

15

Fruit-based Snacks

Pears Stuffed with Spiced Cheese

4 large	pears	4 large
3 tbsp	lemon juice, or as required	3 tbsp

Stuffing

170g (6 oz)	Ricotta cheese	¾ cup
30g (1 oz)	raw cane sugar	2 tbsp
¼ tsp	ground cinnamon	¼ tsp
¼ tsp	ground ginger	¼ tsp
¼ tsp	ground allspice	¼ tsp
55g (2 oz)	candied peel, chopped	2 oz

1 Preheat the oven to 350°F/180°C (Gas Mark 4).
2 Using a sharp knife, halve the pears crossways, then core them, removing some of the flesh at the same time so that there is enough room for the filling. Stand the pear halves side by side in a small, ovenproof dish and pour some lemon juice between them. Bake them, covered, in the preheated oven for 40 minutes or until they are tender, basting them occasionally.
3 Meanwhile, make the stuffing. Mix together the cheese, sugar, spices and peel.
4 Transfer the hot pears to 4 small dishes, spoon the stuffing into the hollows in the pears and then serve them at once.

Note: These are delicious served, for example, after soup and wholemeal (whole wheat) rolls for a light lunch. You can use other soft cheeses instead of Ricotta and nuts instead of the candied peel, or top them with flaked (slivered) nuts. Apples are also very good prepared in this way.

Tofu Strawberry Cream

455g (1 lb)	strawberries	1 lb
455g (1 lb)	silken tofu, drained	2 cups
2-3 tbsp	maple syrup or honey	2-3 tbsp
½ tsp	vanilla essence (extract)	½ tsp
30g (1 oz)	pecan nuts, chopped	¼ cup

1 Wipe the strawberries and hull them. Put them into a blender with the other ingredients, except the pecans, and make a smooth cream. Pour it into 4 small dishes, top with the pecans and serve at once.

Note: This nutritious cream is ideal when you are too rushed to eat, yet need something to fill a gap as well as give you energy. It is also good for those who cannot face breakfast. Make it when strawberries are in season and cheap as it is a good way to use up those that are less-than-perfect. Try it with other fruit too, such as pineapple, raspberries, bananas or dried fruit, such as prunes or apricots.

Hot Grapefruit Cinnamon Crunch

2 large	grapefruits	2 large
2 tsp	ground cinnamon	2 tsp
30g (1 oz)	dark raw cane sugar	2 tbsp
30g (1 oz)	almonds, coarsely chopped	¼ cup
30g (1 oz)	honey toasted bran (see note)	2 tbsp

1 Use a sharp knife to halve the grapefruits, then cut around the segments to loosen them.
2 Sprinkle each cut face with some of the cinnamon, sugar and almonds. Grill (broil) them for 5 minutes. Add the honey toasted bran and heat them for 5 more minutes, then serve at once.

Note: Honey toasted bran is sold as a breakfast cereal in most wholefood stores and is crunchy and sweet. If you cannot find it, you could crumble an oat bar and use that instead. Serve the grapefruits at breakfast or as the first course for a dinner party.

Ginger Melon Starter

2 small	melons (Cantaloupe, Honeydew)	2 small
2	kiwi fruit	2
4	pieces preserved (candied) stem ginger (see note)	4
4 tbsp	orange juice	4 tbsp

1 Halve the melons and use a melon baller to scoop out little balls of flesh, or cut the flesh free with a sharp knife and then dice it.
2 Peel the kiwi fruit and slice them. Finely chop the ginger. Mix the ingredients together and divide the mixture between 4 small glasses. Mix the orange juice with some of the syrup in which the ginger is preserved and spoon some of it into each glass. Chill the melon mixture well before serving.

Note: This is a simple but elegant starter. You can, of course, serve it in the melon shells rather than in glasses, which makes it look even more impressive. Ginger preserved in honey is particularly delicious.

Fruit Salad Mould

570ml (1 pt)	apple juice	2½ cups
2 tsp	agar agar	2 tsp
114g (4 oz)	white grapes, halved	⅔ cup
2 medium	bananas, sliced	2 medium
1 medium	orange, peeled and segmented	1 medium
1 medium	pear, diced	1 medium
2 tbsp	lemon juice	2 tbsp
55g (2 oz)	coconut flakes, roasted	⅔ cup
½ bunch	watercress	½ bunch
1	chicory (endive), sliced	1

1 Bring the apple juice to a gentle simmer, then whisk in the agar agar and continue cooking for a few minutes. Set this mixture to one side to cool. When it is just beginning to set, stir in the fruit, lemon juice and coconut flakes.
2 Rinse a ring mould (tube pan) with cold water, and pour in the jelly. Leave it to cool, then chill it for at least 2 hours or until it is set.
3 When you are ready to serve, dip the mould briefly in hot water before putting a plate over it, inverting it, and lifting off the mould to leave the jelly ring on the plate.
4 Mix together the watercress and chicory and fill middle of the ring with it.

Note: Though this makes a lovely lunch (with granary bread and nut butter, for example), it can also be served as a sweet, in which case, try adding some natural (unsweetened) yogurt or fromage frais.

Pineapple Granola Crêpes

285ml (½ pt)	pancake batter of your choice (see pages 154-155) vegetable oil, for frying	1⅓ cups

Filling

395-g (14-oz)	tin (can) pineapple pieces in natural juice	14-oz
55g (2 oz)	granola	½ cup
55g (2 oz)	brazil nuts, chopped	½ cup

Sauce

1 tbsp	lemon juice	1 tbsp
1 tbsp	maple syrup or honey	1 tbsp
1 generous tsp	arrowroot	1 generous tsp

1 Make the pancake batter according to the instructions and chill it for at least 30 minutes.
2 Meanwhile, make the filling. Drain the pineapple pieces, reserving the juice. Coarsely crush the pineapple and mix in the granola and nuts.
3 Now make the sauce. In a small pan, combine the lemon juice, maple syrup or honey and about 200ml

(⅓ pt/¾ cup) of the reserved pineapple juice. Stir and heat it gently. Mix the arrowroot into another spoonful of juice and add this to the pan. Continue heating the sauce and gently stirring it continually until the sauce thickens, adding more juice or water if necessary.

4 Whisk the pancake batter and adjust the consistency if necessary to that of single (light) cream. Heat some oil in a pan and add just a little batter, tipping the pan to spread it out (the crêpes should be as thin and light as possible). When lightly browned, turn the crêpe to cook the other side, then set it aside and keep it warm. Continue in this way until all the batter has been used up. Put a spoonful of the filling on each crêpe, roll it up, trickle some of the sauce over the top and serve at once.

Note: Granola is a baked cereal usually eaten at breakfast time. You can either buy it ready-made or make your own (see Spiced Pear Granola, page 151).

Other fruit crêpes can be made in the same way, mixing the moistened fruit with nuts only, if you prefer, or with dried fruit.

Grapefruit Sorbet

140ml (¼ pt)	water	⅔ cup
285ml (½ pt)	grapefruit juice	1⅓ cups
2 tbsp	grapefruit peel, finely grated	2 tbsp
55g (2 oz)	raw cane sugar, or to taste	⅓ cup
2	free-range egg whites lemon slices, to garnish	2

1 Combine the water, juice, peel and sugar in a saucepan, bring the mixture to the boil and simmer it for 10 minutes. Then set it to one side to cool.

2 When it is cool, strain the syrup to remove the peel, then pour it into a freezer proof shallow container and freeze it for 1 hour or until it becomes mushy. Tip it into a bowl and beat it lightly to break up the ice crystals. Whisk the egg whites until they are stiff, stir them into the grapefruit mush and return the mixture to the freezer. Freeze it until it has frozen hard.

3 When you want to use it, transfer it to the refrigerator for an hour before serving to soften it slightly. Serve it in individual bowls, garnished with the slices of lemon.

Note: Though sorbets are usually served at the end of a meal, they also make an unusual starter – particularly the sharper-flavoured ones. Alternatively, serve your sorbet part way through a meal to freshen the palate. Other flavours can be made in the same way: try lemon, orange, mango, kiwi.

Mango and Feta Cheese Starter

3 medium	mangoes	3 medium
2 tbsp	lemon juice	2 tbsp
170g (6 oz)	Feta cheese	6 oz

1 Use a sharp knife to carefully peel the mangoes. Then cut them into even slices and sprinkle the lemon juice over them.

2 Thinly slice the cheese and arrange it on 4 small plates, overlapping it alternately with the slices of mango. Chill them briefly before serving.

Note: Another very simple but impressive starter, with the subtle flavour of the mangoes making an excellent contrast to the salty cheese. The mangoes should be ripe but still firm, and take care when removing the stone (pit), which can be difficult to do without tearing the flesh. If you cannot find mangoes in your local shops, look out for fresh figs, which make a good alternative. Failing that, use melon.

Autumn Fruit Bake

Topping

115g (4 oz)	wholemeal (whole wheat) flour	1 cup
85g (3 oz)	cottage cheese, drained	⅓ cup
55g (2 oz)	raw cane sugar	⅓ cup
2 tsp	ground coriander	2 tsp

Base

680g (1½ lb)	cooking (tart) apples, peeled and thickly sliced	5 cups
225g (8 oz)	blackberries, washed	1½ cups
55g (2 oz)	raw cane sugar, or to taste	⅓ cup

1 Preheat the oven to 350°F/180°C (Gas Mark 4).

2 First, make the topping. Put the flour into a bowl and rub in the cottage cheese, then mix in the sugar and coriander.

3 Next, make the base. In a lightly greased ovenproof dish, layer the apple and blackberries and sprinkle each layer with sugar (this dish should not be over sweet, but use more sugar if you wish). Sprinkle the crumble topping over the top and press it down lightly. Bake it in the preheated oven for 20 minutes or until cooked.

Note: This is a nutritionally balanced dish that you can serve instead of a savoury one when there is a glut of autumn fruit – or when you just feel like eating something sweet.

Dried Fruit Soufflés

225g (8 oz)	*dried apricots, cooked*	*1¾ cups*
85g (3 oz)	*raw cane sugar, or to taste*	*½ cup*
4	*free-range egg whites*	*4*

1 Preheat the oven to 325°F/170°C (Gas Mark 3).
2 Drain the apricots well and either blend them or press them through a sieve to make a thick purée. Add the sugar to the mixture.
3 Whisk the egg whites until they are stiff then use a metal spoon to fold them into the apricot mixture. Pour it into 4 lightly greased ramekins and bake them in the preheated oven for about 25 to 30 minutes or until they have risen. Then serve them at once.

Note: These are surprisingly good eaten together with a chunk of cheese!

For an even quicker dish, do not cook the dried fruit mixture. It then tastes rather like a mousse. Other fruit purées can be used instead of the apricot - try strawberries, gooseberries or prunes.

Banana Fritters

115g (4 oz)	*wholemeal (whole wheat) flour*	*1 cup*
pinch	*sea salt*	*pinch*
1	*free-range egg, beaten*	*1*
140ml (¼ pt)	*milk*	*⅔ cup*
4 medium	*firm bananas*	*4 medium*
2 tbsp	*lemon juice*	*2 tbsp*
	vegetable oil, for frying	
	sugar to taste (optional)	
	ground cinnamon to taste (optional)	

1 Sift together the flour and salt. Gradually add the egg and then the milk and keep beating until you have a smooth, light batter. Chill it for 30 minutes.
2 Cut the bananas into chunks, then halve them lengthways. Heat enough oil in a deep pan to deep fry the banana pieces. Before cooking, dip them into the batter, then fry them for 3 to 5 minutes or until they are golden. Drain them well before serving them hot. Though sweet enough as they are, you could add a sprinkling of sugar mixed with cinnamon to make them that bit more special.

Note: This is the kind of snack children love and it's healthier than most, too. Try preparing other fruit in the same way.

Exotic Fruit Salad with Coconut Cream

2	*fresh kiwi fruit*	*2*
8	*fresh lychees*	*8*
1	*fresh star fruit*	*1*
4	*fresh satsumas*	*4*
115g (4 oz)	*fresh dates*	*1 cup*
4	*fresh pineapple rings*	*4*
115ml (¼ pt)	*pineapple* or *orange juice*	*⅔ cup*

Coconut cream

115g (4 oz)	*creamed coconut, grated (shredded)*	*4 oz*
200ml (⅓ pt)	*hot water*	*¾ cup*
	milk or *soya milk, as required*	
55g (2 oz)	*raw cane sugar, finely ground*	*⅓ cup*

1 Peel the kiwi fruit, slice them, then halve the slices. Peel the lychees and remove the stones (pits). Slice the star fruit, and peel and segment the satsumas. Remove the stones (pits) from the dates and coarsely chop them.
2 Combine all the fruit in a bowl, pour the pineapple or orange juice over them, stir the salad gently and then chill.
3 Meanwhile, make the Coconut Cream. Stir the coconut into the hot water so that it dissolves. Then add enough milk to make the mixture the consistency of single (light) cream, adding sugar to taste. Coconut cream is best prepared just before you use it, otherwise it may become firm, but if this happens, just add a little hot water and stir it well. Serve it in a jug for people to help themselves.

Note: Any fruits can be used in this kind of fruit salad, of course. As the more exotic ones can be expensive, for an everyday mixture you might prefer to use the cheaper fruits, adding just one exotic variety (star fruit is one of the prettiest) to give the mixture a lift. If you haven't time to make the Coconut Cream, just serve it with natural (unsweetened) yogurt. Fruit salad makes an ideal snack in summer.

Prune and Apple Compote

225g (8 oz)	*dried prunes, soaked overnight*	*1¾ cups*
115g (4 oz)	*dried apple rings, soaked overnight*	*¾ cup*
55g (2 oz)	*raisins*	*⅓ cup*
200ml (⅓ pt)	*apple juice*	*¾ cup*
1 tbsp	*lemon peel, grated*	*1 tbsp*
½ tsp	*ground cinnamon, or to taste*	*½ tsp*

¼ tsp	ground cloves, or to taste	¼ tsp
55g (2 oz)	brazil nuts, chopped	½ cup

1 Drain the prunes and apple rings and put them in a saucepan together with the raisins, apple juice, lemon peel and spices. Simmer the mixture, covered, for about 10 minutes or until the fruit is just tender. Leave it to cool, then stir in the brazil nuts and serve.

Note: This is good eaten for breakfast or whenever you fancy a sweet snack. You can add natural (unsweetened) yogurt, either dairy or soya, for protein or sprinkle granola or muesli over it.

Avocado and Grapefruit with Mayonnaise

2 large	grapefruits	2 large
1 large	avocado	1 large
4 tbsp	mayonnaise (dairy or soya)	4 tbsp
	seasoning to taste	
30g (1 oz)	walnuts (English walnuts), coarsely chopped	¼ cup
	watercress, to garnish	

1 Halve the grapefruits, carefully scoop out all the flesh and cut it into large pieces. Peel the avocado, remove the stone (pit) and dice the flesh, then mix it with the grapefruit. Stir in enough mayonnaise to moisten the mixture and season it well.
2 Pile the mixture back into the grapefruit shells and sprinkle some of the walnuts over each one. Chill them before serving, garnished with the watercress.

Note: This original combination is great for serving to guests as a first course. Alternatively, pile the mixture onto a bed of shredded crisp lettuce and eat it with wholemeal (whole wheat) rolls for a light and refreshing lunch.

Chilled Fruit Soup

225g (8 oz)	ripe fresh apricots, peeled and stoned (pitted)	2 cups
2 medium	apples, cored and peeled	2 medium
285ml (½ pt)	white grape juice	1⅓ cups
2 tbsp	lemon juice	2 tbsp
2-3 tbsp	raw cane sugar	2-3 tbsp
good pinch	ground cinnamon	good pinch

1 Finely chop the fruit and put it into a saucepan with the grape juice, lemon juice, sugar to taste (how much

you will need will also depend on the sweetness of the fruit) and the cinnamon. Bring the mixture just to the boil, then cover the pan and simmer it for 10 minutes or until the fruit begins to disintegrate. Cool it briefly and chill well before serving.

Note: This is a delicious and different starter on a hot summer's day. Water can be used instead of the grape juice, maybe adding some concentrated apple or orange juice for flavour. For a thicker soup, mix a teaspoon of cornflour (cornstarch) with an extra tablespoon of liquid and stir this into the fruit mixture, simmering it for a few minutes until it thickens.

Summer Pudding

225g (½ lb)	raspberries	1½ cups
225g (½ lb)	blackberries	1½ cups
225g (½ lb)	blackcurrants	1½ cups
115g (4 oz)	redcurrants	¾ cup
6 thin	slices wholemeal (whole wheat) bread, or as required	6 thin

Cashew Milk

170g (6 oz)	ground cashew nut pieces	1½ cups
140ml (¼ pt)	concentrated soya milk	⅔ cup
1 tsp	vanilla essence (extract), or to taste	1 tsp

1 Put the fruit into a saucepan, just cover it with water and simmer it gently for 10 to 15 minutes or until cooked.
2 Meanwhile, line the base and sides of a small bowl with most of the slices of bread, arranging it carefully so that there are no gaps. Pour in the fruit and some of the juice and cover the top with the remaining slices of bread. Put a saucer or small plate on top and weigh it down. Chill the pudding overnight or for 24 hours.
3 When it is ready, remove the weighted saucer or plate, put the serving plate over the bowl, invert them and then carefully remove the bowl.
4 Now make the Cashew Milk. Whisk together the ground cashew, soya milk and vanilla and serve wedges of the pudding topped with the Cashew Milk.

Note: This classic British dish is both tasty and filling – perfect for a snack on a sultry day. Ring the changes by using other fruits, which means you will also be able to make it at other times of year. Take care to include a number of dark or red fruits – such as plums, rhubarb and strawberries – to give the pudding its beautiful colour.

16
Pies and Pasties

Broccoli and Feta Pies

340g (12 oz)	wholemeal (whole wheat) pastry of your choice (see pages 152-153)	12 oz

Filling

1 tbsp	vegetable oil	1 tbsp
1 small	onion, sliced	1 small
55g (2 oz)	mushrooms, sliced	1 cup
1 large	crown broccoli, broken into florets	1 large
170g (6 oz)	Feta cheese, diced	2 cups
2-3 tbsp	sour (soured) cream	2-3 tbsp
	seasoning to taste	
	beaten egg or milk, to glaze (optional)	

1 Make the pastry as instructed, then chill it.
2 Preheat the oven to 400°F/200°C (Gas Mark 6).
3 Meanwhile, make the filling. Heat the oil and sauté the onion in it for 5 minutes or until it has softened. Stir in the mushrooms and cook them for 5 minutes. At the same time, lightly steam the broccoli florets for a few minutes until tender (do not overcook them). Drain them and the onion and mushroom mixture and mix them together in a bowl. Stir in the cheese and cream and season to taste.
4 Roll the pastry out and use just over half of it to make 4 circles (rounds) to line Yorkshire pudding tins (patty or muffin pans). Pile in the filling. Roll out the remaining dough, cut 4 more circles (rounds), brush the edges of the pastry with water and place them over the filling, pressing the edges of the top and bottom pieces of pastry together to seal. Use any extra pieces of pastry to decorate the pies, then make a cut in the top of each pie. Brush the tops with the beaten egg or milk, if using.

5 Bake the pies in the preheated oven for 20 to 30 minutes or until the tops are golden brown. Let them cool slightly in the tins (pans), then carefully remove them and serve.

Note: These creamy pies are delicious both hot and cold and so are good for buffets.

Lentil Cornish Pasties

225g (8 oz)	wholemeal (whole wheat) pastry of your choice (see pages 152-153)	8 oz

Filling

55g (2 oz)	split red lentils	¼ cup
1 medium	potato, diced	1 medium
1 medium	onion, sliced	1 medium
1 medium	carrot, sliced	1 medium
1 medium	swede (rutabaga), diced	1 medium
	seasoning to taste	
	beaten egg or milk, to glaze (optional)	

1 Preheat the oven to 400°F/200°C (Gas Mark 6).
2 Make the pastry as instructed and chill it.
3 Meanwhile, make the filling. Cook the lentils in boiling water until they are tender, then drain them well.
4 Also, lightly steam the vegetables until they are just tender, then drain them well. Mix them with the lentils and season to taste.
5 Roll out the dough and cut out 4 large circles (rounds). Divide the mixture between them. Moisten the edges with water, fold the pastry circles (rounds) in half and press the edges firmly together so that they are well

sealed. Brush the tops of the pasties with beaten egg or milk, if using. Transfer the pasties to a lightly greased baking sheet and bake them in the preheated oven for 20 to 30 minutes or until they are cooked.

Note: This is everyone's favourite picnic pasty – and is excellent for lunch boxes, too. Usually made with meat, this version uses lentils in its place to add protein. Alternatively, use 'beef'-flavoured TVP mince or soya flakes. Coarsely ground nuts also go well in these pasties.

Ratatouille Pie with Cheese Pastry

Pastry

225g (8 oz)	wholemeal (whole wheat) flour	2 cups
85g (3 oz)	margarine	⅓ cup
85g (3 oz)	Cheddar cheese, grated	¾ cup
good pinch	paprika	good pinch
	cold water, to mix	

Filling

1 small	aubergine (eggplant), diced	1 small
	sea salt	
2 tbsp	vegetable oil	2 tbsp
1 medium	onion, sliced	1 medium
1 medium	green pepper, sliced	1 medium
1	clove garlic, peeled and crushed	1
395-g (14-oz)	tin (can) tomatoes, chopped	14-oz
115g (4 oz)	sweetcorn, fresh or canned	⅔ cup
1 tsp	dried thyme	1 tsp
1 tsp	dried parsley	1 tsp
	seasoning to taste	

1 First, make the pastry. Put the flour into a bowl, rub in the margarine until the mixture resembles breadcrumbs. Mix in the cheese and paprika, then use a knife to mix in just enough water to make a soft dough. Wrap the pastry in polythene or clingfilm (plastic wrap) and chill it for at least 30 minutes.
2 Meanwhile, make the filling. Put the aubergine (eggplant) onto a plate, sprinkle salt over it and leave it for 30 minutes or until the bitter juices have oozed out. Then rinse it well, drain it and pat it dry.
3 Preheat the oven to 400°F/200°C (Gas Mark 6).
4 Heat the oil and sauté the onion, green pepper and garlic for a few minutes to soften them. Stir in the aubergine (eggplant) and cook for a few minutes more. Add the tomatoes, sweetcorn and herbs and season to taste. Cover the pan and simmer the vegetables gently for 20 minutes or until they are just cooked.
5 Pile the filling into a medium-sized shallow ovenproof dish. Roll out the pastry and use it to make a lid to cover the vegetables. Make a cut in the top, then bake the pie in the preheated oven for 20 minutes or until the pastry is crisp and golden brown. Serve the pie at once.

Note: This is a good way to turn ratatouille into a satisfying lunch dish. You can add cooked beans instead of the sweetcorn or a handful of chopped walnuts (English walnuts). The pastry can, of course, be used with most other vegetable fillings. Also try it using different cheeses.

Fennel and Peas Pasties

225g (8 oz)	wholemeal (whole wheat) pastry of your choice (see pages 152-153)	8 oz

Filling

30g (1 oz)	margarine	2½ tbsp
2 small	fennel bulbs, trimmed and chopped	2 small
1 small	onion, sliced	1 small
170g (6 oz)	peas, fresh or frozen	1 cup
140ml (¼ pt)	water	⅔ cup
200ml (⅓ pt)	thick White Sauce (see page 156)	¾ cup
55g (2 oz)	curd cheese (cottage cheese, mashed)	¼ cup
	seasoning to taste	
	beaten egg or milk, to glaze (optional)	
1 tsp	fennel seeds (optional)	1 tsp

1 Make the pastry as instructed and chill it.
2 Preheat the oven to 400°F/200°C (Gas Mark 6).
3 Meanwhile, melt the margarine and lightly sauté the fennel and onion in it for a few minutes. Stir in the peas and water, bring the liquid to the boil, then cover the pan and cook the mixture for 10 to 15 minutes or until the vegetables are tender, then drain them well.
4 Mix the vegetables into the White Sauce, add the cheese and stir it in well, then season the mixture to taste.
5 Roll the pastry out and cut it into 4 squares. Divide the filling between them, then moisten the edges of the pastry and fold it over the filling to make triangles, pressing the edges together firmly. Transfer the pasties to a lightly greased baking sheet. If you are using the fennel seeds, brush the pasties with a little beaten egg or milk and sprinkle them over the top. Bake the pasties in the preheated oven for 20 minutes or until they are golden brown and serve them hot.

Note: The creamy filling makes these pasties less suitable for packed lunches, but ideal for guests who join you for lunch.

Red Cabbage, Apple and Cheese Slices

225g (8 oz)	wholemeal (whole wheat) flaky pastry of your choice (see pages 152-153)	8 oz

Filling

30g (1 oz)	margarine	2½ tbsp
½ small	red cabbage, finely grated	½ small
2	green apples, coarsely grated	2
170g (6 oz)	Cheshire cheese, crumbled	1½ cups
1 tbsp	whole caraway seeds, or to taste	1 tbsp
	beaten egg or milk, to glaze (optional)	
	watercress, to garnish	

1 Make the pastry as instructed and chill it.
2 Preheat the oven to 400°F/200°C (Gas Mark 6).
3 Meanwhile, make the filling. Melt the margarine, add the cabbage, stir, and cook it gently until it softens, then drain it well.
4 Roll out half the pastry into a rectangle about 10 by 15 cm (4 by 6 in) and put it on a lightly greased baking sheet. Spread the cabbage, apples and cheese evenly over it, then sprinkle the caraway seeds over the top, if using. Roll out the remaining pastry to the same size and lay it over the filling, dampening the edges and pressing them together to seal. Brush the top with the egg or milk, if using.
5 Bake it in the preheated oven for 20 to 30 minutes or until it is golden brown cooked. Slice it on the diagonal to serve and garnish the slices with sprigs of watercress.

Note: Though simple and inexpensive to make, this dish is very attractive. Serve it at a buffet, making up at least double the quantity.

Other ingredients can be used to fill these slices, for example lentil purée, ground nuts mixed with vegetables, or chopped, hard-boiled (hard-cooked) eggs with beansprouts and mayonnaise.

Celery Almond Pie

Pastry

55g (2 oz)	flaked (slivered) almonds, crushed	½ cup
115g (4 oz)	wholemeal (whole wheat) flour	1 cup
115g (4 oz)	margarine	½ cup
	cold water, to mix	

Filling

55g (2 oz)	margarine	¼ cup
1 large	head celery, chopped	1 large
1 small	onion, sliced	1 small
1 large	red pepper, sliced	1 large
30g (1 oz)	wholemeal (whole wheat) flour	¼ cup
115g (4 oz)	ground almonds	1 cup
200ml (⅓ pt)	vegetable stock	¾ cup
	seasoning to taste	
	beaten egg or milk, to glaze (optional)	

1 First, make the pastry. Mix together the almonds and flour, then using your fingertips, rub in the margarine until you have a fine crumb-like mixture. Stir in just enough cold water to make a firm dough. Knead briefly then wrap it in clingfilm (plastic wrap) and chill it.
2 Preheat the oven to 400°F/200°C (Gas Mark 6).
3 Meanwhile, make the filling. Melt the margarine and sauté the celery, onion and red pepper in it, cooking them gently for 5 minutes. Cover the pan and simmer them for 10 more minutes, or until they are tender. Stir in the flour and ground almonds, cook them briefly, then gradually add the vegetable stock, stirring all the time, and bring it to the boil so that the sauce thickens. Season it generously.
4 Spoon the filling into a shallow, ovenproof dish. Roll out the pastry, lay it over the top, and make a cut in the centre. Brush it with egg or milk, to glaze, if using, then bake the pie in the preheated oven for 20 minutes or until the pastry is golden brown.

Note: You can, of course, use ordinary pastry with this filling, but the almond pastry is especially good. Delicious at lunch-time.

Tofu Turnovers

Pastry

1 tsp	dried yeast	1 tsp
2 tbsp	warm water	2 tbsp
1 tsp	raw cane sugar	1 tsp
340g (12 oz)	wholemeal (whole wheat) flour	3 cups
1 tbsp	vegetable oil	1 tbsp
4 tbsp	warm milk, or as required	4 tbsp

Filling

285g (10 oz)	tofu, drained	1¼ cups
1 large	carrot, grated (shredded)	1 large
6	spring onions (scallions), chopped	6
2 tbsp	fresh oregano, chopped	2 tbsp
2 tbsp	fresh parsley, chopped	2 tbsp
55g (2 oz)	sunflower seeds	⅓ cup
30g (1 oz)	sesame seeds	2 tbsp
55g (2 oz)	beansprouts	1 cup
1 large	free-range egg, beaten seasoning to taste	1 extra large

1 First, make the pastry. In a small bowl, dissolve the yeast in the warm water, mix in the sugar, then leave the mixture in a warm spot for 10 to 15 minutes until it is frothy. When it is ready, stir the mixture into the flour. Stir in the oil with just enough milk to make a fairly firm dough, knead it briefly, then put it in an oiled bowl, cover it, and leave it in a warm spot until it has doubled in size.

2 Divide the dough into 12 small, evenly sized balls, then cover them and leave them for 30 more minutes. Preheat the oven to 400°F/200°C (Gas Mark 6).

3 Meanwhile, make the filling. Mash the tofu and mix it with the carrot, spring onion (scallion), herbs and seeds. When they are thoroughly mixed together, add the beansprouts and, finally, the egg and seasoning to taste.

4 Roll out each of the pastry balls to form a circle (round) about 10 to 13 mm (4 to 5 in) across. Spoon equal quantities of the filling into the middles, dampen the edges of the pastry, fold it over the filling and press the edges together to seal them. Transfer the turnovers to lightly greased baking sheets and bake them in the preheated oven for 20 minutes or until they are golden brown.

Note: This yeasted pastry is lighter than shortcrust, and also goes further, making it ideal for when you are entertaining. Make at least 12 turnovers at a time, or even more as they freeze well. They can be served cold, but are even tastier when hot and flaky. For a party, make them in advance and simply warm them in the oven briefly before serving. Vary the fillings as desired.

Cauliflower and Tomato Pie

340g (12 oz)	wholemeal (whole wheat) pastry of your choice (see pages 152-153)	12 oz

Filling

1 medium	cauliflower, broken into florets	1 medium
30g (1 oz)	margarine	2½ tbsp
1 medium	onion, sliced	1 medium
1-2	cloves garlic, peeled and crushed	1-2
2 tbsp	wholemeal (whole wheat) flour	2 tbsp
200ml (⅓ pt)	vegetable stock	¾ cup
2 tbsp	tahini, or to taste	2 tbsp
2 tbsp	fresh parsley, chopped seasoning to taste	2 tbsp
4 medium	tomatoes, quartered beaten egg or milk, to glaze (optional)	4 medium

1 Make the pastry according to the instructions and chill it for at least 30 minutes.

2 Meanwhile, make the filling. Steam the cauliflower for just a few minutes so it softens, but does not become mushy, and then drain it well.

3 Preheat the oven to 400°F/200°C (Gas Mark 6).

4 Heat the margarine and sauté the onion and garlic in it for 5 minutes. Stir in the flour, cook it briefly, then gradually add the vegetable stock, stirring constantly over a medium heat until the sauce thickens. Add the tahini and parsley and season the sauce to taste, then gently stir in the cauliflower and tomato.

5 Roll the pastry out and use just over half of it to line the base and sides of a shallow ovenproof dish. Bake the pastry case (shell) blind (see page 152) in the preheated oven for 10 minutes. Leave the oven on. Then, spoon the filling in and cover the pie with the remaining pastry, dampening the edges and pressing them together to seal. Brush the top with egg or milk, if using. Make small cuts in the lid and bake the pie in the oven for 20 minutes or until the pastry is crisp. Serve the pie at once, cut into wedges.

Note: This is a filling pie – ideal for lunch on cold winter's days. Try using a cream or cheese sauce, too, instead of the tahini. You can make individual pies instead of one large and make double the amount needed, freezing the extra pies for another time.

Garlic Mushroom Strudel

30g (1 oz)	margarine	2½ tbsp
2	cloves garlic, peeled and crushed (minced)	2
340g (12 oz)	mushrooms, chopped	6 cups
2 tbsp	fresh chives, snipped	2 tbsp
	soya 'bacon' bits (optional)	
	seasoning to taste	
6	rectangular sheets filo pastry	6
4 tbsp	warmed vegetable oil or melted butter, or as required	4 tbsp
1 medium	tomato, sliced, to garnish	1 medium
¼	cucumber, sliced, to garnish	¼

1 Preheat the oven to 375°F/190°C (Gas Mark 5).
2 Melt the margarine and sauté the garlic and mushrooms gently for 5 minutes or until they are tender. Drain them well, pressing them into a sieve (strainer) to remove as much moisture as possible. Then, stir in the chives and 'bacon' bits, if using, and season to taste.
3 Lightly grease a baking sheet. Lay 1 sheet of filo pastry on it, brush it lightly with oil or butter, then repeat this with the remaining pastry, laying the sheets on top of each other.
4 Spread the mushroom mixture evenly across the top sheet. Fold the sides in to hold the filling in place, then carefully roll the pastry up. Lay it back on the baking sheet with the join underneath and brush the top with the remaining oil or butter.
5 Bake the strudel in the preheated oven for 20 to 30 minutes or until it is golden brown. Garnish the strudel with the tomato and cucumber slices, overlapping and alternating them along the top, then serve it cut into slices.

Note: This makes an attractive starter as it is light and yet tasty. You can stir some sour (soured) cream or cream cheese or creamed tofu in with the mushrooms, if liked. The 'bacon' bits make a crunchy contrast, but you could replace them with nuts cooked in soy sauce for a slightly different but equally tasty combination.

Autumn Vegetable Pie

340g (12 oz)	wholemeal (whole wheat) pastry of your choice (see pages 152-153)	12 oz

Filling

2 medium	potatoes, scrubbed and cleaned	2 medium
2 medium	leeks, cleaned and sliced	2 medium
2 medium	carrots, scrubbed and	2 medium
2 medium	parsnips, peeled and diced	2 medium
285ml (½ pt)	Tomato Sauce (see page 156)	1⅓ cups
4	free-range eggs, hard boiled	4
	seasoning to taste	
	beaten egg to glaze	
30g (1 oz)	sesame seeds	2 tbsp

1 Make the pastry according to the instructions, then chill it for at least 30 minutes.
2 Meanwhile, make the filling. Steam the potatoes, leeks, carrots and parsnips until they are just tender. Drain well. Make up the Tomato Sauce and cook it gently until it thickens. Shell and slice the eggs.
3 Preheat the oven to 400°F/200°C (Gas Mark 6).
4 Roll out the pastry and use just over half of it to line a medium-sized ovenproof dish. Spread some of the vegetables across the base, cover with some of the sauce, season, add half the eggs. Repeat this to use up all the ingredients.
5 Use the remaining pastry to make a topping for the pie. Make a cut in the pastry, brush lightly with beaten egg, add a sprinkling of sesame seeds. Bake the pie in the preheated oven for 20 minutes, or until crisp and nicely browned.

Note: Cut into thick wedges to serve – excellent for lunch. Can be served hot or cold. If preferred, use tinned tomatoes. Other fresh vegetables can be used at other times of the year.

Chestnut Pasties

225g (8 oz)	wholemeal (whole wheat) pastry of your choice (see pages 152-153)	8 oz

Filling

225g (8 oz)	fresh chestnuts	8 oz
225g (8 oz)	Brussels sprouts, trimmed	8 oz
1 tbsp	vegetable oil	1 tbsp
225g (8 oz)	mushrooms, chopped	4 cups
2 tsp	arrowroot	2 tsp
2 tbsp	water	2 tbsp
	soy sauce to taste	
	seasoning to taste	
	beaten egg or milk, to glaze (optional)	

1 Make the pastry according to the instructions, then chill it for at least 30 minutes.
2 Meanwhile, make the filling. Cut a cross in the top of each of the chestnuts, put them in a pan, cover them with water and boil them for 10 minutes. Cool them slightly, then use a sharp knife to carefully remove the shell and the inner skin. The chestnuts may well be tender, but if they are not, drop them into fresh water and cook them for a little longer until they are. Drain them well and coarsely chop them.
3 Preheat the oven to 400°F/200°C (Gas Mark 6).
4 Steam the Brussels sprouts until they are tender, then drain and chop them. Heat the oil and sauté the mushrooms in it until they are just cooked. Stir the arrowroot into the water and add the mixture to the pan, heating it gently until it just thickens. Then add the chestnuts, Brussels sprouts and soy sauce and season to taste. If the mixture is very dry, add another spoonful or two of water.
5 Roll the pastry out and cut into 4 large circles (rounds). Divide the filling between them, dampen the edges of the pastry, fold it over the filling and press the edges together to seal. Glaze the pasties with egg or milk, if using. Put the pasties on a greased baking sheet and bake them in the preheated oven for 20 minutes or until they are golden brown.

Note: Use dried chestnuts if you cannot find fresh, or replace them with cooked butter (lima) beans, which have a similar taste and texture when they are chopped and mixed with the vegetables.

Yogurt, Corn and Pepper Pie

225g (8 oz)	wholemeal (whole wheat) pastry of your choice (see pages 152-153)	8 oz

Filling

1	stick celery, sliced	1
1 large	green pepper, sliced	1 large
1 large	red pepper, sliced	1 large
225g (8 oz)	sweetcorn, fresh or frozen	2 cups
55g (2 oz)	walnut (English walnut) pieces	½ cup
15g (½ oz)	margarine	1 generous tbsp
1 medium	onion, sliced	1 medium
1 tbsp	wholemeal (whole wheat) flour	1 tbsp
200ml (⅓ pt)	natural (unsweetened) yogurt	¾ cup
85g (3 oz)	Cheddar cheese, grated	¾ cup
1 tbsp	fresh mint, chopped	1 tbsp
1 tbsp	lemon juice	1 tbsp
	seasoning to taste	
	beaten egg or milk, to glaze (optional)	

1 Make the pastry according to the instructions and chill it.
2 Meanwhile, make the filling. Put the celery, green and red peppers and sweetcorn into a saucepan, cover them with water, bring to the boil, then simmer the vegetables for 10 minutes or until they are just tender. Drain them well, then stir in the walnuts.
3 Preheat the oven to 400°F/200°C (Gas Mark 6).
4 Melt the margarine and sauté the onion in it for 5 minutes until they have softened. Whisk the flour into the yogurt, then add the mixture to the pan and cook it gently for a minute. Remove the pan from the heat and stir in the cheese, mint and lemon juice and season to taste. Combine the sauce with the vegetables. Spoon the filling into a shallow, ovenproof dish and smooth the top.
5 Roll the pastry out and lay it across the dish, pressing the edges lightly to seal and using any extra trimmings to decorate the top. Brush it with egg or milk, if using, then bake it in the preheated oven for 20 to 30 minutes or until the pastry is crisp and golden brown. Serve the pie hot.

Note: This is a delicious lunch-time dish, the yogurt giving it a subtle and yet sharper flavour than would a cheese sauce. Adding the flour to the yogurt helps stop it curdling. You can, of course, use other vegetables and sauces.

Egg and Watercress Triangles

225g (8 oz)	wholemeal (whole wheat) pastry of your choice (see pages 152-153)	8 oz

Filling

15g (½ oz)	margarine	1 tbsp
5 large	free-range eggs, beaten	5 extra large
2 tbsp	wheatgerm	2 tbsp
	seasoning to taste	
pinch	cayenne pepper	pinch
1 bunch	watercress, washed, drained and coarsely chopped	1 bunch
	beaten egg or milk, to glaze (optional)	

1 Make the pastry according to the instructions, then chill it for at least 30 minutes.
2 Preheat the oven to 400°F/200°C (Gas Mark 6).
3 Meanwhile, melt the margarine, add the beaten eggs and wheatgerm and stir continuously until the eggs are cooked. Season to taste and add the cayenne. Stir the watercress into the pan.
4 Roll the pastry out and cut it into 4 squares. Put a spoonful or two of the filling in the middle of each, dampen the edges of the pastry, fold the pastry over the filling to make a triangle, and press the edges together to seal. Glaze them with egg or milk, if using, and put them onto a lightly greased baking sheet. Bake them in the preheated oven for 20 minutes until they are golden brown, then serve them hot.

Note: These tasty triangles are also good served cold. For buffets, you can cut the pastry into 8 squares to make tiny, bite-size triangles. As they are also fairly firm in texture, they are good for picnics and packed lunches, too.

Hazelnut Roll

Pastry

225g (8 oz)	wholemeal (whole wheat) flour	2 cups
85g (3 oz)	margarine	⅓ cup
140ml (¼ pt)	sour (soured) cream	⅔ cup

Filling

55g (2 oz)	hazelnuts, chopped, plus extra for topping	½ cup
55g (2 oz)	raisins	⅓ cup
2	sticks celery, chopped	2
4	spring onions (scallions), chopped	4
55g (2 oz)	margarine, melted	¼ cup
55g (2oz)	wholemeal (whole wheat) breadcrumbs	1 cup
1 tbsp	fresh chives, chopped	1 tbsp
1 tbsp	fresh parsley, chopped	1 tbsp
	seasoning to taste	
	vegetable stock or orange juice, if necessary	
	beaten egg, to glaze	
285ml (½ pt)	Tomato Sauce (see page 156), hot	1⅓ cups

1 First, make the pastry. Put the flour into a bowl, rub in the margarine, until the mixture looks like fine breadcrumbs, then stir in the cream. When pressed together this should make a firm dough, but if it is too dry, stir in a little cold water. Wrap the dough in polythene or cling film (plastic wrap) and chill for at least 30 minutes.
2 Preheat the oven to 375°F/190°C (Gas Mark 5).
3 Meanwhile, make the filling. Mix together the hazelnuts, raisins, celery and spring onions (scallions). Combine the melted margarine and breadcrumbs, then stir the mixture into the nut mixture, adding the herbs, too, and season to taste. Mash the mixture briefly to make a thick paste, adding a spoonful or two of stock or orange juice if it is too dry.
4 Roll the pastry out to form a rectangle 20 by 25 cm (8 by 10 in). Spread the hazelnut filling evenly across it, leaving a small margin along the edges. Dampen the edges, then carefully roll the pastry up from the longer side and press the edges together to seal them. Transfer the roll to a lightly greased baking sheet, making sure that the seam lies underneath. Brush with egg and sprinkle the extra hazelnuts over the top.
5 Bake the roll in the preheated oven for 20 to 30 minutes. Cut it into generous slices and serve them accompanied by the Tomato Sauce.

Note: This roll is perfect for lunch and much easier to make than it looks. You can use other fillings, too, but make sure that they are fairly dry.

Red Dragon Pies

225g (8 oz)	wholemeal (whole wheat) flaky pastry (see pages 152-153)	8 oz

Filling

115g (4 oz)	dried aduki beans, soaked overnight (see page 9)	½ cup
30g (1 oz)	margarine	2½ tbsp
1 medium	onion, sliced	1 medium
1	clove garlic, peeled and crushed	1
2 medium	carrots, sliced	2 medium
2 medium	sticks celery, sliced	2 medium
1 large	green pepper, sliced	1 large
200-g (7-oz)	tin (can) tomatoes, chopped	7-oz
½ tsp	ground cumin	½ tsp
½ tsp	chilli powder, to taste	½ tsp
1 tbsp	fresh parsley, chopped seasoning to taste beaten egg or milk, to glaze	1 tbsp
4 tsp	sesame seeds	4 tsp

1 Make the pastry according to the instructions, then chill it for at least 30 minutes.
2 Preheat the oven to 400°F/200°C (Gas Mark 6).
3 Meanwhile, make the filling. First, cook and drain the aduki beans.
4 Melt the margarine and sauté the onion and garlic together in it for 5 minutes. Add the carrot, celery and green pepper and cook them for a few minutes. Stir in the tomato, cover the pan and simmer the mixture for 5 to 10 minutes or until the vegetables are tender. Add the aduki beans, spices and parsley and season to taste. Spoon the mixture into 4 individual ovenproof dishes.
5 Roll the pastry out, cut out circles big enough to cover the tops of the dishes. Dampen the edges of the circles, put them over the dishes and press the edges gently against the dishes to seal them. Make small cuts in the tops and brush the pastry with egg or milk. Sprinkle the sesame seeds over the tops of the pies.
6 Bake the pies in the preheated oven for 20 to 30 minutes or until the pastry is golden brown. Serve the pies hot.

Note: These filling pies are good for lunch. Make double the number and freeze them so you have them ready for unexpected guests or when time is limited.

Ricotta Pasties with Carrot Sauce

225g (8 oz)	wholemeal (whole wheat) pastry of your choice (see pages 152-153)	8 oz

Filling

170g (6 oz)	Ricotta cheese	¾ cup
30g (1 oz)	grated (shredded) Parmesan cheese	¼ cup
1	free-range egg, beaten	1
8	green pimiento stuffed olives, chopped	8
1 tbsp	fresh parsley, chopped	1 tbsp
1 tbsp	fresh basil, chopped	1 tbsp
1 small	courgette (zucchini), grated (shredded) seasoning to taste	1 small

Sauce

2 large	carrots, sliced	2 large
285ml (½ pt)	vegetable stock	1⅓ cups
1 tsp	arrowroot or cornflour (cornstarch)	1 tsp
½ tsp	raw cane sugar, or to taste seasoning to taste	½ tsp

1 Make the pastry according to the instructions, then chill it.
2 Preheat the oven to 400°F/200°C (Gas Mark 6).
3 Meanwhile, make the filling. Mash together the Ricotta and Parmesan cheeses, then add the egg, olives, herbs and courgette (zucchini) and season the mixture generously.
4 Roll the pastry out and cut out 4 circles (rounds). Divide the mixture between them, dampen the edges of the pastry, fold the pasty over the filling and press the dampened edges together to seal them. Make a small cut in each pasty, then transfer them to a lightly greased baking sheet and bake them in the preheated oven for 20 minutes or until they are golden brown.
5 While the pasties are cooking, make the sauce. Cook the carrot in most of the stock and, when it is tender, blend it with the cooking stock to make a smooth sauce. Mix the arrowroot or cornflour (cornstarch) with the remaining stock and stir the mixture into the sauce, together with the sugar and seasoning to taste. Cook gently, stirring, until the sauce thickens.
6 Either serve the pasties with a few spoonfuls of sauce on the side of the plate, or serve the sauce in a jug and put it on the table for diners to help themselves.

Note: If you do not like olives, use pine nuts or other nuts instead. A Tomato Sauce (see page 156) could be served instead of the carrot sauce. These pasties firm up when they are cold, but they are equally delicious.

Sweet and Sour Butterbean Pie

Pastry

170g (6 oz)	barley flour	1½ cups
55g (2 oz)	soya flour	½ cup
115g (4 oz)	margarine	½ cup
	cold water, to mix	

Filling

2 tbsp	vegetable oil	2 tbsp
2 medium	leeks, cleaned and sliced	2 medium
1 medium	parsnip, peeled and diced	1 medium
170g (6 oz)	butter (lima) beans, cooked and drained	1 cup
285ml (½ pt)	Sweet and Sour Sauce (see page 157)	1⅓ cups

1 First, make the pastry. Sift together the flours, then use your fingertips to rub the margarine into them until the mixture resembles fine breadcrumbs. Add just enough cold water to make a fairly firm dough, then chill it briefly.

2 Preheat the oven to 400°F/200°C (Gas Mark 6).

3 Heat the oil and sauté the leek for a few minutes, then add the parsnip and a little water. Cover the pan and cook the vegetables for 5 to 10 minutes or until they are tender. Drain them and mix them with the beans and Sweet and Sour Sauce. Spoon the mixture into a shallow, ovenproof dish.

4 Carefully roll the pastry out (it will be crumbly so do not try to make it too thin), lay it over the vegetables and trim off the excess. Bake the pie in the preheated oven for 20 minutes or until the pastry is golden brown. Serve it at once.

Note: This pastry is ideal for anyone who cannot eat wheat. Use it with other fillings, too, such as spinach in a creamy sauce or ratatouille with nuts. However, it is not suitable for pasties.

17

Ideas from Around the World

Chinese-style Tofu Vegetable Rolls

Pastry

225g (8 oz)	wholemeal (whole wheat) flour	2 cups
1	free-range egg, beaten cold water, to mix	1

Filling

2 tbsp	vegetable oil	2 tbsp
4	spring onions (scallions), chopped	4
1 small	crown broccoli, broken into florets	1 small
2	water chestnuts, coarsely chopped	2
115g (4 oz)	beansprouts	1 cup
115g (4 oz)	tofu, drained and crumbled	½ cup
	soy sauce to taste	
	seasoning to taste	
	vegetable oil, for frying	
285ml (½ pt)	Sweet and Sour Sauce (see page 157)	1⅓ cups

1 First, make the pastry. Put the flour into a bowl, add most of the egg and enough water to make a fairly firm dough. Knead this briefly, then cover it with polythene and chill it for 30 minutes.

2 Meanwhile, prepare the filling. Heat the oil and lightly sauté the spring onions (scallions) for a few minutes, then add the broccoli florets, stir well, cover the pan and cook them for a few minutes. Add the water chestnuts, beansprouts and tofu and flavour it well with soy sauce and seasoning. Continue cooking and stirring the mixture for 5 more minutes. Drain off any excess liquid.

3 Roll the pastry out and cut it into 12 equal-sized squares. Divide the filling between them, then fold the sides of each one in first so that the filling stays in place, and roll them up to form small packets. Use the remaining egg to dampen the edges, pressing them firmly to seal.

4 Heat enough oil to deep fry the rolls for 3 to 4 minutes or until they are crisp, then drain them well and serve them hot, with the Sweet and Sour Sauce.

Note: Any combination of vegetables can be used in these rolls, providing you chop them finely. Try mushrooms, sweetcorn, carrot and cauliflower. For more authentic rolls, replace the pastry with the special pastry wrappers you can buy frozen from Chinese or speciality shops, or try using filo pastry.

Spinach Gnocchi

455g (1 lb)	*fresh spinach, well washed*	*1 lb*
30g (1 oz)	*margarine*	*2½ tbsp*
pinch	*ground nutmeg*	*pinch*
	seasoning to taste	
170g (6 oz)	*Ricotta cheese*	*¾ cup*
2	*free-range eggs, beaten*	*2*
85g (3 oz)	*Parmesan cheese, grated*	*¾ cup*
30g (1 oz)	*wholemeal (whole wheat) flour*	*¼ cup*

1 Wash and shred the spinach and cook it, covered, without adding more water, until it begins to wilt. Drain it well, chop it finely, then squeeze it until it is as dry as possible.
2 Heat the margarine, add the spinach, nutmeg and season to taste, then cook the mixture over a low heat for a few minutes. Stir in the cheese and cook for a minute more.
3 Tip the spinach mixture into a bowl and leave it to cool slightly before beating in the eggs, half the Parmesan and most of the flour. When the ingredients are well blended, chill the mixture for at least an hour, preferably longer.
4 With floured hands, break the mixture into even-sized pieces and roll them into balls. Bring a large pan of salted water to simmering point, drop in the balls a few at a time, and cook them gently for 5 to 8 minutes or until they float to the top. Scoop them out with a slotted spoon and keep them warm while you cook the remaining balls. Serve them hot, with the remaining cheese sprinkled over them.

Note: These make a delicious start to a meal, or serve them at a buffet, spiking each one with a cocktail stick (toothpick) so they are easy to eat.

Creamy Refried Beans in Taco Shells

170g (6 oz)	*kidney beans, soaked overnight (see page 9)*	*1 cup*
1 medium	*onion, chopped*	*1 medium*
1	*clove garlic*	*1*
1	*green chilli pepper*	*1*
2 tbsp	*vegetable oil*	*2 tbsp*
	water or vegetable stock, as required	
	seasoning to taste	
70ml (⅛ pt)	*sour (soured) cream*	*¼ cup*
8	*taco shells*	*8*
	soya 'bacon' bits to taste (optional)	
	crisp lettuce, shredded, to serve	
	small piece cucumber, sliced, to serve	
	onion rings, to serve	

1 Cook and drain the beans. Then add the onion, garlic and chilli pepper. Cover the pan and simmer them for about an hour or until the beans are tender (do not use too much water, but, at the same time, make sure that the pan doesn't boil dry). Remove the garlic and chilli pepper, then mash the beans to a coarse purée.
2 Heat the oil, add the beans with a few spoonfuls of water or stock, and season to taste. Continue cooking and stirring the bean paste for 10 to 15 minutes to make a thick, dryish paste. Stir in the sour cream.
3 Divide the hot, refried bean paste between the taco shells, top each with the 'bacon' bits, if using, plus a little shredded lettuce, cucumber slices and onion rings, then serve them at once.

Note: Taco shells are fried and shaped corn pancakes and you can buy them in supermarkets as well as wholefood and speciality shops. Mexican in origin, crisp and spicy, they go especially well with these beans (which are cooked twice in order to enhance the flavour). If liked, stir yogurt into the bean paste instead of sour cream, or add grated (shredded) cheese as a topping. These are ideal for picnics, just keep all the ingredients separate until needed, then put them together when you are ready. For how to make your own tacos, see page 72.

Individual Vegetable Moussakas

2 large	*aubergines (eggplants)*	*2 large*
	sea salt, as required	
2 tbsp	*vegetable oil*	*2 tbsp*
1 small	*onion, sliced*	*1 small*
1	*clove garlic, peeled and crushed*	*1*
395-g (14-oz)	*tin (can) tomatoes, chopped*	*14-oz*
¼ small	*white cabbage, shredded*	*¼ small*
2 medium	*carrots, diced*	*2 medium*
115g (4 oz)	*peas*	*⅔ cup*
	seasoning to taste	
¼ tsp	*cayenne pepper*	*¼ tsp*
115g (4 oz)	*Mozzarella cheese, sliced*	*4 oz*
	parsley sprigs, to garnish	

1 Cut the aubergines (eggplants) in half lengthways and use a sharp knife to carefully cut out as much of the flesh as possible, keeping the skins intact. Chop the flesh and sprinkle both the flesh and shells with salt, then leave them for 30 minutes or until the bitter juices ooze out. Rinse them well with cold water, drain them well, then pat them dry.

2 Preheat the oven to 350°F/180°C (Gas Mark 4).

3 Heat the oil and sauté the onion and garlic in it for 5 minutes until they have softened. Add the tomato and stir in the aubergine (eggplant) flesh, cabbage, carrot and peas. Cover the pan and simmer the vegetables gently for about 15 minutes or until they are all tender. Season the mixture to taste, then stir in the cayenne.

4 Stand the aubergine (eggplant) shells close together in a small, shallow baking tin (pan), and fill each one with some of the mixture. Top them with the slices of Mozzarella, then bake them in the preheated oven for 20 minutes or until the skins are tender. Serve them at once, garnished with the parsley.

Note: Other vegetables can be used, and you can top the moussakas with slices of Feta, grated Cheddar or chopped nuts if you prefer. They make an excellent start to a Greek-style meal, or a special-occasion lunch.

'Beef' Martinique

2 tbsp	vegetable oil	2 tbsp
1 large	onion, sliced	1 large
½ tsp	ground mixed spices	½ tsp
¼ tsp	ground cloves	¼ tsp
30g (1 oz)	wholemeal (whole wheat) flour	¼ cup
2 tbsp	medium strength mustard	2 tbsp
2 tbsp	vegetarian Worcestershire sauce	2 tbsp
225g (8 oz)	TVP 'beef'-flavoured chunks, rehydrated and drained	2 cups
425ml (¾ pt)	vegetable stock	2 cups
1 large	carrot, sliced	1 large
115g (4 oz)	green beans, trimmed and sliced	¼ cup
1 large	banana, sliced	1 large

1 Heat the oil and sauté the onion for 5 minutes. Add the spices and flour and cook them briefly. Add the mustard and Worcestershire sauce, stir in the TVP chunks so that they are coated in the mixture and cook them for a minute.

2 Add the vegetable stock, carrot and beans. Bring the liquid to the boil then lower the heat and cover the pan. Cook the mixture gently for about 20 minutes or until the TVP chunks and carrot are cooked. Add the banana and cook it just long enough to heat it through, then serve at once.

Note: This unusual combination makes a delicious and filling lunch. Serve with hot rolls.

Polenta Fries

850ml (1½ pt)	vegetable stock or water	3¾ cups
225g (8 oz)	fine polenta	8 oz
1 tbsp	fresh chives, snipped	1 tbsp
55g (2 oz)	hazelnuts, roasted and coarsely chopped	½ cup
	seasoning to taste	
	vegetable oil, for frying	

1 Bring the stock to the boil, then, using a wooden spoon, gradually stir in the polenta. Simmer it, stirring frequently, for 20 to 30 minutes. When the mixture is thick and smooth, add the chives, nuts and seasoning to taste. Spoon the mixture into a shallow tin (pan), smooth the top and leave it to cool.

2 Cut the polenta into even-sized squares, then cut these across diagonally. Heat enough oil to shallow fry the polenta triangles. Fry them for about 5 minutes on each side or until they are crisp and golden brown, then drain them well and serve them hot.

Note: Polenta is Italian cornmeal, and comes in various grades. Cooked like this it makes a quick and nutritious snack. It can also be served with scrambled eggs, tofu, baked beans and/or salad to make a light meal. The mixture can also be shaped into balls and fried, making an attractive nibble to serve for a buffet. Add onion and garlic if liked.

Onion Bhajis

55g (2 oz)	wholemeal (whole wheat) flour	½ cup
30g (1 oz)	rice flour	¼ cup
1 tsp	ground turmeric	1 tsp
1 tsp	ground cumin	1 tsp
1 tsp	garam masala	1 tsp
4-6 tbsp	cold water	4-6 tbsp
1 small	onion, finely chopped	1 small
	vegetable oil, for frying	
	fresh parsley, coarsely chopped, to garnish	

1 Sift together the flours and spices. Add just enough cold water to mix the ingredients to a thick paste, then add the onion. Shape the mixture into small balls.

2 Heat a pan of oil until it is hot enough for a cube of bread to brown in 30 seconds. Gently add the balls, a few at a time, and cook them for about 3 minutes, moving them about so that they colour evenly. Drain them well and serve them garnished with the fresh parsley.

Note: These spicy fried balls make a delicious snack. They are also good served cold, so add them to a lunchbox or picnic hamper. Adjust the spices to suit your own taste and maybe add some chopped cashew nuts.

Spicy Vegetable Triangles (Samosas)

Pastry

225g (8 oz)	white self-raising (self-rising) flour	2 cups
55g (2 oz)	margarine or vegetable ghee	¼ cup
2 tbsp	water	2 tbsp
	vegetable oil, for frying	

Filling

1 large	potato, scrubbed and halved	1 large
½ small	broccoli	½ small
115g (4 oz)	sweetcorn, fresh or frozen	⅔ cup
1 tbsp	vegetable oil	1 tbsp
1 small	onion, chopped	1 small
1	clove garlic, peeled and crushed	1
½ tsp	ground turmeric	½ tsp
¼ tsp	chilli powder	¼ tsp
1 tbsp	curry powder	1 tbsp

1 First, make the pastry. Put the flour into a bowl and use your fingertips to rub in the margarine or ghee to make a crumb-like mixture. Add just enough water to make a fairly firm dough. Knead it for 5 minutes or until it is smooth and elastic, then cover the bowl and chill the dough for at least 30 minutes.

2 Meanwhile, make the filling. Steam the potato briefly, then add the broccoli and cook both until they are just tender. Dice the potato. Cook the sweetcorn.

3 Heat the oil and sauté the onion and garlic in it for 5 minutes to soften them. Add the spices, cook them for a moment, then stir in the cooked vegetables, coating them well with the spicy mixture.

4 Break the dough into 12, evenly sized pieces. Roll these out into thin circles (rounds) and brush them with milk. Put 1 teaspoon of the filling in the middle of each, fold the pastry in half over the filling and then fold it again to form a triangle. Press the edges together to seal them well and chill the samosas for 15 minutes.

5 Heat some vegetable oil and either shallow or deep fry the samosas for 5 to 10 minutes until they are crisp and golden brown. Drain them well and serve them hot.

Note: This very popular Indian snack can be eaten as it is or dipped into yogurt or chutney. Though best when eaten hot, they are also still very tasty when cold, making them ideal for parties or picnics. Vary the filling to suit what you have to hand.

Chilli Con Soya

3 tbsp	vegetable oil	3 tbsp
1 small	onion, chopped	1 small
2	sticks celery, chopped	2
2 medium	carrots, chopped	2 medium
170g (6 oz)	soya bean flakes	1½ cups
1 small	green chilli, deseeded and chopped	1 small
½ tsp	ground paprika	½ tsp
½ tsp	ground cumin	½ tsp
395-g (14-oz)	can tomatoes, chopped	14-oz
2 tbsp	tomato purée (paste)	2 tbsp
1 tbsp	lemon juice	1 tbsp

1 Heat the oil and sauté the onion, celery and carrot for 5 minutes, stirring frequently. Add the soya flakes, chilli and spices and cook the mixture for a few minutes. Stir in the tomato, tomato purée and lemon juice. Bring the mixture to the boil, then lower the heat, cover the pan and cook it gently for 20 to 30 minutes or until the vegetables and soya flakes are tender.

Note: A bowl of chilli makes a cold day lunch that cannot be beaten. It is good with French bread or cornbread (see page 91) for a change.

For a creamier, milder chilli, reduce the amount of chilli pepper and stir in some grated (shredded) cheese, yogurt or sour (soured) cream.

Chilli keeps well so make twice the amount and freeze the extra.

Soya flakes – which can be found in most wholefood shops – are packed with protein and cook in minutes, so make an ideal substitute for meat in this recipe. If you cannot find them, use kidney beans instead.

Lemon Dhal

170g (6 oz)	dried spit red lentils	⅔ cup
570ml (1 pt)	water	2½ cups
2 tbsp	margarine or vegetable ghee	2 tbsp
1 small	onion, sliced	1 small
1	clove garlic, peeled and crushed	1
1 tsp	ground coriander	1 tsp
1 tsp	ground ginger	1 tsp
¼ tsp	ground turmeric	¼ tsp
¼ tsp	cayenne pepper	¼ tsp
2	tomatoes, finely chopped	2
2 tbsp	lemon juice, or to taste	2 tbsp
	fresh coriander (cilantro) leaves, chopped, to garnish	

1 Put the lentils into a saucepan with the water and cook them for 30 minutes or until they are tender, adding

more water if necessary. Drain and mash them well.

2 Heat the margarine or ghee and sauté the onion and garlic in it for 5 minutes to soften them. Stir in the spices and cook them for 5 minutes. Add the mashed lentils and mix them in well. Stir in the tomato and add enough lemon juice to give the dhal a slightly lemony taste. Serve at once, with the fresh coriander (cilantro) sprinkled over the top.

Note: Though traditionally served as part of a main meal, dhal can also make an unusual snack. Serve it in small bowls with Indian breads, such as crisp poppadoms or the softer, fluffier chapatis. If you cannot get fresh coriander leaves, use parsley or mint instead.

Any leftover dhal may be frozen for another time.

Boston Baked Beans

225g (8 oz)	haricot (navy) beans, soaked overnight (see page 9)	1 cup
2 tbsp	vegetable oil	2 tbsp
2	onions, chopped	2
455g (1 lb)	tomatoes, peeled and chopped	2⅔ cups
3 tbsp	molasses	3 tbsl
1 tsp	mustard powder	1 tsp
1 tbsp	cider vinegar	1 tbsp
¼ tsp	ground cloves	¼ tsp
¼ tsp	ground cinnamon seasoning to taste	¼ tsp

1 Cook and drain the beans.

2 Preheat the oven to 300°F/150°C (Gas Mark 2).

3 In a clean saucepan heat the oil and sauté the onions in it until they have softened. Stir in the tomatoes, molasses, mustard, vinegar and spices and season to taste. Drain the beans and add them to the sauce, stirring them in well, then transfer the mixture to an ovenproof casserole dish. Pour in just enough water for the sauce to cover the beans.

4 Cover the dish tightly and bake the beans in the preheated oven for 3 to 4 hours or until the beans are tender. Stir them every now and again, adding a little more liquid if necessary.

Note: The slow cooking is important as it allows the beans to absorb all the flavour of the sauce. Traditionally, Boston Baked Beans contain brown sugar. Add some if you wish, though this more savoury version is equally delicious. Cook more than you need and store any extra in the refrigerator or freezer for another day. Bought tinned (canned) baked beans pale into insignificance!

Falafels with Yogurt Tahini Sauce

170g (6 oz)	field beans, soaked overnight (see page 9)	1 cup
1 medium	onion, chopped	1 medium
2	cloves garlic, peeled and chopped seasoning to taste	2
1 tsp	ground turmeric	1 tsp
1 tsp	ground cumin	1 tsp
1 tsp	ground coriander	1 tsp
1 tbsp	fresh coriander (cilantro) leaves, chopped vegetable oil, for frying	1 tbsp
1	free-range egg, lightly beaten (optional)	1

Sauce

200ml (⅓ pt)	natural (unsweetened) yogurt	¾ cup
3 tbsp	tahini, or to taste	3 tbsp
1 tbsp	fresh chives, snipped, or to taste	1 tbsp
1 tbsp	lemon juice	1 tbsp
¼ tsp	ground cumin	¼ tsp

1 Cook the field beans for approx 1 hour and drain them well (reserving the water in which they were cooked) and, when they are cool enough to handle, mash them coarsely.

2 Put the mashed beans into a bowl and mix in the onion and garlic, spices and coriander (cilantro) leaves, making sure all the ingredients are thoroughly mixed together. Add just a few spoonfuls of the reserved water to bind the mixture together. For firmer textured Falafels, mix in the egg.

3 With floured hands, divide the mixture into small, evenly sized pieces and roll them into balls. Chill them for 30 minutes.

4 Heat the oil and deep or shallow fry the Falafels until they are crisp and golden brown on the outside. Drain them well, then either keep them warm or let them cool.

5 Meanwhile, make the sauce. Simply combine all the sauce ingredients (the flavour improves if it can be left to stand for a short while). Transfer the sauce to a jug and serve it with the Falafels.

Note: If you cannot get fresh coriander (cilantro) leaves, use parsley. Adjust the spices to suit yourself. Replace some of the beans with wholemeal breadcrumbs for milder, softer textured Falafels. Falafels are traditionally made with chick peas – try these for a change as well as other pulses such as black or kidney beans.

Spanakopita

30g (1 oz)	margarine	2½ tbsp
½ small	onion, sliced	½ small
455g (1 lb)	fresh spinach, well washed and shredded	10 cups
2	free-range eggs, lightly beaten	2
115g (4 oz)	Feta cheese, crumbled	scant cup
115g (4 oz)	cottage cheese	½ cup
1 tbsp	fresh mint, chopped	1 tbsp
1 tsp	lemon juice	1 tsp
	seasoning to taste	
140g (5 oz)	filo pastry	5 oz
2 tbsp	warmed oil, or as required	2 tbsp

1 Melt the margarine and sauté the onion in it until it has softened. Add the spinach, stir, cover the pan and cook it just long enough for it to soften. Drain it well and then chop finely.
2 Preheat the oven to 400°F/200°C (Gas Mark 6).
3 Put the spinach into a bowl and add the eggs, Feta and cottage cheeses, mint and lemon juice and season to taste.
4 Lightly grease a shallow, rectangular baking tin (pan). Cover the base and sides with a sheet of filo pastry, brush it lightly with the warmed oil, add a further sheet and more oil. Continue this way until you have used about ⅔ of the pastry.
5 Add the spinach mixture, spreading it evenly. Lay the remaining pastry on top, oiling each layer (use more oil if necessary). With a sharp knife, score it into even-sized portions (a diamond shape is especially attractive), then bake it in the preheated oven for 30 minutes or until the pastry is golden brown. Cut it along the score lines and serve the Spanakopitas either hot or cold.

Note: This Greek spinach pie is delicious as a starter. The flavour can be varied by changing the balance of the cheeses and adding garlic and/or pine nuts. A less traditional version can be made using puff instead of filo pastry.

Cassoulet with Chestnuts

225g (8 oz)	dried flageolets, soaked overnight (see page 9)	1 cup
1 large	onion, chopped	1 large
2	cloves garlic, peeled and crushed	2
2	bay leaves	2
2	sticks celery, chopped	2
395-g (14-oz)	can tomatoes	14-oz
2 tbsp	tomato purée (paste)	2 tbsp
1 tbsp	fresh oregano, chopped	1 tbsp
1 tbsp	fresh parsley, chopped	1 tbsp
425ml (¾ pt)	vegetable stock	2 cups
115g (4 oz)	dried chestnuts, soaked overnight	4 oz
	seasoning to taste	
115g (4 oz)	wholemeal (whole wheat) breadcrumbs	2 cups

1 Preheat the oven to 350°F/180°C (Gas Mark 4).
2 Cook the beans, then drain them well.
3 In a casserole dish, combine the beans, onion, garlic, bay leaves, celery, tomato, tomato purée, herbs, vegetable stock and chestnuts and season well. Cover the casserole dish and bake it in the preheated oven for about 1 hour, stirring every now and again and ensuring that it doesn't get too dry (add more stock if necessary). Remove the bay leaves, sprinkle the breadcrumbs over the cassoulet and cook it, uncovered, for 30 more minutes or until all the ingredients are tender. Serve it at once.

Note: Cassoulet is usually made with meat, but the chestnuts are an excellent substitute. Serve it at lunch-time.

It is a good idea to make extra and keep it in the refrigerator or freezer for a quick meal another day.

Tempura Vegetables

Batter

115g (4 oz)	wholemeal (whole wheat) flour	1 cup
1-2 tsp	soy sauce	1-2 tsp
2	free-range eggs	2
	cold water, to mix	
455g (1 lb)	mixed vegetables (see note)	1 lb
	wholemeal (whole wheat) flour, for coating	
	vegetable oil, for frying	

Sauce

140ml (¼ pt)	water	⅔ cup
2 tbsp	soy sauce, or to taste	2 tbsp
1 small	piece fresh ginger, peeled and shredded	1 small piece
1 tsp	arrowroot	1 tsp
	seasoning to taste	

1 First, make the batter. Whisk together the flour, soy sauce and eggs. Add just enough water to make the batter the consistency of double (heavy) cream, then chill it briefly before using.
2 Put the vegetable pieces into a bag with some flour and shake it so that they are lightly coated with the flour. Then dip each piece into the batter and deep fry it in hot oil until crisp and evenly browned. Drain the cooked vegetables well and keep them warm while you

cook the remaining vegetables in the same way.

3 Meanwhile, make the sauce. Combine the water, soy sauce and ginger in a saucepan and cook the mixture gently for 5 minutes. Mix the arrowroot with a little water, then add the mixture to the pan and stir continually until the sauce thickens slightly. Adjust the seasoning to taste and add more soy sauce if liked.

4 Serve the hot, battered vegetables with the sauce to dip into.

Note: Choose vegetables such as green beans, celery, button mushrooms, parsnips and carrots, cutting them into small pieces. They can be used raw, although the harder root vegetables could be boiled for just 5 minutes to soften them. Drain them well before using.

These vegetables are great at parties or as a starter for a special meal. You can add some sake or sherry to the dipping sauce.

If you prefer not to eat eggs, omit them and replace some of the wholemeal (whole wheat) flour with buckwheat flour, which has binding qualities.

Russian Cabbage

285ml (½ pt)	sour (soured) cream	1⅓ cups
1 tsp	paprika	1 tsp
30g (1 oz)	margarine	2½ cups
455g (1 lb)	white cabbage, shredded	4 cups
455g (1 lb)	red cabbage, shredded	4 cups
2 tsp	whole caraway seeds seasoning to taste	2 tsp
4	free-range eggs, hard-boiled and peeled	4
4	spring onions (scallions), finely chopped, to garnish fresh parsley, chopped, to garnish	4

1 Mix the sour (soured) cream with the paprika and set the mixture to one side.

2 In a large pan, melt the margarine and gently sauté the white and red cabbage, stirring it frequently, for 5 minutes. Pour in the sour cream, add the caraway seeds, and season to taste. Cover the pan and cook the mixture gently for 30 minutes or until the cabbage is tender. Spoon it into a serving dish.

3 Coarsely chop the eggs and sprinkle them over the cabbage, together with the spring onions (scallions) and parsley to garnish. Serve at once.

Note: This is a tasty snack, especially if it is served with thick slices of fresh rye bread. Alternatively, make the recipe more filling by adding a topping of mashed potatoes or pastry.

Mattar Paneer

30g (1 oz)	vegetable ghee or margarine	2½ tbsp
small piece	fresh ginger, peeled and finely chopped	small piece
1	clove garlic, peeled and chopped	1
1 tsp	ground coriander	1 tsp
½ tsp	ground turmeric	½ tsp
½ tsp	crushed cardamom pods	½ tsp
½ tsp	chilli powder	½ tsp
70ml (⅛ pt)	water	¼ cup
340g (12 oz)	peas, fresh or frozen	2 cups
225g (8 oz)	Paneer, (Indian cheese), diced	1 cup
2 large	tomatoes, peeled and chopped	2 large
1 tbsp	fresh parsley, chopped	1 tbsp

1 Melt the ghee or margarine and sauté the ginger and garlic in it for 5 minutes. Add the spices and cook them for a few minutes more. Add the water and peas and cook until the peas are tender (add a little more water if the mixture seems dry, though do not add more than is necessary).

2 Add the cheese, tomatoes and parsley and stir them in well, then cook the mixture just long enough to heat through. Serve it at once.

Note: This is an unusual cheese and vegetable dish that is good with Indian breads or fresh wholemeal baps (whole wheat burger buns). Paneer is a mild-flavoured vegetarian cheese and is available from speciality shops. If you cannot obtain it, though, try other cheeses such as a mild Cheddar, Gruyère or Edam. Or use plain tofu instead.

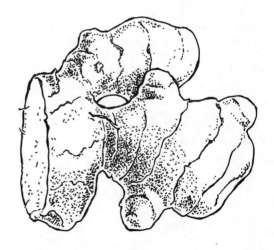

Courgette Vol-au-vents

225g (8 oz)	rough puff pastry (see page 153)	8 oz
1	free-range egg, beaten	1

Filling

1 tbsp	vegetable oil	1 tbsp
1 small	onion, sliced	1 small
1	clove garlic, peeled and crushed	1
1 tbsp	dried rosemary	1 tbsp
2 medium	courgettes (zucchini), coarsely chopped	2 medium
115g (4 oz)	garlic and herb cream cheese	½ cup
	seasoning to taste	
4	tomatoes, sliced	4

1 Make the pastry, according to the instructions, then chill it for 30 minutes. Preheat the oven to 400°F/200°C (Gas Mark 6).
2 Roll the pastry out on a lightly floured surface to a thickness of about 1.25 cm (½ in). Cut circles (rounds) about 7.5 cm (2½ in) in diameter and remove smaller circles (rounds) of dough from half of them, reserving these pieces. Brush the edge of the complete circles with the beaten egg and place the others on top. Brush the tops with egg, also the reserved small central circles (rounds). Put the vol-au-vents and little circles (rounds) on dampened baking sheets, and bake them in the preheated oven for 15 to 20 minutes or until they are cooked (cover them with foil if they are browning too quickly).
3 Meanwhile, make the filling. Heat the oil and sauté the onion and garlic in it for 5 minutes. Add the rosemary and drained courgettes (zucchini). Cover the pan and simmer the mixture until the courgettes (zucchini) are just tender (do not overcook them). Drain them well, then stir in the cheese so that it melts to make a sauce. Season generously.
4 Fill the vol-au-vents with the warm courgette (zucchini) mixture and top each one with the little circles (rounds). Serve at once, garnish with tomato slices.

Note: If you do not want to make your own pastry, use frozen puff pastry instead as there are many good vegetarian ones available in both wholefood shops and supermarkets. (Using a low-fat cheese instead of making a sauce saves even more time!)

Although usually considered to be party fare, vol-au-vents also make a very acceptable starter and can be filled with a variety of mixtures. Use whatever vegetables you like, adding a white, cheese or nut sauce and serve them either hot or cold. The cases can be made a few days in advance.

Dolmades

16	vine leaves (see note)	16
2 tbsp	olive oil	2 tbsp
1 small	onion, sliced	1 small
115g (4 oz)	mushrooms, chopped	2 cups
55g (2 oz)	pine nuts	½ cup
8 tbsp	cooked brown rice	8 tbsp
1 tbsp	fresh parsley, chopped	1 tbsp
	seasoning to taste	
	wholemeal (whole wheat) flour, for dusting	
285ml (½ pt)	vegetable stock	1⅓ cups

1 Rinse the vine leaves, then cook them in boiling water for 5 to 10 minutes. Drain them well and put them to one side.
2 Preheat the oven to 350°F/180°C (Gas Mark 4).
3 Heat the oil and sauté the onion in it for 5 minutes, then add the mushrooms and cook them gently until they soften. Stir in the pine nuts, brown rice and parsley and season to taste. Cook the mixture briefly, then drain it.
4 Put about 2 teaspoonfuls of the mixture in the middle of each leaf, then roll them up like small parcels, turning in the sides so that the filling stays in place. Arrange the parcels in a shallow, ovenproof dish , with the join underneath, dust them lightly with flour, then pour the stock over them and bake them in the preheated oven for about 20 minutes. Remove them from the stock and serve them either hot or cold.

Note: These are great as a starter or for a buffet.
Vine leaves are available from speciality shops and some supermarkets, but as an alternative, use cabbage or lettuce leaves to wrap these savoury parcels.
You can also adapt the filling, of course. For example, mix another grain such as bulgar with nuts, raisins and chopped spring onions (scallions). Alternatively, use wholemeal (whole wheat) breadcrumbs as the main ingredient in your filling.

18
Cooking Outdoors

Foil-baked Vegetables

4 small	potatoes, scrubbed	4 small
4 small	corn on the cob, in their husks	4 small
4 small	onions, whole and unpeeled	4 small
170g (6 oz)	button mushrooms, wiped	3 cups
	margarine, as required	
	olive oil, as required	
	seasoning to taste	

1 If large, halve the potatoes then wrap them loosely in the foil. Do the same with the corns and onions. Fold the ends securely.
2 Divide the mushrooms into 4 portions, add a little margarine to each, and wrap them in foil as before.
3 Cook all the vegetables directly on the coals of the fire. The time needed for them to cook will vary from about 15 minutes for the mushrooms, to an hour for the potatoes.
4 Serve them straight from the foil, leaving it to everyone to remove the husks from the corn, the outer skins from the onions. They can also add their own margarine, oil and seasoning to taste.

Note: Most vegetables can be cooked in the same way. You can also make up small packets of mixed vegetables, adding fresh herbs to taste.

Oriental Vegetables with Almonds

170g (6 oz)	mange-tout (snow peas), trimmed	6 oz
4	spring onions (scallions), chopped	4
a few	water chestnuts, sliced	a few
115g (4 oz)	beansprouts	2 cups
55g (2 oz)	almonds, coarsely chopped	½ cup
1 tbsp	fresh ginger, peeled and shredded	1 tbsp
2 tbsp	vegetable oil	2 tbsp
2 tbsp	soy sauce	2 tbsp

1 Mix together the vegetables, then add the almonds and ginger. Pour the oil and soy sauce over them and stir.
2 Spoon the mixture onto 4 foil squares and fold the foil loosely around the vegetables, securing it carefully.
3 Cook the packetes on the coals, turning them occasionally. They should be ready in about 15 minutes.

Note: Use ½ to 1 teaspoon ground ginger instead of the fresh if you prefer. Other vegetables to try are finely chopped celery, carrots and peppers. You could replace the nuts, if you like, with crumbled tofu.

Lemon Bread

1 medium	wholemeal (whole wheat) loaf	1 medium
	olive oil, as required	
	lemon juice, as required	
	seasoning to taste	

1 Cut the bread into thick slices and lay them flat. Trickle a little oil over each slice, add a good squeeze of lemon juice and season them generously. Put the loaf back together again and wrap it in foil. (If liked, you can divide the loaf into 2 separate packets or individual ones.)
2 Bake the bread over hot coals for 15 minutes or until the bread is hot right through.

Note: This deliciously flavoured bread goes well with kebabs and foil-baked vegetables. Try it, too, spread with hummus or topped with slices of hard-boiled (hard-cooked) eggs.

Avocado Garlic Bread

1	French bread	1
115g (4 oz)	butter or margarine	½ cup
2	cloves garlic, peeled and finely chopped	2
2 medium	avocados	2 medium
	lemon juice, as required	

1 Cut the bread into thick slices, stopping just short of the bottom so they stay attached. Blend together the butter or margarine and garlic and press some down between each of the cuts. Wrap the loaf in foil.
2 Bake the bread over hot coals for about 15 minutes or until it is hot and soft. Peel and slice the avocados, sprinkling them with lemon juice to stop them discolouring.
3 Divide the bread into slices, top each one with some avocado and hand them round at once.

Note: If you prefer, the avocado can be mashed to make a purée. This is nice with a spoonful or two of sour (soured) cream or yogurt added. As an alternative, try serving garlic bread topped with slices of Mozzarella cheese.

Quick Sage and Onion 'Sausages'

170g (6oz)	dry 'sausage' mix	6 oz
½ small	onion, finely chopped	½ small
1 tbsp	fresh sage, chopped	1 tbsp
	vegetable oil, as required	

1 Rehydrate the mix according to the instructions on the packaging. Blend in the onion and sage. Divide the mix into even-sized portions and mould them into 'sausages' shapes with your hands. Brush each one lightly with oil then grill them on the barbecue, turning them carefully every now and again so that they brown evenly.

Note: The actual taste of your 'sausages' will vary enormously depending on which mix you choose, so try different ones until you find your favourite. For 'sausages' that hold together, try chilling them before cooking them. Also, adding an egg with the water will help.

Vegetable and Tofu Kebabs

Marinade

2 tbsp	soy sauce	2 tbsp
4 tbsp	dry sherry (sherry wine)	4 tbsp
2 tbsp	vegetable ol	2 tbsp
¼ tsp	garlic salt	¼ tsp
¼ tsp	chilli powder	¼ tsp
¼ tsp	ground ginger	¼ tsp
1 tbsp	fresh parsley, chopped	1 tbsp
285g (10 oz)	tofu, drained	1¼ cups
2 small	courgettes (zucchini), cut into chunks	2 small
225g (8 oz) sliced	mushrooms, thickly	4 cups
1 large	yellow pepper, cut into squares	1 large
1 large	onion, quartered bay leaves, as necessary	1 large

1 First make the marinade. Simply combine the marinade ingredients in a screw top jar and shake it well.
2 Cut the tofu into cubes, lay them in a shallow pan and cover them with the marinade. Leave them for 1 to 2 hours, turning the cubes every now and again.
3 Push the tofu cubes and vegetables onto 4 skewers, alternating them so that they look attractive, adding a bay leaf every now and again. Brush all the ingredients with any remaining marinade. Grill them on the barbecue, turning them frequently, for 5 to 10 minutes or until they are just cooked. Serve them hot.

Note: Make up double or an even larger quantity of the marinade and keep it in the refrigerator until it is needed. You can vary it by adding tomato purée (tomato paste), more herbs and fewer spices. In an emergency, use a simple salad dressing of oil, lemon juice and herbs as a marinade.

Quorn Kebabs

12 small	new potatoes, scrubbed and halved	12 small
1 large	carrots, cut into chunks	1 large
1 small	cauliflower, divided into large florets	1 small

225-g (8-oz)	tin (can) pineapple pieces, drained, juice reserved	8-oz
225g (8 oz)	Quorn chunks	8 oz
Marinade		
6 tbsp	white wine vinegar	6 tbsp
1 tbsp	soy sauce	1 tbsp
¼ tsp	garlic salt, or to taste	¼ tsp
¼ tsp	ground ginger	¼ tsp
8	cherry tomatoes	8

1 Lightly steam the potato and carrot until they are just cooked (they should be firm), then drain and cool them. (If liked, do the same with the cauliflower florets, though take care to cook them only for a minute or two or they will fall apart when you skewer them.)
2 Thread all the ingredients onto 4 skewers, alternating them as you do so. Lay them gently on a tray or plate.
3 Now make the marinade. Stir together the marinade ingredients, plus 3 tablespoons of the reserved pineapple juice. Trickle this over the kebabs and set them aside briefly.
4 Cook them gently over the barbecue, turning them occasionally. After about 10 minutes add a cherry tomato to each end of the skewers and cook them for a few more minutes before serving.

Note: Quorn, a textured vegetable protein, is excellent when marinated this way and its texture makes it ideal for kebabs. If you cannot find it in your local shops, use unflavoured TVP chunks instead, rehydrating them first and then draining them well.

Crunchy Vegetable and Cheese Kebabs

2 thick	slices wholemeal (whole wheat) bread	2 thick
1 small	aubergine (eggplant), diced	1 small
	sea salt, as required	
1 medium	green pepper, cut into squares	1 medium
2 large	sticks celery, cut into chunks	2 large
2 tbsp	vegetable oil	2 tbsp
225g (8 oz)	Haloumi cheese, diced	8 oz
	vegetable oil, as required	
	garlic salt to taste	
	seasoning to taste	

1 Toast the bread then cut into large dice.
2 Lay the aubergine (eggplant) on a plate, sprinkle sea salt over it and leave it for 30 minutes or until the bitter juices have oozed out. Rinse with cold water, then steam for just 5 minutes. Pat dry and leave to cool.
3 Thread all the ingredients onto 4 skewers, alternating them so that they look attractive. Trickle a little oil over them and generously sprinkle garlic salt and seasoning over them.
4 Grill them briefly over a hot barbecue, turning them frequently (the celery and pepper should be almost raw still and the cheese just beginning to melt). Serve them at once.

Note: To make these especially quick to prepare, replace the aubergine (eggplant) with quarters of large firm tomatoes, or baby sweetcorn. Instead of the Haloumi (a Cypriot cheese) you can use Mozzarella.

Soya Bean Burgers

225g (8 oz)	soya beans, soaked overnight (see page 9)	1 cup
115g (4 oz)	mixed nuts, coarsely ground	¾ cup
1 small	leek, cleaned and finely chopped	1 small
1 small	red pepper, finely chopped	1 small
½ tsp	dried oregano	½ tsp
½ tsp	dried parsley	½ tsp
	seasoning to taste	
2 small	free-range eggs, beaten	2 small
	vegetable oil, for brushing	
8	wholemeal baps (whole wheat burger buns)	8
	pickles and relishes, to serve	

1 Cook and drain the soya beans then grind them coarsely (this is easiest to do in a small electric grinder, though it can be done using a mortar and pestle, providing the beans are well cooked).
2 Mix together the beans, nuts, leek, red pepper and herbs and season to taste. When thoroughly combined, stir in the eggs to bind the mixture. Use your hands to shape small handfuls of the mixture into burgers. Brush them lightly with oil and grill them over the barbecue for 10 minutes or until they are cooked, turning them once half way through the cooking time.
3 Serve them tucked into a warmed bap (burger bun) topped with a selection of pickles, relishes and chutneys or mayonnaise and salad.

Note: A ring of sweet, raw onion or a slice of cheese also make good toppings for these burgers.
To ring the changes, use other beans in this recipe. Add other finely chopped vegetables, too, or a spoonful or two of soya 'bacon' bits. Also, try replacing the herbs with spices for a hot burger.

Tomato Herb Relish

1.4 k (3 lb)	ripe tomatoes, peeled and coarsely chopped	3 lb
1 large	onion, finely chopped	1 large
1 medium	red pepper, finely chopped	1 medium
1 medium	green pepper, finely chopped	1 medium
	sea salt, for sprinkling	
3	cloves garlic, peeled and crushed (minced)	3
1 tsp	mustard powder	1 tsp
1 tbsp	curry powder	1 tbsp
1 tbsp	wholemeal (whole wheat) flour	1 tbsp
2 tbsp	fresh basil or tarragon, chopped	2 tbsp
425ml (¾ pt)	white wine vinegar	2 cups
170g (6 oz)	raw cane sugar	1 cup

1 Combine the tomato, onion and red and green peppers, sprinkle salt over them, cover them and leave them overnight. The next day, drain the vegetables well, then put them into a large saucepan, together with the garlic, and cook them for 5 minutes.
2 In a small bowl mix together the spices, flour and 2 tablespoons of the vinegar, stirring them well to make a smooth paste. Dissolve the sugar in the remaining vinegar.
3 Add the sugar and vinegar mixture to the vegetables, bring it to the boil and then simmer it for 30 minutes. Add the spice paste, mix it in well and cook for 5 more minutes, stirring continually.
4 Pour the mixture into warmed, sterilized jars, cover the top of the relish with circles of waxed or greaseproof paper and leave to cool, then put on the lids and store the jars in a cool, dry place.

Note: This is a popular way to use a glut of tomatoes. Serve the relish with burgers, curries, salads, omelettes, sandwiches. It can also be stirred into soups or stews to add an unusual flavour.

Piccalilli

1.15 k (2 lb)	chopped, mixed vegetables (e.g. cauliflower, green beans, pickling/pearl onions, peppers)	2 lb
	sea salt, for sprinkling	
1.15 l (2 pt)	cider vinegar	5 cups
55g (2 oz)	raw cane sugar	⅓ cup
1 tsp	ground turmeric	1 tsp
1 tsp	mustard seeds, coarsely crushed	1 tsp
1 tsp	ground ginger	1 tsp
½ tsp	chilli powder	½ tsp
1	clove garlic, peeled and finely chopped	1
2 tbsp	wholemeal (whole wheat) flour	2 tbsp

1 Put the vegetables into a bowl, generously sprinkle salt over them, cover them and leave them for 24 hours, stirring them occasionally. Rinse the vegetables well and dry them.
2 In a large saucepan, combine the vinegar, sugar, spices and garlic. Bring the mixture to the boil, then add the vegetables, bring the liquid to the boil again, then simmer the vegetables for 10 minutes.
3 Leave the vegetable mixture to cool in the pan, then cover it and leave it for another 24 hours.
4 Strain the vinegar mixture into another pan. Mix 2 tablespoons of this with the flour. Heat the vinegar mixture, then gradually mix in the flour paste, stirring continually, and continue boiling it until it thickens into a sauce. Stir the vegetables into the sauce, bring it back to the boil, then lower the heat and simmer the mixture for 5 minutes.
5 Pour the piccalilli into warmed, sterilized jars, cover the tops with circles of waxed or greaseproof paper, and leave them to cool. Then put on the lids and store them in a cool, dry place.

Note: For a sweeter pickle, double the amount of sugar. You can also use unripe pears and apples in place of some of the vegetables.

19
Instead of Meat and Fish

Kidney Bean Burgers

170g (6 oz)	kidney beans, soaked overnight (see page 9)	6 oz
1	stick celery, finely chopped	1
1 small	onion, finely chopped	1 small
2 tbsp	soya flour	2 tbsp
2 tbsp	tomato purée (paste)	2 tbsp
1 tsp	ground cumin	1 tsp
1 tsp	yeast extract seasoning to taste wholemeal (whole wheat) flour, for coating vegetable oil, for frying	1 tsp
4	wholemeal baps (whole wheat burger buns) pickles, relishes, etc., to serve	4

1 Cook and drain the beans well and mash them to make a thick purée.
2 Stir in the celery, onion, soya flour, tomato purée, cumin and yeast extract and season to taste. Divide the mixture into small, evenly sized pieces and shape them into burgers. Dip them in flour.
3 Heat enough oil in a frying pan (skillet) to shallow fry the burgers, turning them so that both sides are crisp. Drain them on paper towels. Serve the burgers hot with the baps and a selection of pickles, relishes and other favourite toppings.

Note: These burgers are the perfect anytime snack for both children and adults!
   You can use other beans for a change and, for a crisper coating, dip the burgers in breadcrumbs or oats, too, before frying them. To make burgers with a firmer texture, add an egg to the mixture.

Goulash

140g (4 oz)	TVP 'beef'-flavoured chunks	1 cup
30g (1 oz)	wholemeal (whole wheat) flour	¼ cup
1 tbsp	ground paprika seasoning to taste	1 tbsp
2 tbsp	vegetable oil	2 tbsp
2 large	onions, thinly sliced	2 large
4 medium	tomatoes, quartered	4 medium
285ml (½ pt)	vegetable stock	1½ cups
140ml (¼ pt)	natural (unsweetened) yogurt gherkins or cucumber sticks, to garnish	⅔ cup

1 Rehydrate, the TVP chunks, then drain them well. Mix together the flour and paprika and season to taste.
2 Heat the oil and cook the onion in it for 5 minutes, stirring it occasionally. Add the seasoned flour mixture, stir it in and cook it for a few minutes. Add the tomato, the stock and the TVP. Bring the mixture to the boil, then cover the pan and simmer it for 20 minutes. If the mixture gets dry, add a little more stock.
3 Gently stir in the yogurt and simmer it gently until it is just heated through.
4 Serve the Goulash in 4 small dishes, garnished with the gherkins or cucumber sticks.

Note: This is a tasty lunch, served with warm wholemeal (whole wheat) rolls. This basic recipe can be adapted by adding vegetables. Mushrooms are especially good. You can also use beans to replace the TVP.

Individual Cottage Pies

140g (5 oz)	TVP 'mince' (TVP 'ground round')	generous cup
2 tbsp	vegetable oil	2 tbsp
1	clove garlic, peeled and crushed (minced)	1
1 medium	leek, cleaned and sliced	1 medium
1 tbsp	wholemeal (whole wheat) flour	1 tbsp
2 tbsp	tomato purée (paste)	2 tbsp
285ml (½ pt)	vegetable stock	1⅓ cups
1	bay leaf	1
115g (4 oz)	peas, cooked and drained	⅔ cup
1 tsp	vegetarian Worcestershire sauce, or to taste	1 tsp
455g (1 lb)	potatoes	1 lb
30g (1 oz)	margarine	2½ tbsp
2 tbsp	cream, dairy or soya seasoning to taste	2 tbsp

1 Rehydrate the TVP 'mince' ('ground round').
2 Heat the oil and sauté the garlic in it for 5 minutes. Add the leek and cook it for a few minutes. Stir in the flour. Drain the TVP and add it together with the tomato purée, stock, bay leaf, peas and Worcestershire sauce to taste, stirring until they are well combined. Cover the pan and cook the mixture for 15 minutes.
3 Preheat the oven to 375°F/190°C (Gas Mark 5).
4 Meanwhile, peel and dice the potatoes, then steam them until they are just soft. Drain them well, add the margarine, cream and season to taste, then mash them well. Divide the vegetable and TVP mixture between 4 small, ovenproof dishes, spread the mashed potato evenly over the tops, fluffing the surface up with a fork.
5 Bake them in the preheated oven for 20 minutes or until they are beginning to brown on top, then serve them at once.

Note: This Cottage Pie is perfect for lunch - especially when everyone is eating at different times. It is worth making extra ones to keep in the freezer, they are so useful. For a richer topping, add a couple of egg yolks to the potatoes when you are mashing them.

Jambalaya with Quorn

2 tbsp	vegetable oil	2 tbsp
1 medium	onion, sliced	1 medium
1	clove garlic, peeled and crushed	1
2	sticks celery, sliced	2
½ tsp	chilli powder	½ tsp
1 tsp	ground cumin	1 tsp
1 tsp	dried basil	1 tsp
225g (8 oz)	Quorn chunks	2 cups
395-g (14-oz)	can tomatoes, chopped	14-oz
2 tsp	vegetarian Worcestershire sauce	2 tsp
200ml (⅓ pt)	vegetable stock	¾ cup
115g (4 oz)	brown rice seasoning to taste fresh parsley, chopped, to garnish	½ cup

1 Heat the oil and sauté the onion, garlic and celery in it for 5 minutes or until they begin to soften. Stir in the spices and basil, cook them briefly, then add the Quorn chunks, coating them in the spice mixture. Stir in the tomato, Worcestershire sauce, vegetable stock and rice.
2 Bring the mixture to a boil, then cover the pan, lower the heat, and simmer it for 20 minutes or until the rice is just tender (check it from time to time so that it doesn't boil too dry, adding a little more liquid if necessary). Adjust the seasoning to taste, then serve at once in small bowls, garnished with plenty of the parsley.

Note: This is a filling lunch dish. Serve it with bread fresh from the oven. If you cannot get, or do not like, Quorn, replace it with unflavoured TVP chunks, or vegetarian 'sausages' chopped into small pieces.

Fried Tofu Steaks with Onions

455g (1 lb)	tofu, drained	2 cups
2 tbsp	soy sauce	2 tbsp
2 tbsp	tomato purée (paste)	2 tbsp
1	clove garlic, peeled and crushed	1
1 small	green chilli pepper, deseeded and chopped	1 small
1 tbsp	fresh parsley, chopped	1 tbsp
1-2 tsp	honey (optional)	1-2 tsp
2 tbsp	vegetable oil	2 tbsp
2 medium	onions, sliced	2 medium
1 tsp	cornflour (cornstarch) parsley sprigs, to garnish	1 tsp

1 Cut the tofu into 8 evenly sized rectangles.
2 Use a blender to combine the soy sauce, tomato purée, garlic, chilli, parsley and honey, if using. Pour the mixture into a shallow tin (pan) and marinade the tofu steaks in it for 1 hour, turning them occasionally.
3 Heat half of the oil and fry the onions in it until they are well cooked. Remove them with a slotted spoon and put them to one side, keeping them warm. Drain the tofu steaks if necessary, then add them to the pan and cook both sides. Remove them and keep warm. Mix the cornflour (cornstarch) into a little cold water and add

the mixture to the pan with any remaining marinade. Cook it briefly to thicken it into a smooth sauce, adding a little more water if it is too thick.

4 Serve the tofu steaks onto 4 small plates, pour a little of the marinade sauce over each and top them with the onions. Garnish with sprinkling of parsley over each plate and serve at once.

Note: These are good for a snack, but can also make an unusual starter at a dinner party (in which case garnish them with radish flowers and watercress for a splash of colour). For a crunchy coating, the marinated tofu can be dipped in flour, beaten eggs and then breadcrumbs before being fried.

Bean and Herb 'Sausages'

115g (4 oz)	dried haricot (navy) beans, soaked overnight (see page 9)	½ cup
1 small	onion, chopped	1 small
1 tbsp	lemon juice	1 tbsp
1 tbsp	fresh parsley, chopped	1 tbsp
1 tsp	fresh oregano, chopped	1 tsp
1 tsp	fresh sage, chopped seasoning to taste	1 tsp
1	free-range egg, beaten	1
55g (2 oz)	wholemeal (whole wheat) breadcrumbs vegetable oil, for frying	1 cup

1 Cook and drain the beans, mash them well, then add the onion, lemon juice and herbs and season the mixture generously, mixing everything together well. Chill the mixture for an hour before using.

2 Divide the mixture into 8 equal pieces and, with floured hands, roll them into sausage shapes. Dip each one in the egg, then coat them with the breadcrumbs.

3 Shallow fry the sausages in hot vegetable oil, turning them frequently, for 5 to 10 minutes or until they are crisp and golden brown. Drain them on paper towels, then serve them hot.

Note: Just add tomatoes and mushrooms for a delicious snack or tuck each sausage into a roll and top it with relish. As they also taste good cold, they are excellent for parties and picnics. Also, any herb combination you like can be used and if fresh herbs are not available, use dried ones (not forgetting to halve the quantities as they are stronger in flavour).

'Sausage' Rolls

| 225g (8 oz) | rough puff pastry (see page 152) | 8 oz |
| 6 | vegetarian 'sausages' (see note) vegetable oil, for frying | 6 |

1 Make the pastry according to the instructions, then chill it for 30 minutes.

2 Meanwhile, fry the 'sausages' in some hot oil until they are well browned on all sides, then drain them well on paper towels.

3 Preheat the oven to 425°F/220°C (Gas Mark 7).

4 Divide the pastry in half and roll each piece out to form 2 narrow rectangles. Cut the 'sausages' in halves or thirds. Space the 'sausage' pieces evenly along 1 of the pastry strips and dampen the edges with water. Then lay the second strip over the top and press the edges together to seal. Cut between the 'sausages' and seal the new edges in the same way. Make 1 or 2 small cuts across the top of each roll.

5 Place the rolls on lightly greased baking sheets and bake them in the preheated oven for about 20 minutes or until the pastry has puffed up and is golden brown. Eat these 'Sausage' Rolls hot or cold.

Note: You can use the Bean and Herb 'Sausages' (see previous recipe), tinned (canned) 'sausages' that are ready made and just need to be drained and patted dry, or 'sausages' made from dry mixes. If you prefer, use shortcrust or flaky pastry (see pages 152–153).

Everyone's favourite party fare, these little rolls are also good with bread and salad for lunch and perfect for lunchboxes or picnics.

'Meat' and Pepper Loaf

170g (6 oz)	dry 'burger' mix	6 oz
1 large	red pepper, chopped	1 large
1 small	onion, chopped	1 small
1 tbsp	fresh parsley, chopped	1 tbsp
½ tsp	dried sage, or to taste	½ tsp
1 large	free-range egg, beaten seasoning to taste	1 extra large

1 Preheat the oven to 375°F/190°C (Gas Mark 5).

2 Rehydrate the dry mix as directed on the packaging. Stir in the red pepper, onion, herbs and egg and season to taste.

3 Transfer the mixture to a small, lightly greased loaf tin (pan), smooth the top and bake it in the preheated oven for 30 minutes.

Note: Eat this while it is still hot for lunch with French bread and a selection of pickles, or leave it to cool and serve it cold in thick slices with a salad garnish and Melba toast as a starter at a dinner party.

Pasta Hotpot with 'Beef'

115g (4 oz)	TVP 'beef'-flavoured chunks	1 cup
1 medium	parsnip, peeled and diced	1 medium
2 medium	carrots, peeled and diced	2 medium
2 medium	onions, sliced	2 medium
115g (4 oz)	sweetcorn, fresh or frozen	⅔ cup
2 tsp	dried mixed herbs	2 tsp
285ml (½ pt)	vegetable stock seasoning to taste	1⅓ cups
115g (4 oz)	wholemeal (whole wheat) macaroni	2 cups
4	tomatoes, quartered fresh parsley	4

1 Preheat the oven to 350°F/180°C (Gas Mark 4).
2 Rehydrate the TVP chunks, then drain them well.
3 Put the vegetables into a saucepan together with the herbs and vegetable stock and season to taste. Bring it to the boil and cook it for 5 minutes. Add the macaroni and TVP chunks and bring the mixture to the boil. Transfer it to an ovenproof dish, cover and bake it in the preheated oven for 30 minutes or until the pasta and TVP chunks are just tender. Adjust the seasoning if necessary, then stir in the tomatoes, cover the dish again and leave it for just a few minutes more for them to heat through.
4 Serve the hotpot in 4 bowls, garnished with a generous sprinkling of parsley.

Note: This dish is so easy to prepare and yet tasty and filling. It is perfect for a family lunch on a winter's day and another plus is that – should someone be late – you can just lower the heat and leave their share simmering gently while the rest of you tuck in.

'Pork' in Chinese Sauce

Sauce

3 tbsp	cornflour (cornstarch)	3 tbsp
3 tbsp	raw cane sugar	3 tbsp
4 tbsp	malt vinegar	4 tbsp
285ml (½ pt)	vegetable stock	1⅓ cups
1 tbsp	soy sauce	1 tbsp
4 tbsp	tomato purée (paste) seasoning to taste	4 tbsp
225g (8 oz)	Quorn chunks	8 oz
55g (2 oz)	mung beansprouts	1 cup

1 First make the sauce. Whisk together the cornflour, sugar, vinegar, stock, soy sauce and tomato purée and season to taste. Heat gently until the sauce thickens then adjust the flavouring and seasoning if necessary.
2 Coarsely shred the Quorn chunks, then add them to the sauce with the beansprouts and heat them through gently. Serve it hot.

Note: Quorn is a meat substitute of vegetable origin. It is white, firm-textured and has a subtle flavour that makes it ideal as a replacement for meats such as pork or chicken. If you cannot find it locally, use unflavoured TVP chunks instead, first rehydrating them in water and cooking them briefly before draining and adding them to the sauce. Serve this dish when a special snack is called for, maybe accompanying it with some rice in keeping with the Oriental style of the dish.

Nutty Croquettes

55g (2 oz)	margarine	¼ cup
55g (2 oz)	wholemeal (whole wheat) flour	½ cup
425ml (¾ pt)	vegetable stock	2 cups
1 tsp	dried sage	1 tsp
1 tsp	dried chives	1 tsp
55g (2 oz)	wholemeal (whole wheat) breadcrumbs	1 cup
115g (4 oz)	mixed nuts, coarsely ground	1 cup
1 tsp	soy sauce, or to taste seasoning to taste	1 tsp
1	free-range egg, beaten	1
55g (2 oz)	dried wholemeal (whole wheat) breadcrumbs vegetable oil	½ cup

1 Melt the margarine, stir in the flour, cook it for a minute or two, then gradually add the stock and bring the mixture gently to the boil, stirring continually. Lower the heat and simmer until the sauce thickens.
2 Stir in the herbs, breadcrumbs, nuts and soy sauce and season to taste. Mix them in well and, if the mixture seems very dry, add a little more stock. Divide the mixture into small, evenly-sized pieces and shape them into croquettes. Dip each croquette in the egg, then roll it in the breadcrumbs, coating it evenly.
3 Heat enough oil to deep fry the croquettes. Cook them until they are crisp and golden brown. Drain them well on paper towels, then serve them hot.

Note: These are a delicious and quick snack. The same mix can also be shaped into small balls, deep fried and served cold at a drinks party.

Keema Curry

140g (5 oz)	TVP 'beef'-flavoured mince (round ground)	generous cup
2 tbsp	vegetable oil	2 tbsp
1 medium	onion, sliced	1 medium
1	clove garlic, peeled and crushed	1
2 tsp	ground ginger	2 tsp
½ tsp	chilli powder	½ tsp
1 tbsp	garam masala, or to taste	1 tbsp
200-g (7-oz)	tin (can) tomatoes, chopped	7-oz
140ml (¼ pt)	vegetable stock seasoning to taste	⅔ cup
140ml (¼ pt)	natural (unsweetened) yogurt	⅔ cup
1 tbsp	fresh coriander (cilantro) leaves, chopped	1 tbsp

1 Rehydrate the TVP mince (TVP ground round), then drain it well.
2 Heat the oil and sauté the onion and garlic in it for a few minutes until they have softened. Add the spices, stir and cook them for a minute. Add the TVP mince (TVP ground round) and add it to the pan with the tomato and vegetable stock and season to taste. Bring the mixture to the boil then cover the pan, lower the heat and cook it for 20 more minutes.
3 Stir in the yogurt and heat it gently for just a minute more. Taste, and add more garam masala if liked. Spoon the curry into 4 small bowls, sprinkle the coriander (cilantro) over the top to garnish, then serve at once.

Note: This is a satisfying lunch snack. Indian breads go well with this or try crisp rice cakes for a change. Though the coriander (cilantro) leaves are more authentic, you can use parsley instead.

'Chicken' à la King

85g (3 oz)	margarine	⅓ cup
1 medium	red pepper, sliced	1 medium
55g (2 oz)	mushrooms, chopped	1 cup
30g (1 oz)	wholemeal (whole wheat) flour	¼ cup
200ml (⅓ pt)	milk seasoning to taste	¾ cup
115g (4 oz)	Quorn chunks	1 cup
4 thick	slices wholemeal (whole wheat) bread paprika, to garnish	4 thick
8	pimiento stuffed green olives, chopped, to garnish	8

1 Melt half the margarine and sauté the red pepper in it for 5 minutes. Add the mushrooms and cook them for 5 minutes. Remove the vegetables with a slotted spoon and put them to one side. Add the remaining margarine to the pan, melt it, then stir in the flour and cook it for a minute or two. Gradually add the milk and heat it gently, stirring continually, until the sauce thickens, then season it generously.
2 Coarsely shred the Quorn and add it to the sauce, together with the pepper and mushrooms. Simmer the mixture for 5 minutes to heat everything through.
3 Toast the bread, top the slices with the sauce, garnish with a sprinkling of paprika and the olives, then serve.

Note: Although this makes a good lunch, it is also delicious as a starter. For a special touch on such occasions, the bread can be pressed into Yorkshire pudding tins (patty or muffin pans) and baked to make shaped cases into which you can spoon the filling. The sauce is also excellent served in vol-au-vents cases (see page 134), but chop the ingredients finely. (For more information about Quorn and alternative suggestions for those who cannot find it in local shops, see page 137.)

Rice 'Meatballs' with Egg and Lemon Sauce

4 tbsp	cooked brown rice	4 tbsp
1	free-range egg, beaten	1
115g (4 oz)	dried burger mix	4 oz
1 tbsp	fresh tarragon, chopped, plus extra to garnish cold water, to mix	1 tbsp
Sauce		
1 tbsp	cornflour (cornstarch)	1 tbsp
2 tbsp	lemon juice	2 tbsp
1	free-range egg, beaten	1
200ml (⅓ pt)	vegetable stock vegetable oil, for frying	¾ cup

1 Mix the rice with the egg, then add the burger mix and herbs. Add just enough cold water to make a thick paste. Set aside briefly, then divide it into equal-sized pieces and roll them into balls.
2 Next, make the sauce. Whisk together the cornflour (cornstarch), lemon juice and egg. Heat the stock and add the cornflour (cornstarch) mixture, still whisking, until it thickens, then simmer it.
3 Meanwhile, deep fry the Rice 'Meatballs' until they are crisp and golden brown. Drain them well on paper towels, then serve them hot on 4 small plates with the sauce on the side. Sprinkle the tarragon over the balls to garnish.

Note: Dried burger mixes vary slightly, so you may need to adjust the method and amount of water used. Read the instructions on the packaging first. The rice extends the mixture as well as making for a more satisfying snack.

Stir-fried 'Pork' with Broccoli

4 tbsp	vegetable oil	4 tbsp
455g (1 lb)	broccoli, broken into florets	1 lb
1 medium	onion, sliced	1 medium
1 medium	yellow pepper, sliced	1 medium
225g (8 oz)	mushrooms, sliced	4 cups
225g (8 oz)	Quorn chunks	8 oz
1 tbsp	soy sauce, or to taste seasoning to taste	1 tbsp
30g (1 oz)	flaked (slivered) almonds, roasted	¼ cup

1 Heat half the oil and stir-fry the broccoli in it for a few minutes. Remove it from the pan with a slotted spoon and keep it hot. Add the remaining oil, cook the onion and yellow pepper for a few minutes, stirring continually, then add the mushrooms and continue stir-frying until they begin to colour.
2 Add the Quorn, stir it for a minute, sprinkle the soy sauce over it, season to taste and return the broccoli to the pan. Continue stir-frying just long enough to heat the broccoli through, then divide the mixture between 4 bowls, sprinkle the almonds over them to garnish and serve at once.

Note: This is a delicious snack, or serve it as a starter for a Chinese meal. If you cannot find Quorn, try using one of the milder flavoured tinned (canned) nutmeats for this recipe. Cut into cubes and stir-fried with vegetables, it will have a similar texture to the Quorn, even though the taste will be different.

Tofu 'Fish' Cakes

455g (1 lb)	potatoes	1 lb
225g (8 oz)	smoked tofu, drained	1 cup
2	free-range eggs	2
1 tbsp	lemon juice seasoning to taste	1 tbsp
55g (2 oz)	dried wholemeal (whole wheat) breadcrumbs vegetable oil, for frying	½ cup
2	tomatoes, sliced, to garnish parsley sprigs, to garnish	2

1 Peel the potatoes, then finely grate (slice) them. Wrap the potato in a clean cloth and squeeze it to remove as much moisture as possible.
2 Mash the tofu and mix it with the potato, plus 1 of the eggs, the lemon juice and season to taste. The mixture should be fairly dry, but if it is sticky, add a little flour.
3 Shape the mixture into 4 large or 8 small burger shapes (patties). Beat the remaining egg and dip each 'Fish' Cake into it then coat it in breadcrumbs. Heat enough oil to shallow fry them. Cook them, turning them once, until they are crisp and golden brown, then drain them on paper towels. Serve them garnished with the tomato slices and parsley.

Note: Not an alternative to meat but to fish! It is the smoked tofu that gives these cakes their distinctive salty taste and smooth, slightly oily texture. They are excellent as a snack, served with rolls. You can also make 'fish' fingers in much the same way, just change the shape.

20
Snacks for a Sweet Tooth

Coconut Barfi

570ml (1 pt)	milk	2½ cups
170g (6 oz)	desiccated (shredded) coconut	2 cups
85g (3 oz)	raw cane sugar	½ cup
½ tsp	ground cardamom	½ tsp
1 tbsp	rosewater	1 tbsp

1 Bring the milk gently to the boil, then lower the heat and simmer it for 15 minutes, stirring frequently.
2 Add the coconut and cook it for a minute, then add the sugar, cardamom and rosewater and continue cooking the mixture over a low heat, stirring frequently.
3 When the mixture becomes thick and dry, pour it into a shallow, lightly greased tin (pan) and smooth the top. Mark it into squares, then leave the mixture to cool and become firm. Cut it into the marked squares when it is completely cold. This delicately flavoured Indian sweet can be stored, covered, in the refrigerator for a few days, but is best eaten when fresh.

Note: Traditionally, Barfi is made with khoya, which is the thick residue left when milk is boiled for at least an hour, so, if you have the patience to do this, the results will be more authentic. Khoya can also be made from full-fat powdered milk.

Apricot and Hazelnut Truffles

115g (4 oz)	dried apricots	1¼ cups
55g (2 oz)	wholemeal (whole wheat) cake crumbs	1 cup
55g (2 oz)	roasted hazelnuts, coarsely ground	½ cup
1 tbsp	orange peel, grated	1 tbsp
2 tbsp	concentrated orange juice	2 tbsp
2 tbsp	honey or syrup or maple syrup (optional) hazelnuts, chopped, for coating	2 tbsp

1 Soak the apricots in boiling water for 15 minutes, then drain them well and chop or mash them.
2 In a bowl, mix together the apricot purée, cake crumbs, ground hazelnuts, orange peel and stir in enough of the orange juice to bind the mixture together. For a sweeter truffle, add the honey or syrup, adding less orange juice so that the mixture is not too wet (it should be thick and firm).
3 Break the mixture into even-sized pieces and shape into balls. Roll each one in some of the chopped nuts then chill the finished truffles well before serving.

Note: These nutritious truffles – an ideal everyday alternative to sweets – can be topped with an extra nut or piece of apricot and served in paper cases as a dessert or with after-dinner coffee.

Carob Raisin Nut Clusters

225-g (8-oz)	carob bar	8-oz
85g (3 oz)	raisins	½ cup
85g (3 oz)	brazil nuts, chopped	⅔ cup

1 Break up or coarsely grate (shred) the carob bar and put the pieces into the top part of a double boiler, or in a bowl resting over a saucepan of boiling water (do not let the bowl actually touch the water). Stir it gently until it melts.

2 Add the raisins and nuts, mixing them in well so that they are evenly distributed and, if the mixture seems too dry, add a spoonful of vegetable oil and stir it in well. Using a metal spoon, make evenly-sized little mounds of the mixture on waxed paper or in individual petit fours cases. Leave them to cool and harden. If stored in an airtight container in a cool spot, these Carob Raisin Nut Clusters will keep for a few weeks, though they are best when eaten fresh.

Note: You can use other dried fruit and/or nuts as you like and crystallized ginger is delicious. Instead of carob, you can use plain or milk chocolate bars.

Soya Sesame Balls

85g (3 oz)	candied peel, finely chopped	3 oz
55g (2 oz)	sesame seeds	⅓ cup
55g (2 oz)	soya flour	⅓ cup
½ tsp	ground cinnamon	½ tsp
1-2 tbsp	honey or syrup or maple syrup	1-2 tbsp

1 Mix together the peel, sesame seeds, soya flour and cinnamon. Stir in just enough honey or syrup to bind the ingredients together without making the mixture too sticky. If necessary, add more seeds, flour or honey to adjust the consistency.

2 Use your hands to roll evenly sized pieces of the mixture into small balls, put them on a small serving dish and chill them before serving.

Note: These can be made without the candied peel if you prefer, replacing it with chopped sultanas or other dried fruit. As they firm up well, they are particularly suitable as a high-energy nibble when you are out walking or on picnics.

Toffee Apples

115g (4 oz)	butter or margarine	½ cup
455g (1 lb)	raw cane sugar	2½ cups
2 tbsp	water	2 tbsp
8 small	eating apples	8 small

1 In a large saucepan combine the butter or margarine, sugar and water and heat the mixture gently, stirring it continually with a wooden spoon, until the sugar dissolves. Then bring the mixture to the boil and continue boiling gently until the toffee reaches the soft crack stage. (To test this, drop a little of the mixture into a small dish of cold water. It will be ready when the toffee separates into threads which break easily.)

2 Meanwhile, wipe the apples and if the skin is very shiny, roughen it a little with a fine grater (shredder). Remove the stalks and spear each apple through the core with a small stick.

3 As soon as the toffee mixture is ready, remove it from the heat and dip the apples into it 1 at a time, tipping the saucepan if necessary to coat each apple completely and evenly. Then dip the apples briefly into a bowl of very cold water. Arrange the apples on a greased tray or stand the stick in a jar and leave them to dry.

4 These toffee apples are best eaten within a day or two.

Note: This old-fashioned favourite is still popular with children – even those who do not like fruit!

Date 'Fudge'

170g (6 oz)	dried dates	1 cup
2 tbsp	lemon juice	2 tbsp
140ml (¼ pt)	water	⅔ cup
1 tsp	vanilla essence (extract)	1 tsp
55g (2 oz)	margarine	¼ cup
55g (2 oz)	wholemeal (whole wheat) flour	½ cup

1 Chop the dates and put them into a saucepan together with the lemon juice, water and vanilla. Cook them gently for about 5 minutes, then mash them to make a thick purée.

2 Melt the margarine, add the flour and cook it gently for a few minutes. Stir the date purée into the pan with a wooden spoon, making sure that all the ingredients are well blended and there are no lumps.

3 Spoon the mixture into a small, shallow tin (pan), press it down evenly and smooth the top. Leave it to cool before cutting it into small squares. If it is not to be eaten at once, transfer it to an airtight container and store it in the refrigerator where it will keep for a few days.

Note: This unusual 'fudge' can be dressed up by adding chopped nuts, coconut flakes, chopped crystallized ginger and so on when it is going to be served at the end of a dinner party. For a *really* luxurious version, replace the flour with the same amount of ground almonds.

Treacle Oat Bars

85g (3 oz)	margarine	1/3 cup
2 tbsp	milk	2 tbsp
1 tbsp	molasses	1 tbsp
1 tsp	raw cane sugar	1 tsp
85g (3 oz)	wholemeal (whole wheat) flour	3/4 cup
1/2 tsp	bicarbonate of soda (baking soda)	1/2 tsp
1 tsp	ground ginger	1 tsp
85g (3 oz)	rolled oats	3/4 cup

1 Preheat the oven to 325°F/170°C (Gas Mark 3).
2 Put the margarine, milk, molasses and sugar into a saucepan and heat the mixture gently, stirring it with a wooden spoon until the margarine melts.
3 Combine the remaining ingredients. Stir this dry mixture into the syrupy mixture. The resulting paste should be thick and slightly moist (adjust the consistency if necessary). Divide it into 12 evenly sized pieces, shape them into bars and put them on foil-lined baking sheets.
4 Bake them in the preheated oven for 20 minutes or until they are just firm. Leave them to cool on the baking sheets briefly before transferring them to wire cooling racks. They should be completely cold before being put away.

Note: This basic recipe can be adapted in many ways. Try, for instance, adding spices, seeds, finely chopped nuts, some dried fruit, crumbled banana chips or whatever else you have to hand. The molasses can be replaced with honey, syrup or maple syrup for a milder taste.

Carrot Cake with Coconut Topping

340g (12 oz)	carrots, peeled and grated	2 cups
115g (4 oz)	sultanas (golden seedless raisins)	2/3 cup
85g (3 oz)	margarine	1/3 cup
225g (8 oz)	raw cane sugar	1 1/3 cups
285ml (1/2 pt)	water	1 1/3 cups
285g (10 oz)	wholemeal (whole wheat) flour	2 1/2 cups
1 good tsp	bicarbonate of soda (baking soda)	1 good tsp
1 tsp	ground mace	1 tsp
1 tsp	ground allspice	1 tsp
1 tsp	ground cinnamon	1 tsp
1 tsp	vanilla essence (extract)	1 tsp
85g (3 oz)	desiccated (shredded) coconut	1 cup

Topping

115g (4 oz)	creamed coconut boiling water, as required	4 oz
55g (2 oz)	raw cane sugar, finely ground roasted coconut flakes, to finish	1/3 cup

1 Preheat the oven to 350°F/180°C (Gas Mark 4).
2 Put the carrot into a large saucepan together with the sultanas (golden seedless raisins), margarine, sugar and water. Bring the mixture gently to the boil, then lower the heat and simmer it for a few minutes. Leave the mixture on one side to cool slightly.
3 Meanwhile, in a bowl mix the flour, bicarbonate of soda (baking soda) and spices. Stir the vanilla into the carrot mixture, then pour it onto the dry ingredients and mix it in thoroughly. Stir in the coconut.
4 Grease a small, shallow square or rectangular tin (pan), pour the mixture into it, smooth the top and bake it in the preheated oven for 20 to 30 minutes or until a sharp knife inserted in the middle comes out clean. Leave the cake to cool in its tin (pan) briefly, then transfer it to a wire rack to finish cooling.
5 Meanwhile, make the topping. Grate (shred) the creamed coconut and then pour a very little boiling water over it, stirring it well so that the coconut dissolves. Add the sugar and stir until it dissolves. The result should be a fairly stiff but spreadable cream. Top the cake with the cream straight away and sprinkle a handful of roasted coconut flakes over the top. When the cake has cooled and the topping hardened, serve it cut into squares.

Maple Pecan Popcorn

2 tbsp	vegetable oil, plus extra as required	2 tbsp
115g (4 oz)	popping corn	4 oz
4 tbsp	maple syrup	4 tbsp
85g (3 oz)	pecan nuts, chopped	2/3 cup

1 In a large saucepan with a well fitting lid, heat just a spoonful of the oil. Then add some of the corn, cover and cook it until it begins to pop. Continue cooking, shaking the pan, until the noise stops. Tip the popped corn into a dish and keep it warm while you repeat the process for the rest of the corn.
2 Make a thin sauce by diluting the maple syrup with a little hot water. Stir in the chopped nuts. When all the corn is ready, trickle the sauce over it and stir it gently to coat it evenly and eat it at once.

Note: Popcorn is a popular snack and far more nutritious than people realize. You can also flavour it with honey and spices or serve it as a savoury snack with salt or soy sauce sprinkled over it.

Wholemeal Waffles

115g (4 oz)	wholemeal (whole wheat) flour	1 cup
pinch	sea salt	pinch
1 large	free-range egg, beaten	1 extra large
200ml (⅓ pt)	milk	¾ cup
30g (1 oz)	margarine, melted	2½ tbsp
30g (1 oz)	raw cane sugar	2 tbsp

1 Sift together the flour and salt, then add the lightly beaten egg. Gradually add the milk, beating it in well so that the batter is smooth. Then, stir in the margarine and sugar.
2 Grease a waffle iron, heat it for 2 to 3 minutes, then pour in just enough of the batter to cover it. Close the waffle iron for 2 minutes, by which time the waffle should be crisp and golden brown.
3 Either serve straight away or keep it warm while you make the rest. Top your hot waffles with honey, low-sugar jam (jelly), maple syrup or fruit purées such as apple, and a generous sprinkling of nuts.

Note: Though not widely used in the UK, waffle irons are available from the larger stores and it is well worth treating yourself to one. Apart from having waffles for breakfast or as a sweet snack as Americans do, you'll also be able to make them into a mini meal by topping them with such savouries as scrambled eggs, ratatouille, baked beans and so on. Make up more than you need and freeze the extra ones. These can then just be heated in the oven for a few minutes when required.

Muesli Shortbread

225g (8 oz)	margarine	1 cup
115g (4 oz)	raw cane sugar	⅔ cup
225g (8 oz)	wholemeal (whole wheat) flour	2 cups
115g (4 oz)	muesli	1 cup
½ tsp	mixed spice	½ tsp
55g (2 oz)	banana chips, broken into small pieces	2 oz

1 Preheat the oven to 300°F/150°C (Gas Mark 2).
2 Cream together the margarine and sugar. Gradually stir in the flour, muesli, mixed spice and banana chips.
3 Grease a small Swiss roll tin (jelly roll pan). Press the mixture into it, smooth the top and bake it in the preheated oven for 30 minutes. Mark it into slices, but leave the mixture to cool and set firm before removing the shortbread from the tin and breaking it along the lines into slices.

Note: The texture and taste of your shortbread will vary considerably depending on the muesli you use. Ideally it will contain some nuts and dried fruit. If you feel you would like more, add them to taste. Butter is often used to make shortbread, which does of course give it a richer flavour, so, if your intake of saturated fats is low, Muesli Shortbread made with butter will do you no harm as an occasional treat.

Date and Apple Bran Muffins

170g (6 oz)	wholemeal (whole wheat) flour	1½ cups
55g (2 oz)	bran	½ cup
2 tsp	baking powder	2 tsp
30g (1 oz)	raw cane sugar	2 tbsp
pinch	sea salt	pinch
55g (2 oz)	dates, finely chopped	⅓ cup
1 medium	apple, grated (shredded)	1 medium
1 medium	free-range egg	1 large
200ml (⅓ pt)	milk	¾ cup
45g (1½ oz)	margarine, melted	4 tbsp

1 Preheat the oven to 425°F/220°C (Gas Mark 7).
2 Sift together the flour, bran and baking powder. Stir in the sugar, salt, dates and apple.
3 Whisk the egg into the milk and add the melted margarine. Gradually pour the liquid into the dry ingredients and stir it gently until it is all mixed in and the dates and apple are evenly distributed.
4 Half fill 12 lightly greased fairy cake tins (muffin pans) and bake them in the preheated oven for 20 minutes or until a fine knife inserted into the middle of a muffin comes out clean. Eat them warm or cold, either plain or spread with butter or low-sugar jam.

Note: Muffins can be flavoured in a variety of ways. Try using other dried fruits, chopped nuts, fruit purées, crushed pineapple, whatever you have to hand. Mashed bananas added to the basic mix and topping the muffins with banana chips makes for a delicious variation. Spice up the muffins with ginger or cloves or other spices of your choice, too.

Lemon Yogurt Tarts

Pastry

225g (8 oz)	81 per cent wholemeal (whole wheat pastry) flour (see note)	2 cups
2 level tsp	baking powder	2 level tsp
115g (4 oz)	margarine	½ cup
2 tbsp	cold water, to mix	2 tbsp

Filling

115g (4 oz)	lemon curd	4 oz
6 tbsp	set natural (unsweetened) yogurt, or as required	6 tbsp
	small piece chocolate, grated (shredded), to garnish	

1 Sift the flour to remove as much of the bran as possible (save it to use in another recipe), then combine the flour with the baking powder. Using your fingertips, rub in the margarine until the mixture resembles fine breadcrumbs. Add just enough cold water to make a firm dough. Knead it briefly, then wrap it in polythene and chill it for 30 minutes.

2 During this time, preheat the oven to 375°F/190°C (Gas Mark 5).

3 When the pastry is ready, roll it out on a floured surface and use a cup or biscuit (cookie) cutter to cut out 12 small circles (rounds). Arrange these in lightly greased tart tins (tartlet pans), prick them lightly, then bake them blind (see page 152) in the preheated oven for 10 minutes. Cool them briefly before carefully removing them from the tins (pans), and then put them on a wire rack to cool.

4 Meanwhile, make the filling. Put the lemon curd into a bowl and stir in enough yogurt to make it pale and creamy. Divide this between the tarts, preparing more of the lemon yogurt if necessary. Sprinkle some of the chocolate over each one. Eat these tarts the same day.

Note: The bran is removed from the flour in this recipe to make the pastry lighter and easier to handle, but you can, of course, leave it in if you prefer. Look out, too, for 81 per cent wholemeal flour (whole wheat pastry flour) that has already had most of the bran removed.

Almond Rhubarb Crumble

1.15 k (2 lb)	rhubarb, washed and cut into small chunks	6½ cups
170g (6 oz)	raw cane sugar	1 cup
¼ tsp	ground cloves	¼ tsp
1 tsp	ground cinnamon	1 tsp
2 tbsp	orange juice, or as required	2 tbsp
1 tbsp	grated orange peel	1 tbsp

Crumble topping

115g (4 oz)	wholemeal (whole wheat) flour	1 cup
55g (2 oz)	rolled oats	½ cup
55g (2 oz)	raw cane sugar	⅓ cup
85g (3 oz)	margarine	⅓ cup
45g (1½ oz)	almonds, chopped	4 tbsp

1 Preheat the oven to 350°F/180°C (Gas Mark 4).

2 Put the rhubarb into a saucepan with the sugar, spices, orange juice and peel. Cover the pan and simmer the mixture gently until the rhubarb is just tender (it should not have disintegrated). If necessary, add a little more orange juice or water if it starts to dry out. Also, check the sweetness and add a little more sugar if it is too sour. Spoon the rhubarb into a small, ovenproof dish.

3 Now make the crumble topping. Combine the flour, oats and sugar, then using your fingers, rub the margarine into the dry ingredients until the mixture resembles fine breadcrumbs. Stir in the nuts, then sprinkle it over the rhubarb, pressing it down lightly.

4 Bake the crumble in the preheated oven for about 30 minutes or until it is crisp and golden brown on top.

Note: Though usually served as a dessert, fruit crumble on its own can make a nutritious snack, especially if served with yogurt. When making one, prepare extra and divide this between individual dishes, then freeze. You can, of course, make them using a variety of fruits and combinations of fruits, including apple and blackberry, mixed red summer fruits, apricots.

Banana Crêpes

285ml (½ pt)	pancake batter of your choice (see pages 154-155) vegetable oil	1⅓ cups

Filling

4 small	ripe bananas	4 small
1-2 tbsp	honey or maple syrup	1-2 tbsp
1 tbsp	lemon juice	1 tbsp
140ml (¼ pt)	sour (soured) cream	⅔ cup
55g (2 oz)	flaked (slivered) almonds, roasted ground cinnamon, to taste	½ cup

1 Make the batter according to the instructions and chill it for 30 minutes.

2 Meanwhile, prepare the filling. Mash the bananas to make a smooth purée, mix in the honey or maple syrup, lemon juice and cream.

3 Heat a small amount of oil in a frying pan (skillet) and cook just a spoonful or two of the batter at a time, swirling the pan to spread it well for small, thin crêpes. Keep them warm while you use the rest of the batter up in the same way.

4 Fill each crêpe with some of the creamy banana mixture, fold it in half over the filling and sprinkle almonds and cinnamon over the top. Serve at once.

Note: Sweet crêpes can make a delicious snack. Boost their nutritional value with nuts, yogurt and so on, or sprinkle a spoonful of granola over them. When time allows, make up extra crêpes and store them, separated with sheets of foil, in the freezer where they should keep for up to 3 months.

Brazil Nut Cookies

115g (4 oz)	margarine	1 cup
115g (4 oz)	raw cane sugar, plus extra for sprinkling	⅔ cup
1 large	free-range egg	1 extra large
115g (4 oz)	brazil nuts, ground, plus extra whole nuts, to garnish	½ cup
175g (6 oz)	wholemeal (whole wheat) flour	1½ cups

1 Preheat the oven to 350°F/180°C (Gas Mark 4).
2 Cream the margarine and sugar together in a bowl using a wooden spoon. Lightly beat the egg and add it to the bowl.
3 In a separate bowl sift together the ground nuts and flour, then stir the mixture gradually into the creamed mixture and blend it in thoroughly.
4 Lightly grease a baking sheet and drop spoonfuls of the cookie mixture onto it. Roughly chop the extra nuts, press down each biscuit lightly, then scatter some of the chopped nuts on top. Sprinkle a little sugar over them for a little extra crunch.
5 Bake them in the preheated oven for 15 minutes or until they are firm to the touch and just golden brown. Cool briefly on the baking sheet, then transfer the cookies to a wire rack to cool completely. Store the cookies in an airtight container until they are needed.

Note: Other nuts can be used in this simple recipe, as can some raisins or sultanas (golden seedless raisins) or chopped, candied fruit. Chocolate chips are also delicious in these cookies.

Tofu Cheesecake

Base

115g (4 oz)	margarine	½ cup
1 tbsp	syrup or maple syrup	1 tbsp
1 tbsp	raw cane sugar	1 tbsp
170g (6 oz)	rolled oats	1½ cups
55g (2 oz)	hazelnuts, coarsely chopped	½ cup
½ tsp	ground mixed spices	½ tsp

Filling

6 tbsp	syrup or maple syrup	6 tbsp
30g (1 oz)	cornflour (cornstarch)	¼ cup
140ml (¼ pt)	water	⅔ cup
225g (8 oz)	tofu, drained	1 cup
6 tbsp	lemon juice	6 tbsp
1 tbsp	grated (shredded) lemon peel	1 tbsp
1 tsp	vanilla essence (extract)	1 tsp

Topping

10	green grapes	10
10	white grapes	10
2	tangerines	2

1 Preheat the oven to 425°F/220°C (Gas Mark 7).
2 First, make the base. In a saucepan, combine the margarine, syrup and sugar and heat the mixture gently for a few minutes. Then stir in the oats, nuts and spices, mixing everything together well. Lightly grease a baking sheet and small ring (loose-bottomed cake pan) and press the mixture evenly across the base and up the sides. Bake it in the preheated oven for 10 minutes or until it has lightly browned, then leave it to cool completely.
3 Meanwhile, make the filling. In another saucepan, heat together the syrup, cornflour (cornstarch) and water, stirring all the time until the mixture thickens to form a sauce. Blend the tofu to a smooth purée and add this to the sauce together with the lemon juice, peel and vanilla. Cook the mixture briefly, then leave it to cool.
4 Pour the tofu filling into the prepared crust, smooth the top and chill it. Halve the grapes, peel and segment the tangerines and use the fruit to decorate the cheesecake before carefully removing it from the ring, then serve.

Note: Maple syrup gives this cheesecake a special flavour. If using ordinary syrup, a spoonful or two of tahini makes an unusual addition. In summer, top the cake with fresh strawberries or make a fruit purée and spread this over the tofu filling.

Frozen Yogurt with Pineapple

70ml (⅛ pt)	lemon juice	¼ cup
70ml (⅛ pt)	honey or maple syrup	¼ cup
425ml (¾ pt)	natural (unsweetened) yogurt	2 cups
115g (4 oz)	pineapple, fresh or canned, drained and juice reserved	4 oz
½ tsp	ground mixed spice	½ tsp
1	free-range egg white	1

1 Mix together the lemon juice and honey or syrup, then stir this into the yogurt. Coarsely crush the pineapple and stir this into the yogurt together with the mixed spice. (If using tinned/canned pineapple, you can replace some or all of the honey or syrup with the reserved juice.)
2 Pour the mixture into a shallow freezer proof tray, cover it and freeze until the mixture is firm, but not solid. Beat the mixture to break up the ice crystals (using an electric mixer makes this job much easier). Add the egg white and continue beating the mixture briefly. Return the mixture to the container and freeze it until it is firm.
3 Remove the frozen yogurt from the freezer for about 10 minutes to soften slightly before serving.

Note: Yogurt prepared this way can also be flavoured with crushed strawberries or other fruits, apple purée, mashed banana, nuts, candied fruit – let your imagination run wild! It is a delicious and healthy alternative to ice-cream.

Carob Calypso Mix

55g (2 oz)	cashew nut pieces	½ cup
55g (2 oz)	sunflower seeds	½ cup
55g (2 oz)	peanuts, raw or roasted	½ cup
55g (2 oz)	dried pineapple	½ cup
55g (2 oz)	dried mangoes, chopped	½ cup
55g (2 oz)	raisins	⅓ cup
55g (2 oz)	banana chips	½ cup
55g (2 oz)	coconut flakes, roasted	¾ cup
115-g (4-oz)	carob bar, grated (shredded)	4-oz

1 Combine all the ingredients except the carob, mixing them gently but well. Use a sharp knife to cut the carob bar into small chunks and add these to the other ingredients.
2 Store the mix in a screw top jar in a cool place, to be dipped into whenever something sweet to nibble is needed. Alternatively, put a snack-sized amount in small bags or containers to add to lunchboxes. It is also delicious added to plain yogurt or sprinkled over frozen yogurt or ice-cream.

Note: This mix can be made using any combination of nuts and dried fruit, so be imaginative and make up your own with whatever ingredients you have to hand. The carob can be omitted altogether or replaced with chocolate if you prefer.

Spiced Pear Granola

115g (4 oz)	margarine	½ cup
140ml (¼ pt)	hot water	⅔ cup
1 tsp	vanilla essence (extract)	1 tsp
455g (1 lb)	mixed cereal base	4 cups
55g (2 oz)	bran	½ cup
115g (4 oz)	raw cane sugar	⅔ cup
1 tsp	ground cinnamon	1 tsp
1 tsp	ground mixed spices	1 tsp
½ tsp	ground ginger	½ tsp
55g (2 oz)	cashew nuts, coarsely chopped	½ cup
55g (2 oz)	walnuts (English walnuts), coarsely chopped	½ cup
55g (2 oz)	sesame seeds	scant ½ cup
115g (4 oz)	dried pears, chopped	scant 1 cup

1 Preheat the oven to 350°F/180°C (Gas Mark 4).
2 Melt the margarine in the hot water and add the vanilla. Stir in the mixed cereal base, bran, sugar, spices, nuts and sesame seeds, making sure that they are evenly distributed.
3 Lightly grease 1 large or 2 small baking sheets and spread the mixture across it/them. If some of it tends to cling together in large lumps, break these down, though some small lumps give the finished Granola its distinctive texture.
4 Bake it in the preheated oven for about 30 minutes, stirring gently every now and again. When it is golden and crunchy, switch the oven off, and stir the pears into the mixture. Leave it in the oven to cool. When completely cold, store the granola in a screw-top jar.
5 Eat it as a breakfast cereal or anytime snack with dairy or soya milk, or as a dry nibble straight from the jar.

Note: Though mixed cereal base is especially nutritious, you can use plain rolled oats instead or jumbo oats for a crunchier texture. Flavour your Granola with other nuts or dried fruits, pumpkin or sunflower seeds. Instead of sugar, you can sweeten it with honey or, for a real treat, maple syrup.

21

Basic Recipes

Pastry

Baking blind

Many of our recipes call for pastry cases to be baked blind, which means without a filling. Pastry made using white flour tends to buckle, so it is necessary to put in a temporary filling to hold it in place (this is usually a foil or greaseproof/waxed paper covering filled with dried beans or rice or ceramic baking beans). Wholemeal (whole wheat) pastry, however, holds its shape better so you need only to prick it with a fork and then bake it empty. However, if you prefer to fill it, do.

Using the pastry

Pastry made using wholemeal (whole wheat) flour will be more crumbly than that made using white flour, though once you get used to using it this is rarely a problem. If it should break, just dampen it and press it together and, in most cases, the join will 'mend' during cooking. However, when a more perfect finish is important, roll the pastry out on polythene, clingfilm (plastic wrap) or foil, then use this to lift the pastry, which will help prevent it breaking.

Shortcrust Pastry

225g (8 oz)	wholemeal (whole wheat) flour*	2 cups
pinch	sea salt	pinch
115g (4 oz)	margarine or butter	½ cup
2-3 tbsp	cold water	2-3 tbsp

1 Sift the flour and salt together into a bowl. Using your fingertips, rub the margarine or butter in until the mixture looks like fine breadcrumbs. Stir in just enough cold water to bind the mixture into a firm dough and knead it briefly. If it seems dry, add a little more water.
2 Wrap it in a polythene bag or foil and chill it for 30 minutes before rolling out and using as required.

* If preferred, use half plain wholemeal (whole wheat) pastry flour, half self-raising (self-rising).

Making extra

The above quantity is sufficient for 1 large flan (deep sweet or savoury tart). As pastry making takes a little time, it is worth making extra and keeping it for instant use when next needed. Either rub the margarine or butter into the flour and store the resulting mixture in an airtight container in the refrigerator, or freeze the dough.

Variations

For savoury pastry, add any of the following: fresh or dried herbs to taste; 55g (2 oz/3 tbsp) sesame or chopped sunflower seeds; 55-85g (2-3 oz/½-¾ cup) finely grated (shredded) Cheddar cheese; 115g/4 oz/½ cup cottage cheese (in which case, use less liquid); 1 egg yolk (also use less liquid). For sweet pastry, add 30g/1 oz/2½ tbsp raw cane sugar. You could also use fruit juice instead of water.

Shortcrust Pastry with Egg

200g (7 oz)	wholemeal (whole wheat) flour	1¾ cups
85g (3 oz)	margarine	⅓ cup
1 medium	free-range egg, beaten	1 large
1 tbsp	cold water	1 tbsp

1 Put the flour and margarine into a bowl and use your fingertips to rub in the fat to make a crumb-like mixture. With a round-tipped knife, stir the beaten egg into the mixture, then add sufficient cold water to form a dough.
2 Knead it briefly, adding more flour if it is sticky, more water if it is too dry. Wrap it in polythene and chill it briefly before rolling it out as required.

Pastry with Oil

225g (8 oz)	wholemeal (whole wheat) flour	2 cups
1 tsp	baking powder	1 tsp
pinch	sea salt	pinch
3 tbsp	vegetable oil	3 tbsp
3 tbsp	cold water	3 tbsp

1 Sift together the flour, baking powder and salt. Whisk together the oil and water. Stir the liquid into the dry mixture and mix it in as thoroughly, but as rapidly as possible.
2 Wrap the pastry in a polythene bag or foil and chill it for at least 30 minutes before rolling it out and using it as required.

Flaky Pastry

225g (8 oz)	wholemeal (whole wheat) flour	2 cups
pinch	sea salt	pinch
2 tsp	baking powder	2 tsp
175g (6 oz)	margarine or butter	¾ cup
	cold water, to mix	

1 Sift the flour, salt and baking powder together into a bowl. Divide the margarine or butter into thirds and rub one of them into the flour, then add enough water to make a soft dough. On a floured surface, roll the dough out into a long, rectangular shape.
2 Flake one of the remaining thirds of margarine or butter over two-thirds of the dough, leaving the bottom third uncovered. Fold the bottom third of the pastry up and the top third down, like an envelope. Seal the open edges by pressing them with a rolling pin. Repeat this process with the last third of margarine or butter after rolling the dough out into a long rectangle again.
3 Turn and roll out the pastry again, making 'ribs' at

intervals with the rolling pin to equalize the pressure of air and help the pastry rise evenly. (If it is still firm to handle, repeat the turning, rolling and folding once more, but if it is sticky, chill it for a while before the final rolling out.)
4 Chill the pastry for at least 30 minutes before using as the cold pastry is easier to handle and will also rise better. Roll it out and use as required.

Making extra

See under Shortcrust Pastry, page 152.

Rough Puff Pastry

115g (4 oz)	wholemeal (whole wheat) flour*	1 cup
115g (4 oz)	white flour*	1 cup
pinch	sea salt	pinch
170g (6 oz)	butter or vegetarian suet	¾ cup
2 tsp	lemon juice	2 tsp
	cold water, to mix	

1 Sift together the 2 flours and salt. Use a knife to cut the fat into pieces and stir it into the flour without breaking up the pieces. Mix the lemon juice and enough cold water into the dry mixture to make a firm dough. Transfer the dough to a floured surface and roll it out into a long rectangle. Fold the bottom third up and the top third down, seal the ends by pressing them down with a rolling pin and make 'ribs' with the rolling pin so that the air pressure is equal and the pastry rises evenly.
2 Give the pastry a half turn. Repeat the rolling and folding process 2 more times (chilling it briefly first if it has become sticky).
3 Chill it again for at least 30 minutes before rolling it out and using.

* This pastry should be light, which is difficult using *just* wholemeal (whole wheat) flour. Mixing it with white flour is an alternative or use unbleached white flour.

Pasta

Pasta shapes

Ravioli Roll out 2 large, thin, rectangular sheets. Mark one into squares, put some of the filling into the centre of each square and dampen the dough along lines. Lay the second sheet of dough over the first and press it down along the lines before cutting out the squares. Although this is the traditional way of making ravioli, pastry made from wholemeal (whole wheat) flour is more crumbly than that made with the more glutinous refined flour, so it might be easier to use 4 smaller sheets or even to cut the pasta into individual squares *before* adding the filling.

Cannelloni Roll the dough out into rectangles about 10 by 13 cm (4 by 5 in) and cook them in boiling water before adding the filling. Then roll them up, put them in a greased ovenproof dish with the seam underneath, cover them with a sauce and bake them briefly in a hot oven.

Tagliatelle Roll the dough out into large, very thin rectangles, flour them lightly, then roll them up loosely into a sausage shape. Slice them with a very sharp knife into 6 mm (¼ in) intervals. Unroll and use as required.

Noodles Make these like the tagliatelle, but make the slices even thinner!

Lasagne Roll the dough out and cut it into sheets about 5 by 20 cm (2 by 8 in). Cook it in boiling water before layering it with the filling of your choice and baking.

Home-made Pasta

340g (12 oz)	wholemeal (whole wheat) flour	3 cups
pinch	sea salt	pinch
2	free-range eggs	2
3 tbsp	olive oil	3 tbsp
2-3 tbsp	cold water, to mix	2-3 tbsp

1 Sift the flour and salt together into a bowl. Whisk together the eggs and oil and add this mixture to the flour with enough cold water to make a smooth, shiny dough. Knead it briefly.
2 Wrap it in a polythene bag and chill it for 30 minutes.
2 On a floured surface, roll out the dough thinly, then cut it into the required shape.
3 To cook, bring a large pan of water to a fast boil, add salt, then add the pasta all at once. Bring the water back to the boil, stir it briefly to separate the shapes, then cook it for about 6 minutes. Pasta is cooked when it is *al dente*, which is just tender and slightly firm in the centre. Drain it and use it at once (bought pasta may take longer to cook so check the instructions on the packaging).

Variations

Home-made pasta can be flavoured with herbs and/or finely chopped garlic or garlic salt. It can also be coloured green or red and, of course, filled with a wide variety of mixtures.

Green pasta is made by adding about 55g (2 oz/scant ¼ cup) puréed and well-drained spinach to the dough at the same time as the eggs. Mix it in very well so that the colour is even, then proceed as usual. For red pasta, add the same amount of tomato purée (paste).

Make a more nutritious pasta by substituting 55g (2 oz/½ cup) of wheatgerm (wheat berries) for the same amount of flour. Pasta can also be made without eggs, though it will be heavier and less easy to handle, so will, therefore, be more suitable for larger, simpler shapes, such as lasagne.

Pancakes

Pancake Batter

115g (4 oz)	wholemeal (whole wheat) flour	1 cup
pinch	sea salt	pinch
1-2	free-range eggs	1-2
285ml (½ pt)	milk or half milk, half water mixed	1⅓ cups

1 Sift the flour and salt into a bowl. Whisk the egg(s) and gradually stir it/them into the flour with the milk or milk and water to make sure that the mixture is smooth and free of lumps. Whisk it well to make a light, creamy batter.
2 Chill the batter for 30 minutes before using, then whisk it again before making the pancakes. The batter should be the consistency of single (light) cream, so add more milk if it seems too thick.

Eggless Pancake Batter

115g (4 oz)	wholemeal (whole wheat) flour	1 cup
55g (2 oz)	soya flour	½ cup
pinch	sea salt	pinch
1 tsp	baking powder	1 tsp
285ml (½ pt)	water	1⅓ cups

1 Sift together all the dry ingredients, then gradually stir in the water. Whisk it well to lighten the mixture and when the batter is smooth and frothy, chill it for 30 minutes. Whisk it again before using, checking that the consistency is that of single (light) cream. If necessary, adjust this by adding a little more water.

Oatmeal Batter

115g (4 oz)	oatmeal	1 cup
30g (1 oz)	wholemeal (whole wheat) flour	¼ cup
pinch	sea salt	pinch
1 tsp	baking powder	1 tsp
200ml (⅓ pt)	milk	¾ cup
1 tsp	vegetable oil	1 tsp
1 small	free-range egg, lightly beaten	1 small

1 Sift together the dry ingredients. Mix together the milk, oil and egg, then gradually add this to the dry ingredients. Beat the batter well and then chill it for at least 30 minutes, preferably longer, before using.

2 Beat the batter again before making the pancakes and, if necessary, adjust the consistency so that it pours easily. Use only the minimum amount to make each pancake, cooking it over a steady heat until it begins to set. As oatmeal pancakes have a heavier texture than those made with flour, serve them either flat or folded just once.

Buckwheat Batter

85g (3 oz)	buckwheat flour	¾ cup
55g (2 oz)	wholemeal (whole wheat) flour	½ cup
pinch	sea salt	pinch
285ml (½ pt)	water	1⅓ cups
1	free-range egg, lightly beaten	1

1 Sift together the 2 flours and salt. Whisk together the water and egg, then gradually add the mixture to the dry ingredients and beat them well to incorporate air into the batter to lighten it. Chill it for at least 30 minutes, preferably longer. Before using, beat the batter well again and, if necessary, adjust the consistency so that it pours easily.

2 Buckwheat pancakes are heavier in texture than those made from flour alone but have a wonderfully nutty flavour.

Pizza

Basic Pizza Dough

15g (½ oz)	fresh yeast	1¼ tbsp
70ml (⅛ pt)	warm water	¼ cup
225g (8 oz)	wholemeal (whole wheat) flour	2 cups
pinch	sea salt	pinch
2 tbsp	olive oil	2 tbsp
2-3 tbsp	milk	2-3 tbsp

1 Crumble the yeast into a bowl and mix it well with the warm water. Leave it in a warm place until it is frothy (about 10 to 15 minutes).

2 Then, sift the flour and salt together into a warmed bowl, make a well in the middle, pour in the yeast mixture and stir until all the dry ingredients have been incorporated. Add the oil and enough milk to make a smooth but firm dough. Knead it for 5 minutes.

3 Put the dough in a clean, floured bowl, cover it with polythene or a damp cloth and leave it in a warm place

for about an hour or until it has doubled in size. Knead the dough briefly again, then divide into half or quarters. Roll each piece out on a floured board to make 2 large or 4 small circles (rounds). Transfer them to a lightly greased baking sheet and proceed as given in the recipe.

Note: If you prefer to use dried yeast, you will need 7g (¼ oz/½ tablespoon).

Crispy Pizza Dough

15g (½ oz)	fresh yeast	1¼ tbsp
140ml (¼ pt)	warm water	⅔ cup
1 tbsp	olive oil	1 tbsp
225g (8 oz)	wholemeal (whole wheat) flour	2 cups
pinch	sea salt	pinch

1 Crumble the yeast into a bowl and mix it well with the warm water. Leave the mixture in a warm place until it begins to bubble (about 10 to 15 minutes).

2 Preheat the oven to 400°F/200°C (Gas Mark 6).

3 Then, add the oil to the yeast mixture. Sift together the flour and salt, make a well in the middle, and pour the yeast mixture into it. Stir until all the flour has been incorporated and you have a smooth but firm dough. Knead it for 5 minutes until it is soft and elastic.

4 Divide the dough into half or quarters and roll each piece out to make 2 medium or 4 small circles (rounds). Put them onto lightly greased baking sheets and prebake them for 5 minutes in the preheated oven. Add the topping as per the recipe and return the pizzas to the oven to cook for about 15 more minutes.

Note: If you prefer to use dried yeast, you will need 7g (¼ oz/½ tablespoon).

Pizza Dough with Easy Blend Dried Yeast

225g (8 oz)	*wholemeal (whole wheat) flour*	*2 cups*
pinch	*sea salt*	*pinch*
1 generous tsp	*easy blend dried yeast*	*1 generous tsp*
200ml (⅓ pt)	*warm water*	*¾ cup*

1 Combine the flour, salt and yeast. Gradually stir in the warm water, using just enough to make a soft dough. Transfer it to a floured surface and knead it for 5 minutes.
2 Put the dough in a clean, floured bowl, cover it with polythene or a clean, damp cloth and leave it in a warm place until it has doubled in size (about 1 hour).
3 Knead it again, divide into half or quarters and roll it out to make 2 medium or 4 small circles (rounds). Put them on lightly greased baking sheets, cover them again and leave them in a warm spot for 30 minutes or until they have puffed up.
4 Add the topping and cook as given in the recipes.

Sauces

Brown Gravy

Makes about 425ml (¾ pt/2 cups)

2 tbsp	*vegetable oil*	*2 tbsp*
1 small	*onion, finely chopped*	*1 small*
30g (1 oz)	*wholemeal (whole wheat) flour*	*¼ cup*
¼ tsp	*dried thyme*	*¼ tsp*
425ml (¾ pt)	*vegetable stock*	*2 cups*
	seasoning to taste	

1 Heat the oil in a pan and fry the onion gently until it begins to colour. Add the flour, stir and then cook it briefly.
2 Add the thyme, then gradually stir in the vegetable stock. Bring it gently to the boil, stirring frequently, then lower the heat and simmer for 10 minutes.
3 Strain the gravy, season to taste and serve at once. If preferred, you can blend the gravy to make it smooth, then reheat it gently before serving. (Thicken or thin it as desired.)

Variations

You can use margarine or butter instead of the oil and, for extra flavour, add yeast extract, soy sauce or miso to taste. Try, too, using different herbs. A small glass of red wine makes a delicious special-occasion gravy.

White Sauce

Makes about 285ml (½ pt/1⅓ cups)

30g (1 oz)	*margarine*	*2½ tbsp*
30g (1 oz)	*wholemeal (whole wheat) flour*	*¼ cup*
285ml (½ pt)	*milk*	*1⅓ cups*
¼ tsp	*ground mace* or *nutmeg*	*¼ tsp*
	seasoning to taste	

1 Melt the margarine in a pan. Sprinkle in the flour, stir and cook it gently for a few minutes.
2 Gradually pour in the milk, stirring quickly and continually so that the sauce is smooth and glossy and begins to thicken.
3 Bring it to the boil, then lower the heat and simmer it for 5 to 10 minutes. Add the spice and season to tase, then serve. (Thicken or thin it as desired.)

Variations

A vegan version of this sauce can be made by using oil instead of the margarine and soya milk instead of cow's. Other variations you might like to try include using butter instead of margarine, adding fresh or dried herbs (e.g. parsley) instead of the spice and using other milk, such as goat's. Try also adding grated Cheddar cheese (shredded New York Cheddar cheese) or chopped, hard-boiled (hard-cooked) eggs to the cooked sauce. Lightly cooked vegetables such as onions, mushrooms or leeks also go well.

Tomato Sauce

Makes about 285ml (½ pt/1⅓ cups)

2 tbsp	*vegetable oil*	*2 tbsp*
1 small	*onion, chopped*	*1 small*
1	*clove garlic, peeled and crushed*	*1*
1 tsp	*wholemeal (whole wheat) flour or cornflour (cornstarch)*	*1 tsp*
140ml (¼ pt)	*water*	*⅔ cup*
455g (1 lb)	*tomatoes, peeled and chopped*	*2⅔ cups*
2 tbsp	*tomato purée (paste)*	*2 tbsp*
1 tbsp	*fresh parsley, chopped*	*1 tbsp*
	seasoning to taste	

1 Heat the oil in a pan and gently cook the onion and garlic in it until they have softened and are begining to colour. Stir in the flour or cornflour (cornstarch) and cook it briefly.
2 Gradually stir in the water, tomato, tomato purée and parsley. Bring the mixture to the boil, then lower the heat and simmer the sauce for 20 to 30 minutes until the tomato has broken down and the sauce has thickened.
3 Sieve or blend it for a smooth sauce. Season to taste and use as needed, thickening or thinning it if necessary.

Variations

For a coarser textured sauce, do not blend it. Any herbs can be used in place of the parsley and try finely chopped leek instead of onion. Tinned (canned) tomatoes may be used instead of fresh ones. For a really creamy sauce, add a few spoonfuls of cream, some cream cheese or tahini.

Sweet and Sour Sauce

Makes scant 285ml (½ pt/1⅓ cup)

200ml (¾ pt)	orange juice	¾ cup
70ml (⅛ pt)	white wine vinegar	¼ cup
1 tbsp	raw cane sugar	1 tbsp
1 tbsp	arrowroot	1 tbsp
pinch	mustard powder	pinch
	soy sauce to taste	
	seasoning to taste	

1 Whisk together all the ingredients, then pour them into a saucepan and heat very gently, stirring continually, until the sauce thickens.

Note: Vegetables, beans, and so on can be simmered in the sauce to cook them, in which case you might need to add more liquid. Alternatively, add the cooked vegetables and simply heat them and the sauce through.

Variations

Use pineapple juice instead of orange, maybe adding some crushed pineapple for a different taste and texture. Cornflour (cornstarch) or even wholemeal (whole wheat) flour can be used instead of the arrowroot to thicken the sauce. Try cider vinegar instead of wine vinegar or adding spices.

Curry Sauce (English Style)

Makes about 715ml (1¼ pt/3 cups)

2 tbsp	vegetable oil	2 tbsp
1	onion, finely chopped	1
1 small	apple, coarsely chopped	1 small
1-2 tbsp	curry powder	1-2 tbsp
55g (2 oz)	wholemeal (whole wheat) flour	½ cup
570ml (1 pt)	vegetable stock or water	2½ cups
1-2 tbsp	tomato purée (paste)	1-2 tbsp
1 tbsp	lemon juice	1 tbsp
1 tsp	raw cane sugar	1 tsp
	seasoning to taste	

1 Heat the oil in a pan and sauté the onion and apple in it for a few minutes to soften them. Add the curry powder and flour, stir and cook them for a few minutes.

2 Gradually stir in the stock or water, then add the tomato purée, lemon juice and sugar and season to taste. Bring the sauce to the boil, then lower the heat and simmer it, stirring occasionally, for 20 to 30 minutes. Leaving the sauce to cool and stand overnight ripens the flavour. Use as needed, thickening or thinning the sauce as needed.

Curry Sauce (Indian Style)

Makes about 285ml (½ pt/1⅓ cups)

3 tbsp	vegetable ghee	3 tbsp
1 large	onion, finely chopped	1 large
1	clove garlic, finely chopped	1
2 tsp	ground coriander	2 tsp
2 tsp	ground cumin	2 tsp
1 tsp	ground turmeric	1 tsp
good pinch	ground cloves	good pinch
2	bay leaves	2
200ml (⅓ pt)	water	¾ cup
4 tbsp	coconut milk*	4 tbsp
½-1 tsp	garam masala, or to taste	½-1 tsp
	seasoning to taste	

1 Melt the ghee in a pan and sauté the onion and garlic in it for 5 minutes. Add the spices and cook them for a few minutes, stirring continually.

2 Add the bay leaves, water and coconut milk. Bring the sauce to the boil, then lower the heat, cover the pan and simmer it for 30 minutes. The resulting sauce should be quite thick (if it is too watery, uncover the pan and cook it for a little longer to dry it out). Remove the bay leaves.

3 Add garam masala to taste, season well and thicken or thin the sauce as needed. The flavour improves if the sauce is made the day before you need to use it, just leaving it to cool and stand in the pan overnight.

* Indian curries often contain the milk from fresh coconuts, which gives them a subtle yet unique flavour. If, however, you cannot find any near you, you can make your own thin version by soaking desiccated (shredded) coconut in boiling water overnight, then straining it. Alternatively, use coconut cream, which is available from supermarkets as well as Indian and wholefood stores. This needs to be grated (shredded) and then dissolved in boiling water before being added to the sauce.

Index